PEOPLE WHO WRITE ARE SO INTERESTING!

[signature]

EVIL AMONG US

EVIL AMONG US

The Texas Mormon Missionary Murders

Ken Driggs

Signature Books
Salt Lake City

Cover design by Ron Stucki

© 2000 Signature Books. All rights reserved. Signature Books is a registered trademark of Signature Books, Inc.

∞ *Evil Among Us: The Texas Mormon Missionary Murders* was printed on acid-free paper and was manufactured in the United States of America.

05 04 03 02 01 2000   6 5 4 3 2 1

LIBRARY OF CONGRESS CATALOGING-IN-PUBLICATION DATA
Driggs, Ken
    Evil among us : the Texas Mormon missionary murders
    / by Ken Driggs.
      p. cm.
    ISBN 1-56085-138-4 (pbk.)
      1. Kleasen, Bob. 2. Murder—Texas—Austin—Case
    studies. 3. Mormon missionaries—Texas—Austin—
    Mortality—Case studies. I. Title.
HV6534.A8 D75 2000
364.15'23'0976431—dc21
                                99-048062

Introduction

About a year after arriving in Texas in 1993 as an attorney, I chanced upon newspaper reports of the incredibly brutal 1974 murders of young Mormon missionaries Gary Darley and Mark Fischer. I recalled hearing about them years earlier in my own LDS congregation when the news first broke, and started investigating the case with an eye toward an article or two. The more I dug, however, the more compelling and heart-rending the story became. Stories, actually, of alleged murderer Bob Kleasen's mental illness and pathetic life, of well-meaning Mormons responding to troubled new converts, of loving families dealing with unimaginable loss, and of a tortuous death penalty case.

In the mid-1970s death penalty law in the United States was unsettled. In 1972 the U.S. Supreme Court had invalidated all death penalty statutes because of the gross racism in how they were applied. Nearly every state was then attempting to enact new constitutional statutes which the Court was just beginning to rule on. This was the situation when Kleasen was brought to trial for killing Darley and Fischer.

Even though there seems to be little doubt Kleasen was the killer, his conviction was reversed on appeal and he was never retried. As a lawyer who specializes in death row cases, I was particularly interested in how the criminal justice system responded to such a situation. All of this clearly added up, I felt, to a story worth reading.

What follows isn't intended to support the death penalty. Personally, I'm opposed to all executions. Nor is it an indictment of the American criminal justice system. In some ways, I realize, justice was frustrated in this case. However, it also illustrates how cases can work out in the real world of criminal law. And while I believe Kleasen was a murderer and, like everyone else, would prefer that he be locked up, I found considerable evidence of the forces that shaped him. I believe that understanding these forces—however much we may want to ignore them or tell ourselves they could never affect us—may help to prevent future Kleasens.

As with many religious and cultural communities, Mormons sometimes have a language of their own and concepts peculiar to Latter-day Saint life. I have attempted to explain these terms and beliefs for non-Mormon readers. Mormonism is more than a religious denomination; in many ways, it is close to an ethnic community.

Much of this book is drawn from Texas, New York, and federal court transcripts. Additional information comes from extensive newspaper coverage of Kleasen over the years. Quotations from those sources don't always translate neatly into writing, so I've occasionally taken the liberty of slightly rewording some to make them read more smoothly. In every instance, however, the plain meaning of the quotes has been preserved. Whenever the quotation is ambiguous, or its language is critical, it is used exactly as found.

This book would have been impossible without the help of many people, some of whom were kind enough to revisit old, often unpleasant memories. I conducted about fifty interviews of varying lengths. For most, recalling events twenty years in the past in great detail was difficult. In many instances recollections didn't always square with the existing documentary record. Whenever such conflicts were present, I chose to rely on the contemporary written record. Periodically, some of the people I spoke with still feared Kleasen or had other reasons for not wanting to be identified. In other instances I felt that some of the parties who couldn't be located wouldn't have wanted to be identified by their real names. For these reasons I've used several fictional names in the book. Each of these instances is identified.

Several Austin Mormons who knew Kleasen offered invaluable insights, along with a few former LDS missionaries who served in Texas and New York. Frank and Norma McCullough, Eddie Davis, Bruce and Ruth Smith, Richard and Lynn Odell, Caleb West (not his real name), and Larry Doty provided important background into Kleasen's Mormon involvement. Lance Chase, now on the faculty at

Brigham Young University in Hawaii, supplied helpful information on Mark Fischer.

In New York several individuals who tracked Kleasen both before and after the murders went out of their way to help. Veteran Wayne County probation officer David Williams prepared thorough PreSentence Investigation Reports on Kleasen. As a result, he was able to supply history critical to this book. New York parole officer Richard Low provided useful insights and documentation. Wayne County public defender Ron Valentine was another helpful interviewee. Retired Buffalo City police officer and district attorney investigator Dick Murphy spent years gathering information on Kleasen which he generously shared. The New York aspects of this book could not have been written without Murphy's generosity.

Veteran Buffalo civil rights lawyer David Jay, who represented Kleasen from 1988 to 1990, was gracious and candid. Several administrators and residents of both the downtown Buffalo City Mission and Lafayette Hotel also willingly talked about a man whose friendship might have embarrassed many people. I appreciate as well one of his unwitting pen pals, Ann-Eliza Young (not her real name) of Northern Ireland.

Retired Austin police lieutenant Colon Jordan spent hours going through records in his possession and reflecting on the 1974 murder investigation he coordinated. Texas wildlife officer Max Hartman, now a state magistrate-judge in Fredericksburg, was helpful in interviews as well, as were Texas game officer Norm Henk, retired FBI agent Joe Butler, and former Austin police officer Doug Ferris.

Several of the Austin attorneys involved with the murder case provided helpful interviews and/or documents. In particular, Pat Ganne and David Bays, junior members of Kleasen's 1975 trial defense team, were generous with their time. Former assistant district attorney Charlie Craig provided invaluable interviews. Phil Nelson, who is still with the Travis County district attorney, and Richard Banks, formerly a Travis County prosecutor and later an assistant United States attorney in Houston, were helpful as well. Travis County district attorney witness-victim assistance counselor Bobbi

Neyland wasn't part of the Kleasen case but provided important insights into the expected experiences of the surviving parents of murdered children.

Very late in the writing process, I also received help from Kleasen's fourth wife, Marie Longley, from Vera Fawden, and from her son Joe Fawden. To the extent they were allowed under British law to discuss their ongoing investigations of Kleasen, several Humberside law enforcement officers made contributions to this book as well.

I spent many days in the clerk's office of the Texas Court of Criminal Appeals studying the lengthy appellate record of the 1975 capital murder conviction. The CCA, as it is known to Texas lawyers, is the state's highest court for criminal matters. (There is a Texas Supreme Court for civil law matters.) Every person in that office went out of his or her way to assist me. Presiding judge Mike McCormick took more than a passing interest in the project and made himself available to bounce ideas off as well as to help locate Texas participants in these events. Clerk of the court Troy Bennett, chief deputy clerk George Miller, and deputy clerks Abel Acosta, Faye Koenig, John Brown, Belva Myler, Louise Pearson, and Greg Ross all helped at one time or another. I thank each for his or her many courtesies. Likewise, the staffs at the Blanco County and Travis County, Texas, courthouses, as well as at the Erie County, New York, courthouse, were consistently helpful. The Austin History Center provided a number of photographs from 1974, 1975, and 1978. These originated with the *Austin American-Statesmen*. This resource added considerably to the book.

I invested considerable effort in gathering public government and law enforcement records on Kleasen. My thanks to the Texas Department of Public Safety and its crime lab; the Freedom of Information Act offices of the Federal Bureau of Alcohol, Tobacco, and Firearms; the U.S. State Department; and the Central Intelligence Agency for records, confirmations, and denials they provided.

The Church of Jesus Christ of Latter-day Saints History Department in Salt Lake City, Utah, has an invaluable file on Kleasen's involvement with the Mormon church in both Denmark and Texas. Its archives also contain useful local records on the Texas San Antonio

Mission and the Austin First Ward (congregation). (As one non-Mormon interviewee said, "Them Mormons, they never throw anything away.") Steven Sorensen, Ronald Barney, William Slaughter, Larry Draper, Linda Haslam, April Williamson, Ronald Watt, and Richard Davis, along with others, steadily assisted me with this and other writing projects.

Sunstone magazine of Salt Lake City published a lengthy article drawn from this book in its December 1997 issue. I appreciate its interest and in particular managing editor Eric Jones's efforts. That article brought several letters from individuals who had firsthand knowledge of these events which added to the book. Among those was retired University of Wisconsin and Brigham Young University law professor Edward L. Kimball, whose help is much appreciated.

Very special thanks to James and Catherine Fischer of Milwaukee. They are the parents of Mark Fischer who had just begun a mission for the LDS church when he was killed. Mark's brothers Matthew and Martin and sister Melissa were also open with their experiences.

The family of the second victim, Gary Darley, was equally gracious. Gary's father David K., his older brother Kelle Darley, and other members of their large family were ready to share their memories. Kelle in particular provided case records and Gary's missionary journals which were indispensable in telling this story. Unfortunately Gary's mother, Jill, passed away in 1994.

I am painfully aware that this book forced both families to relive what has to be the most difficult experience any relative can ever be confronted with. Their tears left me with more than a little guilt about reopening this chapter in their otherwise happy lives. I hope this book will in some small way add to their positive memories of good sons.

Friends at the offices of my former employer, the Texas Resource Center in Austin, helped me in ways they probably don't appreciate. In particular I want to thank Eden Harrington who brought me to Austin where this book was an unintended by-product. Grace Adame translated some Spanish language materials that filled in details. They and a few others there also helped to make this book possible.

Mike and Tracy Graff, friends from the Round Rock Ward of the

LDS church just north of Austin, read through drafts and made a number of useful suggestions. Their questions and insights greatly improved the book.

The events in Great Britain set out at the end of this book came to my attention while I was a senior staff attorney at the Atlanta-based Multicounty Public Defender's Office. At times this last-minute work was an inconvenience for that office, and I would like to thank my co-workers for their tolerance, especially Mike Mears.

Finally, I appreciate the members of my own family for their steady support. My parents, Don F. and Dorothea Heiserman Driggs, of Tallahassee, Florida, my brother Randy, who is a criminal defense lawyer in Los Angeles, and my sister, Patricia Knight, of New Hope, Pennsylvania, all helped me overcome financial binds, writer's block, stress, and frustration. My sister in particular never let me get discouraged about the project or trip over the many hurdles.

Prologue

The early to mid-1970s was a time of paranoia in American history, and the events described in this book are probably best understood in the context of those tumultuous years. Certainly, Bob Kleasen seems a creature manufactured by the worst of that era.

The Vietnam War was raging, and in May 1972 a lunatic shot and paralyzed race-baiting U.S. presidential candidate George Wallace. Later that same year Watergate erupted; House impeachment and Senate investigative hearings followed the next year. Arab terrorists shocked the world with the slaughter of eleven Israeli participants in the summer Olympics in 1973. Patty Hearst was kidnapped by domestic terrorists the following February, then resurfaced as a bank robber working with them. Richard Nixon proved himself a crook and resigned in disgrace on August 9, 1974. Early the next year, another congressional committee began to investigate abuses by both the CIA and the FBI. Teamsters boss Jimmy Hoffa disappeared in July 1975. Two months later two different crazies tried to assassinate U.S. president Gerald Ford less than three weeks apart. Utah murderer Gary Gilmore demanded execution and was shot by a firing squad on January 17, 1977. Elvis Presley died of a drug overdose later that August.

Perhaps the times demanded that Bob Kleasen come into existence. His acts insured that a peaceful Mormon community would not escape the violence of the era.

ONE

ON SUNDAY, NOVEMBER 3, 1974, ELDER GARY SMITH DARLEY, twenty, and his roommate Elder Mark J. Fischer, nineteen, didn't show up for the all-male priesthood meeting at the Austin Ward of the Church of Jesus Christ of Latter-day Saints.

No one had heard from them since late Monday afternoon, October 28. In the thoroughly regulated life of the full-time volunteer Mormon missionary, this was unusual, especially for two dutiful young men. Darley was a district leader responsible for the spiritual and physical well-being of six to ten other young missionaries; Fischer was an earnest "greenie" barely five weeks into his two-year mission.

Alarm bells had begun to ring in the Austin Mormon community a few days earlier. The two missionaries were last seen heading for a dinner engagement at the rural trailer home of Bob Kleasen, a troublesome recent Mormon convert they hoped to reactivate. They were wearing the Mormon missionaries' standard dress: white shirts, ties, dress slacks, and dress shoes. They also wore distinctive black plastic name tags over their breast pockets. Both were tall and thin, the green-eyed Darley standing 6'1" and 150 pounds, while Fischer was 6' and 170 pounds.

Local church authorities had been warned by Mormon headquarters in Salt Lake City that Kleasen might be a con man who should be watched closely. The previous week Kleasen had had an angry confrontation with other church members. He loved firearms and violent talk. The lay bishop of the Austin Ward, Frank McCullough, had advised the young missionaries not to have any further contact with Kleasen. Darley, the more experienced "senior companion," told McCullough they felt obligated to keep this last dinner commitment.

The two missionaries had failed to show up for another dinner on

Tuesday, October 29, with Larry and Sandy Wall, a young Mormon couple near their age. Church members are encouraged to feed the low-budget missionaries often. Their no-show was uncharacteristic and the Walls were immediately concerned. By 9:30 or 10:00 p.m., they were calling other Mormons who knew the missionaries, wondering what had happened to them. One of those calls was to Richard and Lynn Odell, recent converts who'd been taught about Mormonism by Darley. Local Mormons soon learned the missionaries had also missed an appointment with another investigator, Rollo Greene.

The young missionaries' landlady, Dora Jones, became concerned after not seeing them for several days. She contacted Austin Stake president Amos Wright through a relative. (A Mormon stake is roughly the equivalent of a Catholic archdiocese.) Jones had rented a small two- bedroom upstairs apartment in her home to many Mormon missionaries and had come to know how regulated and predictable her tenants' lives were.

"I knew something was wrong," Jones later told a reporter. "Those boys never took off like that before."

Wright contacted the local mission zone leaders, young men of a similar age who supervised the goings and comings of the thirty or thirty-two Mormon missionaries in the Austin area. Elders Conrad Brent Hardcastle and Christopher Warnock made repeated calls to Darley's and Fischer's little 313 West Mary Street apartment but got no answer. They then alerted the headquarters of the San Antonio Mission that something was wrong.

The anxious zone leaders decided to check the missing young men's apartment. What they saw concerned them even more.

The missing elders' luggage, clothing, money, and possessions all were there. University of Texas t-shirts Fischer had bought for younger brothers and sisters the previous Monday were in their store bag on his dresser. Their beds had not been slept in. Mormon missionaries typically limit the number of clothes they take on a mission, including for some a maximum of eight shirts, always white. Hardcastle found seven neatly hung shirts for each missionary in the closet. None were in the laundry even though it was several days since the two could have last done their wash. The apartment suggested that no one had entered it for several days.

Their now very concerned mission president, Ronald Lee Loveland of Idaho, called Hardcastle and Warnock at the apartment for a report. The two told Loveland they'd last seen the missing missionaries on Monday, the 28th. Darley and Hardcastle had been missionary companions earlier and their bond was sufficiently close that they made a point to spend free time together.

Monday is the missionaries' day off, a time to do laundry, write letters home, and get some exercise. Darley, Fischer, Hardcastle, Warnock, and two other missionaries, Charles Rogers and Randall Lomax, met at the LDS institute building on San Antonio Street next to the University of Texas campus. They played ping pong and chess, then walked to a UT gym, Belmont Hall, where Hardcastle worked out with a gymnastics team. On the way Fischer stopped at the Co-op Book Store on Guadalupe Street to buy the Longhorn t-shirts that were found on his dresser.

As the clock drew towards 3:30, Darley and Fischer had left the gym, saying they had a regular dinner engagement with Kleasen set for 5:00. Recently they'd joined the man for Monday night dinners in an effort to befriend him. Active Mormons gather on Monday nights for "Family Home Evening," a time of fellowship and religious discussion. Mormons who aren't part of families often gather together in their own groups, which was why Darley and Fischer joined Kleasen on Mondays.

That Monday afternoon they had invited Hardcastle along. Darley told him, "We're going out to the country to eat venison with a member who feeds us all the time."

But Darley had also told his four missionary friends he "felt uneasy" about the dinner engagement, that he was "apprehensive." He was probably thinking about the recent warning from Bishop McCullough as well as his own growing personal discomfort with Kleasen.

Hardcastle thought about joining them until he remembered a conflicting appointment to teach investigators about the church.

About 4:00 p.m. a neighbor, James Thomas, saw Darley and

Fischer driving west on West Mary Street, toward Kleasen's trailer, in their little white American Motors Hornet. He was the last person—except Kleasen—to see the two alive.

What none of the concerned Texas Mormons knew was that Darley's father, David K., back in Simi Valley, had heard a disturbing message. In the early morning hours of Tuesday, October 29, he'd been awakened by a voice calling out to him, "Dad" or "David." He thought it was his son Clark, the only person in the house with him that night. Groggily, he walked to Clark's room but found the boy asleep. Puzzled, the father returned to bed wondering what he'd heard.

TWO

BOB KLEASEN HAD BEEN A MORMON FOR JUST OVER A YEAR IN late October 1974. He was around six feet, weighed just under 200 pounds, and had an odd stare that could be disconcerting. His thick dark hair, which was beginning to streak gray, was usually combed in a vaguely Elvis Presley style. Kleasen looked rugged, was stocky but not muscular; some found him attractive. He favored jeans and white t-shirts. He'd recently secured work as a carpenter on Austin area building sites.

On Tuesday, October 29, Kleasen didn't seem unusual. He was allowed to live in a twenty-two foot aluminum camper trailer behind the Austin Taxidermy Studio by longtime associate Lem Rathbone who ran the place with his sons. Rathbone was a gruff, crusty character, but his taxidermy skills were much prized by Texas hunters. On most days Rathbone arrived about 7:00 a.m. and was there until 5:00 or 6:00 p.m.

Kleasen often hung around the shop. On Tuesdays he usually left early for a Pentecostal Church meeting, but on this Tuesday he decided not to go. It was a cool rainy day; maybe he didn't want to go out in the weather. Kleasen's cars were notoriously unreliable as well.

That night Kleasen made a collect call to Rev. Rick Rickaby of the Burnet Pentecostal Church. Rickaby refused the call, and Kleasen called back a few minutes later at his own expense. He was agitated because, he said, Rickaby had refused the earlier call. Kleasen said he only wanted Rickaby, an electrician, to wire one of the sheds near his trailer. Two days later Rickaby came to the taxidermy studio and did the work.

That Friday, November 1, Clay Rathbone walked around the grounds of the business looking for deer tracks. He was the son of the taxidermist and had known Kleasen for several years. Lem Rathbone owned the 4.5-acre parcel where his business was located; most of it was undeveloped. About a hundred yards from the buildings near Kleasen's homemade shooting range, Clay noticed a name tag and a little "prayer book" in the grass. Each item had a bullet hole through it, but no powder burns. Inside the prayer book was a folded Mormon temple recommend, a pass faithful Mormons are issued for admission into temples which they consider to be sacred.

Clay took the materials to his father. The temple recommend—he couldn't remember whose name was on it—hadn't expired, so he figured someone would be looking for it. But Lem decided the name tag and papers weren't worth saving and threw them away.

"To me they were just a piece of paper with a hole in it," Lem later said. He agreed it was a bullet hole, but didn't think anything of it because it was found next to Kleasen's homemade shooting range.

Two days later, on Sunday, November 3, Kleasen burned the trash. As soon as Clay read about the missionaries' disappearance in the next day's paper, he started looking for the name tag and prayer book, but couldn't find them.

On Saturday, November 2, Bishop McCullough, a civil engineering and transportation professor at the University of Texas, called Bruce Yarborough, a Mormon FBI agent in his congregation. Yarborough lived near the taxidermy shop. McCullough wanted to know whom to call to report the missing boys. Yarborough answered that since Kleasen lived on Highway 290 West, ten miles outside Austin on the edges of the hill country, he should call the Travis County sheriff's department. McCullough called the sheriff and Travis County deputy John Barton was asked to investigate.

Barton arrived at Kleasen's trailer before midnight on Saturday, November 2. No one was home. He returned at 1:30 in the morning and found Kleasen's American Motors car beside the darkened trailer. The deputy and an accompanying patrolman knocked on the trailer's door. They heard a loud noise, like someone stumbling in the dark. Inside a man yelled a couple times.

After a few moments Kleasen came to the door looking groggy. He sat down on the step to talk to Barton. He said he "fixed up quite a large dinner" for the missionaries, but "they never showed up." After a few minutes the deputy left with no new information on the missionaries' whereabouts.

Later that Sunday morning, mission president Loveland and an assistant, Tim Gines, drove to Austin from San Antonio. They met at the Parker Lane meeting house with stake president Wright, Bishop McCullough, and two men who assisted McCullough, Ed Guyon and Yarborough. Guyon was McCullough's executive secretary and helped with church administrative matters. He was a recent University of Texas law graduate with a new Austin practice. He knew Kleasen and was troubled by him. Yarborough was a ward assistant executive secretary. He'd secured permission from his FBI superiors to investigate the matter in an official capacity. Both were large men.

Also the previous night someone undertook the painful task of notifying each boy's parents that the two missionaries had been missing for almost six days. In Milwaukee that duty fell to Bishop Jack Vogl, a police officer and friend of the Fischer family. (LDS church records spell his name Vogel, while the Fischer family recalls the spelling as Vogl.)

In Simi Valley, California, David Darley was awakened about 6:00 a.m. by his bishop and stake president at his front door, both looking sober and distressed. They'd been called by Salt Lake City church authorities and asked to convey the news that Gary was missing. Darley immediately thought of the voice crying out to him early the previous Tuesday morning.

The Austin group decided Guyon and Yarborough should try to meet with Kleasen, so later in the morning they drove out to the trailer. Guyon, a military veteran, now recalls that both men felt there was substantial risk in the assignment. Yarborough brought his FBI-issued handgun.

The two drove the fifteen miles or so out to the Oak Hill community, parked their car at the taxidermy shop near the crest of a hill, and walked toward the square silver trailer in back. It was about 10:00 a.m. A man came toward them from an area of old sheds on the property. "Can I help you?" he asked.

Yarborough said they were looking for Bob Kleasen. The man replied, "I'm Bob Kleasen." Guyon walked up and they talked at the trailer hitch of the camper, not moving around the property.

"I identified myself to him by showing him my credentials and told him I was a special agent for the FBI. I told him that we were searching for a car that belonged to two missionaries who had been missing for several days and that they were last seen heading for his place to have dinner," Yarborough later testified.

"He [Kleasen] said, 'They did not come.' He said, 'I have no reason to believe that they would have come although they have been here before.'"

Yarborough recalled that Kleasen specifically said "he didn't expect them" on the night of the 28th. Deputy Barton had earlier been told by Kleasen that he prepared a big meal for them.

Yarborough asked if he could look around inside the trailer. Kleasen refused but agreed to let the FBI man look in the windows, and then only after Kleasen went inside to conceal an object in the carpenter's apron he wore.

While Yarborough looked in the windows, seeing nothing, Kleasen talked to Guyon. They set up an appointment for Kleasen to see Bishop McCullough later that afternoon.

Guyon and Yarborough returned to the LDS meetinghouse to report. For the remainder of the day, the group called everyone they could think of who might know something about Kleasen. This resulted in a meeting with a Texas Game and Fish officer. Kleasen was a notorious poacher who hunted year round without regard to seasons or bag limits. Yarborough began assembling a list of the firearms Kleasen had in his possession when game officers encountered him.

Kleasen came to the ward meeting hall at 2:00 p.m. Bishop McCullough had gone on to an outlying congregation and missed him. Kleasen met with one of McCullough's counselors instead. Kleasen's first nervous comment on arriving at the chapel was that he knew nothing of the missing missionaries.

Since returning from Kleasen's trailer, Yarborough had been using his professional contacts to learn what he could about Kleasen.

He found that the 1964 Rambler station wagon parked in front of Kleasen's trailer was registered in Texas to a Richard C. Raadt with an Austin post office box for an address. Texas had issued driver's licenses to both Raadt and Kleasen, both reflecting 1931 birth years.

While Guyon and Yarborough investigated, other church leaders were interviewing any member they could think of who had contact with Kleasen. One was a young member named Jack Paris who, along with his wife Chris, had been encouraged by missionaries to fellowship the man. Paris had been a dinner guest at Kleasen's trailer several times. Stake president Wright and one of Bishop McCullough's counselors caught Paris at church and asked what he knew about Kleasen.

The Parises fed missionaries two or three nights a week and enjoyed their company. Gary Darley was a regular guest. It was through missionaries that Jack met Kleasen and tried to fellowship him. Paris told them about Kleasen's CIA stories and of his once threatening suicide, holding a loaded pistol to his head. The young Mormon had begun to fear Kleasen and was careful not to cross him.

In Simi Valley David Darley, who was a Mormon stake high councilor, had been assigned to visit an outlying congregation that Sunday. He struggled to get through the day, sometimes sobbing and thinking, "Gary's gone, Gary's gone ..."

By Monday, a week after the missionaries had last been seen, fear for them among Mormons increased dramatically.

On Monday, November 4, Loveland and Gines provided local law enforcement, which were starting to treat the matter seriously, with all the information they had.

At the time missing persons cases were handled by the juvenile division. One of the first officers asked to investigate the matter was Doug Ferris.

Lieutenant Colon Jordan heard about the case and knew it could be more than just kids running off. A veteran cop of twenty-two years, Jordan had been in charge of homicide investigations since 1972. He went to police chief Bob Miles and asked to be more involved.

Assistant district attorney David Spencer, the liaison with the police department, was also informed. However, because the matter was unfolding in such an unusual way, the DA's office was not very involved in the early stages of the investigation.

Yarborough continued to work the telephone and his law enforcement contacts. On Monday he talked to missionary Blair Bell who'd labored in Austin but had recently been transferred to Houston. Bell had unwittingly become one of Kleasen's regular pen pals since his transfer.

Yarborough learned from Bell that Kleasen had shown off a driver's license with his photograph but identifying him as Richard C. Raadt. He explained to Bell that he used it for purchases he didn't want traced to him. On one occasion Bell accompanied Kleasen to a local firearms dealer where he purchased reloading components using this identification. Yarborough immediately passed this information on to the federal Bureau of Alcohol, Tobacco, and Firearms.

Then Yarborough talked to Bill Millner, a Texas Department of Public Safety official. Millner had compared the thumb prints accompanying the Raadt and Kleasen driver's licenses and had determined they were from the same person.

Mormon leaders met with local media, and by the evening news the case was a major story. The front page of the evening *Austin American-Statesman* ran the headline "Two Missionaries Reported Missing" with photographs of Darley and Fischer.

"They were good, reliable, dependable young men, or they wouldn't have left their schools and homes and families to come down here," the Mormon leaders told reporters. "We are very much afraid for their lives, and the concern of their parents is tremendous."

The first break in the case had actually come two nights earlier, but had not been reported through police channels until Monday.

It was Austin police sergeant A. P. Lamme who found the missionaries' abandoned car Friday night, November 1. A seven-and-a-half-year veteran of the force, Lamme was in narcotics at the time. Working undercover with an informant, he'd been hanging around the Inwood Apartments on South Lamar. He hadn't been looking for the car, but for the open drug dealing they believed was going on.

About 7:00 that evening, Lamme and his informant started lounging on a curb on the east side of the complex, trying to look as indigenous as possible. He soon noticed what looked like an abandoned American Motors Hornet. "It was sitting on concrete blocks," he recalled, and "appeared to have been sitting there a few days." Lamme noticed "the windshield was dirty, and it was sitting up on those concrete blocks with leaves and dirt piling up on it.

"The leaves apparently had been washed down against the blocks where it collected. You know, it was a little stack like they normally do when you have a rain." It had rained a lot in the past week. There were no license plates, but the hood and trunk were down and the doors were locked. The tires, wheels, and lug nuts were all missing.

Lamme couldn't inspect the car too closely, but made a mental note of it. "You get into a problem of being robbed when you're going out making these buys, and so you want to be kind of familiar with the vehicles that are normally there." He and the informant thought the car was probably stolen, and were "just passing the time while we were waiting for something else to happen." Both men left the area a couple of hours later. Lamme planned to point out the car to their auto theft division. He saw the car again several times on Saturday.

Two days later, on Monday morning, November 4, Lamme read the newspaper article about the two missionaries. The article mentioned that they were last seen driving a white two-door American Motors Hornet sedan. He immediately reported the car to the officers investigating the case. About the same time a Mormon woman named Carol Wise who lived in the apartment complex called police to report the abandoned car.

When officers arrived to inspect the car, the license plate was gone but they noticed a bumpersticker reading "Happiness Is Family Home Evening" given out by the LDS church.

At 4:00 p.m. mission president Loveland was at the FBI office with Yarborough preparing to call church headquarters in Salt Lake City to report on the situation. Before he placed the call, they learned that the missionaries' car had been found. They quickly drove to the Inwood Apartments.

The car was sitting on pumice blocks, some of them streaked with brown stains. Officers had popped the trunk which was empty except for a single Spanish-language missionary pamphlet. The jack and spare tire—an almost new black wall Goodyear—were missing. The inside of the car was likewise empty except for a rag on the floor and gas receipts in the ash tray. When officers opened the hood, they found someone had cut the battery cables, but that the battery remained in place.

Officers first fingerprinted the car, then took dirt samples from the exterior. After it was removed to a police impoundment facility, other officers fanned out through the apartment complex to interview anyone who might have seen something. Those apartment residents who had noticed the car recalled first seeing it on October 28 or 29.

Federal Bureau of Alcohol, Tobacco, and Firearms agent Dale Littleton was assigned the Kleasen case that Monday. ATF agent Roger Bowers had compiled a list of firearms Kleasen possessed during his various encounters with game officers. That information alone did not mean much, but it was a starting point. Littleton was also working with a lead from FBI agent Yarborough that Kleasen had bought guns using the name Richard Raadt.

Littleton took the list and contacted the National Tracing Center in Washington, D.C. With the make and serial numbers of the weapons, the center backtracked through the manufacturers to the retail sellers and from there to required federal paperwork filled out by the buyer.

Meanwhile, Bill Bluntzer, a high school kid who had worked at the Austin Taxidermy Studio for three years and had known Kleasen for half that time, was talking to his friend Jeff Rathbone about the name tag and papers Jeff had found the previous Friday. Bill got curious. Around 9:30 a.m. on Tuesday, November 5, he went out back of the shop to look around in the tall grass and weeds.

Twenty-five or thirty yards from the trailer along a fence where Kleasen had set up a shooting range, Bill found another 3-inch-by-3-inch black-and-white plastic pocket name tag. It read:

Elder M. J. Fischer
Texas-San Antonio Mission
Church of Jesus Christ of Latter-day Saints

There was a hole in the lower right-hand corner; it looked like a bullet hole.

Bluntzer gave the name tag to Lem Rathbone who this time called FBI agent Yarborough. Yarborough called the Austin police. Within minutes Austin police sergeant Doug Ferris drove to the shop to pick it up. Sergeant Harold Bilberry and a police photographer, Richard "Curley" Jones, joined him.

Kleasen was gone for the day.

Bluntzer led Ferris around back and showed him where he'd found the name tag in the tall grass. Ferris quickly called his supervisor, Lieutenant Jordan, to tell him about the find. By 11:00 Ferris was joined at the taxidermist's by Jordan, Sergeant Al Riley, and Texas Ranger Wallace Spillar.

Lem Rathbone consented to a search; no warrant was needed. The officers scoured the shop and grounds without finding anything more, and by 3:30 returned to police headquarters.

Meanwhile Agent Littleton got his first hit from the National Tracing Center. A Browning .22 rifle had been purchased by a Robert E. Kleasen at McBride's Guns in Austin on August 11, 1973. The buyer had filled out forms indicating he was neither under indictment for a felony nor a fugitive from justice. He also answered on the form that he had never been adjudicated mentally defective or been committed to a mental hospital. The printed forms warned that "the making of any false oral or written statement" was a felony. Kleasen had used a Texas driver's license for identification.

By this time Littleton and other investigators had learned that Kleasen had jumped bail on a 1971 Wayne County, New York, felony assault charge. He apparently had shot a man. Later they would learn he also had a history of psychiatric treatment.

With this information Littleton went to federal magistrate Phil Sanders about 4:00 p.m. He sought and got a criminal complaint for the illegal purchase of the Browning .22 rifle, and a search warrant for the trailer.

Just as now, police in 1974 were not allowed to burst into a person's residence to search on a hunch or suspicion. Except in certain limited circumstances—such as when the property owner gives police permission to search, as Rathbone had, or when seized items are already in "plain view"—officers must get a search warrant first, and the issuance of that warrant is subject to later review.

Littleton presented a sworn affidavit in support of the application for a warrant. He alleged that Kleasen had bought a Browning .22 rifle at McBride's gun shop in violation of the 1968 federal Gun Control Act and concealed it in his trailer on the Rathbone property. As substantiation for this claim—"probable cause"—Littleton said an unnamed "reliable citizen who lives near ROBERT KLEASEN" had said within the past week he saw Kleasen shooting a firearm on the property and in possession of other guns. The magistrate quickly issued the search warrant, possibly based on some oral representations by Littleton which were not part of later appellate records.

Littleton brought his search warrant to the taxidermy shop and Kleasen's camper trailer about 6:00 or 6:30 that evening. ATF agent Earl Dunagan accompanied him. The two had asked for "assistance" from local law enforcement and were joined by Jordan, Riley, Bilberry, Ferris, and Jones of the Austin police department and Texas Ranger Spillar. Lieutenant Jordan and Ranger Spillar did not seize any evidence themselves, but supervised.

Littleton first searched the rundown buildings around Kleasen's trailer and found firearms, ammunition, and "component parts" for more guns. Agent Dunagan found a gray suitcase with a slide projector and hundreds of pornographic color slides. In a trailer closet Sergeant Riley found a tooled leather shaving case. It contained several watches, old coins, and photographs. Several photographs were nude black-and-white pictures of young women Kleasen would later claim were previous wives.

One watch was a Seiko with blood spattered on the band. It was self-winding but had stopped at 6:00 p.m., October 30, 1974. Knowing that nothing in the case came within the scope of the search warrant, Riley left it but first showed it to Lieutenant Jordan. Someone later told a newspaper reporter about the watches and they were mentioned in the *Austin American-Statesman* the next morning.

In a drawer under the sink, Riley found a key ring which included one for an American Motors car, a padlock key, and a key to a bicycle lock. Later in the day Sergeant Bilberry took the key ring to where Kleasen's Rambler station wagon was impounded. One opened the door; another fit the ignition. From there he went to the missionaries' Mary Street apartment. Another key fit the padlock the young men used to lock their front door. Still another key was later found to fit the bike lock belonging to one of the missionaries.

In other drawers Riley and Dunagan found a birth certificate and other identification papers for a Richard Carl Raadt. By now officers knew of Kleasen's alias. There was also a driver's license for Don Eugene Carrington of Richardson, Texas, along with passport pictures of Kleasen.

In a drawer under the trailer refrigerator was a short "Dear Brother Kleasen" letter from missing missionary Darley confirming their October 28 dinner engagement. Dated Saturday, October 19, the letter canceled a dinner commitment for the 21, but promised "We'll plan on seeing you Mon. the 28th."

In that same drawer was a letter addressed to John T. Williamson at Kleasen's Austin post office box. It was from the pastor of a Buffalo church saying a Francis Raadt was buried at his church in an unknown year.

There were several books of Mormon scripture, each with the fly page neatly cut out. A few had inscriptions to Kleasen from various Mormon missionaries.

There was also a manuscript typed on yellow paper: "My Thousand Whitetails a Poacher's Notebook," authored by John T. Williamson. It was the work of a braggart, proud of his poaching accomplishments, especially the kills and getting away with it. Part of that manuscript discussed how to dispose of deer carcasses.

In addition, the officers found several written records of Kleasen's purchases of firearms, some fuses, blasting caps, and primer cord. Also, ten firearms and reloading supplies were found in and around the trailer.

With the search, the officers felt they had enough to take Kleasen into custody.

THREE

WHILE THE SEARCH WAS BEING CONDUCTED, OTHER OFFICERS had located Bob Kleasen in Burnet, an hour or so away. He was attending a Pentecostal church's Tuesday night meeting, as was his habit. Lieutenant Jordan, who had coordinated much of the day's raid, had been in touch with the Burnet County sheriff. Jordan knew Kleasen was "packing" and did not want the suspect arrested in church. No one wanted a shoot-out.

About 9:30 p.m. a Burnet County deputy radioed to the search party that the church meeting was breaking up and that now was the time to move on Kleasen. Jordan, Spillar, and Littleton were already on their way.

Before Kleasen could return to his Rambler station wagon, Littleton peered in the windows. On the backseat he saw an open guncase with a Walther .22 Hornet rifle within easy reach of the driver's seat. It was later identified as one of the illegally purchased weapons.

Finally Kleasen came out of the church, apparently without noticing anything unusual. He talked to a few people as he left, got into his car, and headed south on Highway 281 toward his Oak Hill home. There were a hundred or more church people still in the area.

Kleasen drove a mile or a mile and a half before officers surrounded him with police cars and forced him to the side of the road. Everyone had their weapons drawn. An obviously surprised Kleasen muttered, "Why are you after me? I didn't do anything." He surrendered meekly. Officers quickly moved him away from the car and frisked him.

In the front seat right beside Kleasen was a hunting knife with a five- or six-inch blade. It was underneath some Austin newspapers with articles about the missing missionaries. Under the seat and his right leg was a loaded Colt .357 magnum pistol and holster. These were in addition to the rifle in the back seat. Officers first secured the rifle, then the pistol, ejecting the shells. Littleton took the firearms into custody.

Kleasen was arrested and placed in Jordan's police car for the trip back to Austin. Littleton took Kleasen's keys and drove the Rambler to a secure storage facility. Kleasen told him the heater didn't work and it was a cold night out.

When someone is arrested in their car and cannot make arrangements on their own to have it picked up, law enforcement tows and impounds the vehicle. Police often relish this opportunity because it allows them to thoroughly search it without a warrant under the guise of inventorying the contents. The rationale of inventory searches is to protect law enforcement from false claims over property that might turn up missing from an impounded vehicle.

Back at the Austin police department, and after Kleasen was given his Miranda warnings by a state magistrate, Jordan sat down with him. It was now 2:30 or 3:00 in the morning, November 6.

The detective took fingernail scrapings from Kleasen to be used with other trace evidence that might be recovered. He also asked for head hair samples. Kleasen plucked a few strands from his scalp which Jordan put into a small evidence envelope.

By this time Jordan knew about Kleasen's various identities, and was already thinking there might be more than one personality in play here. "I'm not talking to Bob Kleasen right now, I'm talking to Richard Raadt," he started. "Where do you think we should look for the bodies?"

Kleasen thought for a moment and answered with a riddle that still troubles Jordan. He said, "I'd look over the barrel and in the bush." Kleasen was then placed in a jail cell with other inmates. At the time the cramped jail was located on the upper floors of the Travis County Courthouse.

Later that same day Vernon Endicott was placed in the cell with Kleasen and several other black and Mexican males. Kleasen was bragging. He said police were after him for killing two people, but they had no evidence, so they had jailed him for carrying a .22 rifle.

Kleasen went on to say he knew one of the boys who had often been a guest at his dinner table, most certainly Darley, but he didn't know the second one. Endicott talked with Kleasen for about an hour and a half before Kleasen abruptly left for his bunk and went to sleep. He slept most of the remaining time Endicott was in the cell.

Endicott's son-in-law reported all this to the police a few days later; nothing he had to say added to their case.

FOUR

THROUGHOUT THE FIRST PART OF NOVEMBER, MORMONS CON-
tinued to hold out hope for Gary Darley's and Mark Fischer's return. "Our hopes are running high because of the tremendous love we
have for these young men," mission president Loveland told reporters
on Wednesday, November 6. "We have not entirely given up hope."

Loveland also praised law enforcement. "I've never known of
such loyal and great cooperation between the people of Austin and the
police and the members of the LDS church as is occurring at this
time."

Officers and a number of volunteers, including Mormon missionaries, were back searching the taxidermy studio on November 6.
Newspapers reported that eighty people helped, including Fischer's
father, Jim. This new search party fanned out over the rural Hill Country. "We don't know what we're looking for," police told Bishop
Frank McCullough. "We're just looking."

One group of volunteers from the Ft. Hood Army Base flew military helicopters over the area searching for anything that might suggest the missionaries were there.

Thirty-five to forty people combed the grounds around the taxidermy shop. Texas game officer Frank Henzy was among them. He
had been helping out almost from the beginning. On this day he was
responding to a Texas Department of Public Safety request for law enforcement officers to assist with the search.

Henzy didn't enter the trailer but noticed a large metal can close to
it. (The prosecution and defense would later argue over whether the
can was for trash or a sort of laundry drop.) He saw underwear, a pair
of pants, and a combat type jacket stuffed in the can.

Henzy pulled out the wadded clothes and looked them over. He immediately noticed blood stains on the pants and jacket and what looked like hair stuck to the pants. The blood on the pants was around the right knee in a stain about twice the size of a thumbnail. He couldn't tell if it was human blood, but it certainly warranted testing.

Another officer helping was Hays County deputy sheriff Alfred Hohman, who had come over from his home in Dripping Springs. For a time he was among eight to ten people crawling on their hands and knees in the tall grass where Bill Bluntzer had found Elder Fischer's name tag. Hohman and missionary Conrad Hardcastle, Elder Darley's close friend, found some fragments of burned papers and a split black Bic pen about a hundred yards behind the buildings. Fischer had always carried this type of pen. His father had bought him a ten- pack at the University of Utah bookstore shortly before he departed for his mission six weeks earlier.

Among the burned papers was a piece of the ministerial certificates issued to missionaries. There were also bits of the daily planner missionaries used to keep track of their weeks—"We call them our paper brains," the missionary who found the fragments said at trial. Darley's handwriting was clearly recognizable on them.

Another searcher looked under a tarp in one of the sheds near Kleasen's trailer and found a set of tires that later proved to be from the missionaries' car. Searchers also found the car's Texas license plate—HTR-410—in the same shed.

Colon Jordan logged in evidence which turned up in this and other searches. The idea was to simplify chain of custody problems for the anticipated trial.

Back in town that morning, Kleasen was asked to fill out a personal history form for ATF files—"Form 57-a" in bureaucratic jargon. He listed Burnet Pentecostal pastor Rickaby to be notified in an emergency.

The federal court set Kleasen's bond at $10,000 which he was unable to post. At first he remained in the Travis County Jail, but soon was taken to San Antonio and housed in the Bexar County Jail. Initially police would only say this was to treat "medical problems."

Kleasen made a phone call to a lawyer who had recently represented him, Randy Savage of Marble Falls. Savage would not take the case and urged Kleasen to seek a court-appointed lawyer. Kleasen did so and Austin lawyer Sal Levatino was assigned to him.

Another planned aerial search of Lem Rathbone's property and surrounding areas on Thursday, November 7, was called off because of low clouds and more rain.

The next day Texas Ranger Spillar returned to the Austin Taxidermy Studio. Rathbone told him he had several Skill and band saws, including one used to cut off deer horns and bones. Normally the saw had a metal plate attached to it, but on October 29 this had been replaced with a wooden one in anticipation of deer season. Spillar asked for the metal plate, which he took to the Texas Department of Public Safety (DPS) crime lab where tests showed the presence of human blood and head hair later identified with both victims.

Also that day Sergeant Riley accompanied a DPS criminologist to the missionaries' Mary Street apartment to lift fingerprints, hair samples, and anything else of value. There they found Elder Darley's mother, Jill, and two of his brothers, Kelle, himself a former missionary in Texas, and Clark. The Darleys had arrived by car from California on Friday, November 8, just in time to participate in a massive search the following day. (Cathy Fischer had been so distressed she could never bring herself to visit her missing son's apartment.)

They all talked for a while. Kelle described for the officers the Voumaid calendar watch he had given Gary. His description matched the watch seen in and later taken from Kleasen's trailer. The crime technician processed the apartment for fingerprints. He also gathered some papers and a butcher knife with hair on it. None of these proved to be of value.

Riley also found a note on Elder Fischer's desk dated November 1, 7:00, and with a name, address, and phone number. Riley tracked the name down—a married couple where the husband was Mormon and the wife was not. They both knew the missing missionaries but could not explain the note. Maybe Fischer had planned to contact them on that date, the couple suggested. Neither had heard from Fischer or Darley on the 1st or later.

Fearing the worst, law enforcement asked church leaders if they could secure medical records and hair samples to identify any body parts that might turn up.

In California David Darley undertook the painful task of gathering Gary's dental records and hospital x-rays which he forwarded to Texas.

A few days before leaving on his mission in January 1974, Gary Darley's mother Jill cut his shoulder-length hair. His girlfriend Kerrie Hampton was there and scooped up much of the hair from the floor with her fingers, putting it into a plastic bag and saving it along with other mementos of their relationship. She filled half the bag with Gary's hair. David Darley now drove to her home where he secured several locks of Gary's hair which he sealed in an envelope and sent to Texas.

In Milwaukee Mark Fischer's cousin Susan Fischer cut his hair two days before he left for his mission. Mark had gathered it from the floor and taken it to his girlfriend Barbara Bakewell.

Within a week of the initial Oak Hill police search, Lem Rathbone went into the trailer to gather up whatever he thought might be valuable. Lieutenant Jordan had talked with Rathbone and suggested that he collect the case containing the watches, and that if he did, the police might be interested in them. Afterwards Rathbone called Jordan to come get the watches.

On Saturday, November 9, over a thousand volunteers in 170 cars gathered from Corpus Christi, Houston, San Antonio, Austin, and other cities to search the countryside for clues. Lieutenant Jordan had asked for 600 volunteers and got many more. They were joined by off-duty sheriffs' deputies, FBI and ATF agents, game wardens, and ordinary citizens.

The Friday night before, Jordan and other officers met in the LDS meeting house with Mormons who would coordinate their volunteers. "I don't want to tell you what to look for," he told the group, "just look for anything unusual. It might be as small or unexpected as a human finger. This man traveled a lot at night and did some strange things. If we don't search the right way we might be missing a good bit." He cautioned the group not to move anything suspicious, just to mark the spot until police officers could check it out.

Another officer commented that most of Kleasen's recent "activity" had been in the Burnet area.

After Jordan's briefing, stake president Amos Wright told a reporter about Kleasen's letters to a missionary named Bell. "This man talks a lot, and some of his talk is pretty gruesome—about chopping people up and that sort of thing."

On Saturday the Austin meeting house on Parker Lane was the starting point. As drivers pulled through the parking lot, they were organized into teams, with groups of five or six teams reporting to a separate law enforcement officer. They were first instructed on what to look for and what to do if they found anything. Maps were passed out; each team was assigned a two-mile stretch of road.

From the chapel they fanned out over Travis and bordering counties. They walked up one side of the road, then down the other, searching for anything that might provide clues. When something promising was found, volunteers would stay with it until one of their police supervisors, cruising the roads of their assigned areas, came along. The officers then decided on the value of the find. Hundreds of miles of roadside were searched.

About noon two Mormons from Houston found $50,000 in counterfeit $20 bills. Most had the same serial number—K-66485860A. The bogus money was hidden in a trash bag in a brushy area near Highway 71, two miles west of the hamlet of Bee Caves. The Secret Service quickly collected the bills from the searchers but refused to say much about the matter.

The money had nothing to do with the missing missionaries but was just one more freakish event in an increasingly weird story.

Jordan recalls that it was deer season and they found a lot of sacks filled with discarded doe heads and hides. In all several pick-up trucks worth of promising items were saved for further testing, but produced nothing in the crime lab.

After the day's search, the detectives tried to be optimistic. "We're still hunting [for] them," Jordan told a reporter. "We're going to find them."

On Sunday the 10th another helicopter search by LDS servicemen from Ft. Hood was conducted. This would be the end of efforts organized by the church. Afterwards the case was developed by law enforcement alone.

That same day police searched a Burnet County park called Mormon Mills after a nineteenth-century Mormon settlement once located there. The area included a small but deep lake. The search turned up nothing of value.

FBI agent Joe Butler was even dispatched to search a barn in nearby Hayes County that a psychic had connected to the case. He found nothing.

While searchers returned to the rural roads, a police investigator raised Kleasen's impounded Rambler on a grease rack and inspected the underside. He gathered some hair he found on two wheels, along with dirt samples from the fenders. All would be tested at the DPS lab with negative results.

Also on the 11th, Littleton was back in touch with the National Tracing Center. Suddenly the Raadt identification papers became significant. The Walther .22 Hornet rifle seized by Littleton from Kleasen's car the night of his arrest had been purchased on August 25, 1973, from Don's Gun Sales in San Antonio by a Richard C. Raadt. The buyer provided a Texas driver's license for identification—probably the fake license found in Kleasen's trailer. Again the completed federal forms denied any outstanding criminal charges or prior psychiatric hospitalizations. Handwriting experts would later identify the writer as Kleasen.

With the investigation winding down, investigators returned to the trailer on November 11. Sheriff's investigator Robert Nestoroff found the manufacturer's serial number on the left side of the trailer tongue. Number 20296 turned out to be the same serial number as one on a used Twilight Bungalow trailer reported stolen from an Oak Hill mobile home dealer a year and a half earlier.

Deputy Jim Lammers and Sergeant Riley moved inside the trailer, this time without a search warrant. Riley had been part of the earlier

November 4 search. Lammers found cassette tapes and film strips on a counter by the sink—two were *Man's Search for Happiness* and *Meet the Mormons,* both used by missionaries instructing investigators. Lammers inventoried the contents of the trailer as it was being impounded.

The septic tank at the taxidermy studio was also pumped. Police collected hair, bone fragments, and other biological debris from it. Four large plastic bags of suspicious materials were left with the crime lab for testing. None of this would prove to have any value.

Taxidermist Rathbone gave Sergeant Riley the tooled leather shaving kit which had been in a closet next to the camper's refrigerator. It contained several wrist and pocket watches, including a Seiko with a blue face and a gold colored Voumard. Rathbone also turned over several pieces of jewelry, antique coins, some binoculars, and a few other items. There were two inscribed wedding rings, one from Kleasen's first marriage and one apparently from his grandparents.

That would wind up most of the investigation in the field. On November 11 Lieutenant Jordan told reporters they were going to "cool it" for a while and begin a closer examination of the evidence they had gathered. "We have some things in the lab to be examined," he explained. "We've got a lot of laboratory work that we're waiting on." Jordan would not detail everything that was to be tested, but he said they had turned over "barrels and barrels" of articles collected in the Texas Hill Country.

The next day some Mormons searching in Zilker Park on the Colorado River found what they thought were two shallow graves. They were located in thick woods on the west side of the park, a popular downtown recreation area. Police were summoned but concluded they were left over from some fisherman digging for worms.

Sometime during this period Kelle Darley and his brother Clark drove late one night to the taxidermy shop and broke into Kleasen's camper. They saw a number of things the police would later collect as evidence but didn't take anything on their own.

FIVE

JILL DARLEY AND CATHY FISCHER MET SEPARATELY WITH BOB
Kleasen in the Travis County Jail to plead for their sons. Jill visited
him for fifteen or twenty minutes one or two days after her November
10 arrival in Texas.

"I was trying to be courteous to him and see if perhaps he would
talk from the heart to me as Gary's mother," she said. Still holding out
some hope her child was alive if Kleasen would just say where, she felt
enormous pressure meeting with him. She described the experience as
"a mother's heart pleading for her son."

She thought she had begun to develop a connection with Kleasen,
but ten minutes into their conversation Sheriff Raymond Frank came
up and said in a loud voice, "Well, did you get out of him what you
wanted?" She felt that pretty much destroyed the fragile rapport she
had developed.

Jill was accompanied by her son Kelle, who had also served a mission in Texas. Kelle spoke to Kleasen privately, but the mother and
son never learned anything about the fate of the missing Gary.

Jill tried again a few days later, this time meeting with Kleasen for
another fifteen or twenty minutes. She complimented him on his efforts to make the shacks around the trailer habitable. The Darleys had
been part of the thousand-person search on November 9, thus giving
Jill a chance to inspect the taxidermy studio and grounds. Kleasen
went into great detail on how much he'd done and what the efforts
meant to him.

Then Jill took out a leather key case with her name tooled on it.
The gift meant a great deal to her, especially now. She told Kleasen
Gary had made it for her. "He was such a beautiful artist, he did such
beautiful things," she told him. Then wistfully she added, "Isn't it too

bad that Gary won't be able to do this anymore?"

"How can you, his mother, talk about your son as though he were dead?" Kleasen snapped. "I just can't imagine how you could do such a thing being his mother."

Jill began to cry and said how much she loved her son. Kleasen began to cry with her, saying that he loved Gary too.

They talked a little longer, but she couldn't recall just what was said. Again she wept for her son and for her family. She left without having learned anything about Gary's fate.

A few days later Kelle and Clark visited Kleasen. Kelle's hopes of getting some information about his brother were dashed almost immediately when the jailer who brought the suspect to them loudly stated, "Maybe you can get something out of him when everybody else has failed." Kelle was furious.

Kleasen gave the young men a limp handshake and played dumb. "At that point he just wanted to be Mr. Innocent," Kelle recalls. The two brothers left without learning anything new.

Cathy Fischer also tried. After flying from Milwaukee to Austin, Cathy first then Jim a day later, the Fischers stayed in the home of Bishop McCullough and his wife Norma. The bishop accompanied Cathy to the jail but remained at the prisoner's meeting room so that she could meet with Kleasen privately.

Cathy Fischer is a warm, outgoing, deeply religious woman, not threatening in any way. But on this day her natural vivaciousness was subdued—all she could bring with her were sorrow and anxiety. Even face to face with Kleasen whom all believed had killed her son she did not carry any hatred.

She greeted him with a handshake at the visiting room door. She had even brought him cookies and banana nut bread made by Mormon Relief Society women in an attempt to ease her pain, but a jailer at the door would not let her give it to him.

"We talked. He cried for a good part of the time that I was in there," she said of the encounter. "I told him I was concerned about the welfare of my son because the boys had been in short sleeves when they were last seen and it was cold and rainy. He said to me that he didn't think the boys were alive. It was a week and a half since they had been gone. We talked again and I told him that our family didn't have very much materially but that there was a lot of love in our house and I was concerned and I was frightened and I was worried. And he told me that if it was any comfort to me that he would be dead too."

Kleasen told her about cooking venison steaks for the missionaries. At other times he had denied that the missionaries had come to his Oak Hill trailer on October 28. This statement to Cathy suggested otherwise, however, and was probably the only time Kleasen had met Mark Fischer.

The two prayed together before Cathy left. As they parted, Cathy gave Kleasen a Book of Mormon. She wrote her name and address in the book so he could write if he had anything more to say.

Kleasen never wrote.

Like Jill Darley, Cathy Fischer left the jail without learning anything about the fate of her son.

SIX

ON WEDNESDAY, NOVEMBER 13, 1974, HOPES OF FINDING THE missionaries alive were officially abandoned. Robert E. Kleasen was officially charged with the murders of Gary Darley and Mark Fischer.

Chief Bob Miles held a press conference where he confirmed that Kleasen would be charged with capital murder—a murder in the course of a robbery. Asked about the still undiscovered bodies, Miles, said "No, we don't have bodies. We have body parts." He told reporters these body parts had been positively identified as belonging to the two missing missionaries. Police sources confirmed to at least one reporter that these parts were found on a bandsaw in the taxidermy shop.

Miles described the crimes as among the worst murders he had ever seen in Austin. The case "looks as bad as the Cross, Whitman, and Durbin cases," he said. James Cross was convicted of murdering a female University of Texas student in 1965 and was suspected in the murder of another woman. Charles Whitman had shocked the nation on August 1, 1966, when he climbed atop the University of Texas Tower with a high-powered rifle and shot forty-seven people, killing sixteen, before he was finally killed by Austin police officers. Clyde Durbin received life sentences for the 1969 shooting murder of two UT students at a local lover's lane.

Kleasen was brought into federal court that day handcuffed and wearing a blue State University of Buffalo windbreaker. He stared straight ahead, a week's worth of reddish-brown stubble on his heavy jowls.

That day he visited briefly with Linda Miller, a heavy-set piano teacher from Longview, Texas. The two had been introduced through

Pentecostal friends and corresponded for four or five months. Kleasen had kept up a veritable blizzard of mail throughout his incarceration. This was the first time he and Miller had actually met. Kleasen told her he had nothing to do with the disappearance of the two missionaries. He asked Miller to pray with and stand by him.

But Miller wasn't so ready to believe and quizzed him about the evidence. She asked about the incriminating name tag with the bullet hole in it. Kleasen said the three men were horsing around outside the trailer one day; he threw the name tag into the air, then shot a hole in it when it hit the ground.

Afterwards Miller recounted some of their conversation to reporters. She loyally insisted, "I believe him."

Kleasen's bond on the murder charges was set at $100,000.

The next day, the 14th, Texas Ranger Spillar went back to the taxidermy shop to ask Lem Rathbone for the rest of the suspected band saw. Rathbone had given him the metal plate a week earlier. This time Rathbone was less than thrilled, but he surrendered the machine. Back at the crime lab, biological residue was collected from the blade and housing for testing.

Fearing something really ghoulish, Lt. Jordan on the 19th secured a package of meat from one of the freezers which Kleasen had filled with poached deer meat. Jordan had it tested at the DPS Lab.

Some of Kleasen's Pentecostal acquaintances also anxiously brought in packages of deer meat he had given them.

It was only venison.

SEVEN

THE FISCHERS RETURNED TO MILWAUKEE SICK WITH GRIEF.
On Sunday, November 17, Cathy Fischer stood before a deeply
saddened open-microphone ward sacrament meeting to speak briefly
of her son. She read a favorite verse from the Book of Mormon that
spoke to her beloved Mark: "For the Lord suffereth the righteous to be
slain that his justice and judgment may come upon the wicked; therefore ye need not suppose that the righteous are lost because they are
slain; but behold, they do enter into the rest of the Lord their God"
(Alma 60:13).

A memorial service was held in the Milwaukee Stake Center for
their dead son on November 23, 1974. Elder Vaughn Featherstone,
second counselor in the church's Presiding Bishopric and a past president of the Texas San Antonio Mission, flew to Milwaukee to speak at
the service. The Fischer family asked that, rather than flowers, contributions be made to their ward missionary fund.

The Milwaukee Stake Center was filled to overflowing with Mormons, family friends, and supporters. It was a solemn occasion, where
the deep religious conviction of the Fischers and their friends was the
dominant emotion.

Keyte Hanson, Mark's former bishop and a member of the stake
presidency, began the meeting by praying "that we might be com-
forted with the realization and knowledge of Mark's life, purpose,
faith, and belief."

"May we remember, Father," Hanson continued, paraphrasing
Maxwell Anderson's play *Joan of Lorraine*,

> that every man and woman gives his life for what he or she believes.
> Sometimes some give their lives to little or nothing because of little or

nothing to believe in. We have but one life to live on this earth and then it is gone. May we learn to live that we will believe in those things that are everlasting, that we will so live our lives that it will not be wasted. And may memory of this occasion serve to help us live our lives better in the realization that Elders Fischer and Darley had great faith and belief in what they lived for.

Two other men who as bishops had known Mark spoke movingly of what a good young man he was, how devoted he was to his family, and of his commitment to his faith. "He was the kind of young man you hoped and prayed some day your sons would be," Bishop Vogl, himself the father of seven children, said of Mark. Former bishop and now stake patriarch Hans E. Kindt added, "Mark firmly believed that to be of service to Jesus Christ meant to go and proclaim the gospel, to leave comfort and security behind, to go forward."

Throughout the service, a choir, which called itself "the singing mothers of the Milwaukee Ward," and the congregation sang hymns Mark had most loved. The final hymn was a Mormon standard, "A Poor Wayfaring Man of Grief," sung to the Mormon prophet Joseph Smith by a disciple just before his 1844 murder by an Illinois mob. It had been Mark's favorite.

The tearful Fischer family sat in the front of the congregation listening to their son being eulogized but not speaking themselves. Because his body had not been recovered, they were not—and never would be—allowed to say good-bye.

In Utah Spencer W. Kimball, the leader of the Mormon church, was deeply moved by the murders. The night after he had been informed, he was so distressed that a physician was summoned to his home. Kimball was seventy-nine years old at the time. The doctor observed him to be visibly disturbed but could not find anything physically wrong with him. He asked Kimball, who explained that he had just received the news of the slaying of two "fine young missionaries" by a man who was a "lunatic." The doctor recalled "his concern for those missionaries and their families had made him literally ill."

Later in November David and Jill Darley were in Utah for the Thanksgiving holiday, visiting children who lived in the Salt Lake

Valley. On Friday afternoon, the 29th, President Kimball met with the Darley parents privately in his office for two hours. David Darley was surprised to notice a letter on Kimball's desk written by the wife of a friend in California. The letter described the Darleys' agony over the death of their son and urged Kimball to reach out to them. Afterwards, Kimball, a very small man, pulled from a high bookshelf a religious book he had written and inscribed it to the couple.

Their oldest son, Kelle, waited in the hallway chatting with Kimball's wife Camilla during the meeting. He was attending Brigham Young University in Provo at the time. After his parents came out, the Mormon prophet put his arm around Kelle and ushered him into the office for a few more private moments. He urged Kelle to look out for his parents and to comfort them through their difficulties.

EIGHT

WHO WAS THIS GUY KLEASEN?
  On paper there were many Robert Elmer Kleasens. During his life he used several aliases: Charles Kleasen, John T. Williamson, Richard Raadt, and Don Eugene Carrington, among others.

To anyone who would listen, Kleasen said he was a top CIA operative, a big game hunter and outstanding marksman, a brilliant scholar, a world traveler who spoke many languages, and a deeply religious man. Much of his conversation was filled with accounts of these imaginary accomplishments or the trials connected with them. He enjoyed the attention his stories brought to him.

Kleasen rarely made up a complete lie—there was almost always some shred of truth to each of his stories. But the very grandiosity of this imaginary life gives some insight into how pathetic his real existence probably was. He was deeply depressed, his life had been one personal disaster after another, and he had very few real accomplishments to point to. Beyond a handful of temporary high points, he lived a marginal existence.

To Texas and New York law enforcement, as well as eventually to most Mormons, he was an evil man, a completely unrepentant law breaker, a cold blooded killer, a pathological liar, and very dangerous. It is difficult to reconstruct him from interviews with Mormons and law enforcement because across the board they see him as a monster.

Kleasen lived a life surrounded by firearms and punctuated by violent outbursts. He left a trail of victims in his wake, including his own elderly mother. Many people still fear him. Former Travis County district attorney Robert O. Smith in 1988 told reporters, "This guy is probably the most dangerous person I've ever met."

Yet many young adults, inexperienced in life or with people like

Kleasen, seemed fascinated by him and willing to accept his stories. Others felt sorry for him and went out of their way to help. They saw him as lonely and depressed, which was true enough but not the whole picture.

For a time Mormons greeted him as an "investigator" interested in joining their church and later as a new convert to be fellowshipped. Young missionaries, typically youths of nineteen, twenty, or twenty-one, with little exposure to the world, were drawn to his macho stories of guns, spying, and danger. Two young missionaries lost their lives due to just such an attraction.

Nearly all the mental health experts who evaluated Kleasen saw him as disturbed and needing medication which he rarely received when not in custody. He was variously diagnosed as a psychopathic personality with psychosis, as a paranoid schizophrenic possibly with a psychomotor epileptic condition, as suffering from a schizoid personality disorder, as being severely depressed, and as an emotionally unstable personality. He sometimes threatened dramatic suicide. A 1977 death row evaluation concluded that because of his obvious paranoid mental illness he was "an extremely dangerous person who would constitute a threat to society if ever released."

Kleasen was not so severely ill that his condition could be instantly recognizable. The majority of his life appeared to be normal and he did accomplish things. He was a college graduate and had enrolled in graduate courses; he worked as a New York deputy sheriff for two years; he was married and had a child; and was able to impress many people with his talents. He was the kind of unhospitalized schizophrenic who often lives among us, undiagnosed and untreated, one of those difficult people we all have to deal with. But unlike the vast majority of mentally ill, Kleasen was exceptionally dangerous.

Throughout his life, and especially while on parole in Buffalo, New York, he had real friends. More than a few people came forward to describe him as intelligent, courteous, willing to help others, a pretty good guy.

Much of what can be learned about Kleasen comes from the tide of letters he wrote. He pecked away on an old typewriter daily, sending letters to anyone he thought would read them. Many of those letters were saved by his correspondents. At a minimum, they reveal an active fantasy life. But it is hard to say how much of what he wrote he actually believed. They often portray a man who is very difficult to like.

NINE

ROBERT KLEASEN WAS THE ONLY CHILD OF ELMER AND LYDIA Kleasen.

Elmer M. Kleasen was born on July 1, 1891, in Buffalo. His parents were Marine and Adrianna Kleasen. (One of the engraved wedding rings taken from Kleasen's trailer in mid-November was inscribed "M. K. to A. K. June 15, 1887.") Adrianna was born in Germany; Marine was born in the United States. Until his marriage, Elmer lived with his parents at 20 Milnor and later at 186 Oxford Avenue in Buffalo. He was a twenty-two-year-old store clerk when he married.

Lydia Steck was born in Buffalo a few months after her future husband on October 18, 1891. She was twenty-one when she married Elmer. Her parents were George and Louise Velter Steck. Her father was a realtor. Lydia's occupation is listed on the marriage certificate as milliner.

The couple married on September 25, 1913. The wedding was solemnized by Rev. Phillip Haendiges at the Riverside German Methodist Episcopal church. This 1872 church was located at 186 Mortimer and was a landmark in the Buffalo German community until it was torn down in 1924 for a commercial development.

By 1919 the Kleasens were living in a three-story wooden house at 39 Victoria Avenue near the center of Buffalo. It was in a German neighborhood once called Kaisertown. In 1925 George Steck sold the house to his daughter Lydia—Elmer is not listed on the transaction—for $3,500.

For many years Elmer worked as a clerk at a paint, oil, and glass store, F.T. Coppins Company, located at 681 Main Street in the center of the old Buffalo commercial district. He worked there at least until 1931, then lost his job in the Depression. By 1939 he found work as a gardener. Records from 1948 list him as a laborer with the Department of Public Works. By 1952 he had returned to retail work as a clerk in a Buffalo hardware store, Weed and Company.

The Kleasens had no children for the first nineteen years of the marriage, then on September 20, 1932, their only child, Robert Elmer, was born at Deaconess Hospital in Buffalo. His father was forty-two, his mother forty-one. He was born in an uneventful, full-term, caesarean delivery.

Little information is available about Kleasen's childhood. There are indications that both he and his mother were abused by his father, whose behavior became increasingly erratic. In September 1936 Kleasen began public education at Public School 54 in Buffalo which he attended through the eighth grade. He began high school in 1944. In June 1949 he graduated from Emerson Vocational High School where he had studied cabinet making.

Reportedly both of Kleasen's parents were gun enthusiasts, collectors, and hunters. From whatever source, their son had fallen in love with firearms by the time he was a teenager. One mental health expert who examined him recalled hearing stories about how as a youth Kleasen used to go to the Victoria Avenue home attic with his BB gun and plunk away at neighborhood kids up and down the street.

The first indication of Kleasen's mental problems in the public record occurred in December 1950 when he was eighteen. On Christmas Eve Day, a Sunday, Kleasen was out hunting rabbits with a shotgun near Clarence, New York. He was alone. He later described his rabbit hunting approach as jumping into the brush to flush the animals out, then shooting them. When he jumped into one bush, Kleasen drove a rusted nail through his boot and into his foot. He claimed he then got caught in a blizzard and was lost outdoors for three days, during which time gangrene developed. It is apparent Kleasen was injured somehow, but there is no support for his story of exposure and gangrene.

His mother Lydia, then fifty-nine, took him to the Meyer Hospital Emergency Room in Buffalo. When he was not treated immediately, Kleasen went berserk. He started screaming and threatened a clerk. His mother tried to calm him and he struck her.

The youth then rushed out into the parking lot, smashed out the window of his mother's car, and grabbed his shotgun. A watchman tried without success to stop him.

Kleasen stormed back into the hospital brandishing the shotgun. Terrified patients and staff scattered before him. He cornered a twenty-four-year-old nurse and a doctor in an office and fired the shotgun five times into the walls over their heads. Finally he was wrestled to the floor by an intern, an ambulance driver, and an orderly who held him until the police arrived.

Kleasen would have been a minor at the time, but was charged with first-degree felony assault. He could have been sentenced as an adult had prosecutors sought such a conviction. The Buffalo police secured a search warrant for his home. There they seized thirteen rifles, including one with a telescopic sight, a dozen swords and machetes, several Japanese sabers, and a large quantity of ammunition. This would be the first of several raids on Kleasen's residences over the years to seize large caches of weapons.

Initially he was held in the psychiatric ward of the Meyer Memorial Hospital. The courts immediately saw him as a severely ill young man and committed him to the Gowanda State Hospital on January 4, 1951. Prosecutors let the matter drop with his involuntary hospitalization, and Kleasen was not prosecuted further. He was held in Gowanda for treatment over the next eight and a half months. On September 15 he was released to after-care lasting another year. He was not completely discharged until August 28, 1952.

According to Gowanda records, Kleasen was diagnosed as psychotic with a psychopathic personality. Hospital staff concentrated on treating his psychosis by keeping him in a calm, controlled environment and giving him insulin and metrosol, an early psychiatric medication. (This was before Thorazine revolutionized psychiatric medications.) They had enough success to lead to his release. They felt, however, that because of Kleasen's long-standing mental disease, prognosis for full recovery was poor.

Kleasen would later deny that he was prosecuted in the matter and would only say he was in the mental hospital to be "checked out," apparently as part of his fantasy career in the CIA. It may not be significant, but Kleasen later would claim 1952 was the year he began working for the CIA. (Not surprisingly, the CIA denies that Kleasen has ever had any association with it.) He claimed also that beginning in 1950 he was a test pilot for Bell Aircraft in the United States and Korea, as well as flew U2s for the military. He claimed he had his pilot's license by age fifteen, in 1947 or 1948.

In 1951 a cousin, John Townstead Williamson, died. Later in life Kleasen would periodically adopt Williamson's identity as his own.

TEN

BOB KLEASEN'S ADULTHOOD WAS MOSTLY A MATTER OF DRIFT, mental illness-driven anger and violent outbursts, some higher education, and a series of short-term jobs with little to boast about. However, his adult experiences provided a hook upon which he hung his extravagant spy and war hero fantasies.

Kleasen worked for Bell Aircraft in Niagara Falls, New York, from 1951 or 1952 to 1956, as a file clerk. Then he moved to Little Rock, Arkansas, in 1956 and on to Texas around 1957 where he stayed until about 1960.

In Texas Kleasen told people he hoped to find work at a Bell Helicopter plant near Ft. Worth, but then was injured in a car accident which left him walking with a cane. He said he lived off government benefits connected to his prior military service as a pilot in Korea.

He had a pet beagle at the time and often took him to veterinarian Dr. J. P. Jones in Hurst, a suburb of Ft. Worth. Kleasen liked to tell Jones about his military exploits and hunting successes. Kleasen would later tell people he had been a paid helper, but Jones recalls that he was just an odd young man who liked to hang around. Kleasen always wore military jackets and tried to leave the impression he was a retired officer.

Kleasen came to love Texas, especially the many hunting opportunities he found in the beautiful Texas Hill Country west of Austin. While in Texas in 1957, he also "graduated" from the mail order Northwestern School of Taxidermy.

As he came to love hunting, Kleasen also developed a lasting relationship with taxidermist Lem Rathbone. Kleasen had Rathbone mount many of his trophies and corresponded often. "He is a note writer," Rathbone later commented. No matter where he lived, Kleasen came to Texas at least once a year to hunt and, just as regularly, to drop off his kills at Rathbone's Austin Taxidermy Studio.

While in Texas, Kleasen frequently slipped down to Mexico. He married his first wife, Landy Maldonado diBalboa, a Mexican national, in a Mexico City church wedding on September 6, 1961. The second wedding ring taken from Kleasen's trailer in mid-November 1974 was engraved "L.M.B. to Pito R.E.K. 9/6/61 Mex. D.F." Pito was probably a pet name. "Mex. D.F." probably stands for Districo Federal, or Mexico City, where the couple married. After moving to Buffalo, they had a second marriage performed in a Presbyterian church. For a short time afterwards, Kleasen worked at a Buffalo shipping company. The couple moved into his mother's Victoria Avenue home.

On June 6, 1962, Kleasen began work as an Erie County deputy sheriff. The department likely did no background check or they would have discovered the 1950 emergency room shooting incident. Kleasen did not disclose information about the charge on his application. As badge #568, he was a jail guard, a civil service position that did not expose him to the public in the normal course of his work.

In September 1963 Kleasen enrolled in the Erie Technical Institute's police science program, taking classes into 1964. He did fairly well in the sheriff's basic training courses and especially well in two courses on fingerprinting. This may explain why his fingerprints were not found on any of the critical evidence in the murder investigation.

While a deputy sheriff, Kleasen persuaded a newspaper outdoor writer to publish a column about his exaggerated exploits hunting black bear in the Smokie Mountains of northeast Tennessee. "Kleasen's Tale of Two Boars a Tennessee Hair-Raiser," the headline read. Kleasen was still carrying the browned clipping when he was arrested in 1974.

In the early 1960s, the Erie County sheriff's department had a reputation for heavy-handedness, but even so still Kleasen was too zealous. The sheriff's department received numerous complaints about his erratic behavior. One court official later described him as "badge happy" in that "he threatened the use of firearms on several citizens without there being cause to do so."

In winter 1963 Kleasen threatened a young man with his shotgun when the man parked near Kleasen's Victoria Avenue home during a snow storm. The last straw came on June 10, 1964, when Kleasen chased and handcuffed some neighborhood kids to a porch after he caught them setting off firecrackers. The sheriff had finally had enough, telling Kleasen to resign or he would be fired. Kleasen turned in his badge on June 25, 1964, after just over two years in uniform.

Kleasen's marriage to Landy was a stormy one. In 1964 they had a daughter, Yvonne, but the new baby didn't save the union. His wife would later describe him as "a pathological liar" and an extremely violent and dangerous man. Kleasen beat both her and his elderly mother in Landy's presence. After being fired as a deputy sheriff, he began to, in her words, constantly scheme to live without working, using others any way he could.

Finally Landy borrowed money from friends and disappeared. On September 20, 1966, she took their baby daughter and left him for a distant new home. She only told one family in Buffalo where she was going. On May 25, 1967, she divorced him in a Mexican court. She later detailed his violence and extensive gun collection for federal agents, but only when they promised not to reveal her whereabouts.

The day after Landy got her divorce, Kleasen married Laura Salazar-Artiedia, a native of Quito, Ecuador, and a friend of the first wife. She was four years older than Kleasen. At some point he brought her to Hurst, Texas, where she was introduced to the veterinarian.

He had told his new wife his usual self-aggrandizing stories about being an air force veteran and a Korean War pilot. Beginning in June 1967, the couple moved in with Kleasen's elderly mother on Victoria Avenue. In Buffalo Laura worked as a seamstress four days a week.

By 1951 his father's increasingly erratic behavior was interfering with his ability to cope. Finally in July 1956 Elmer Kleasen had what his wife's lawyer would later call "a complete mental breakdown." It took Buffalo police to forcibly remove him from Victoria Avenue to Meyer Memorial Hospital. From there he was committed to the state hospital at Gowanda on July 10, 1956, about five years after the son was treated there. He was diagnosed as psychotic with arteriosclerosis. His wife Lydia visited him there and soon became aware of his attachment to another patient named Edwin Storey.

The father was discharged from the hospital in 1961. But Lydia would not let him return to Victoria Avenue to live with her, her son, and new daughter-in-law. Elmer lived out his days in rooming houses on Social Security checks, his best friend being Storey. He died in a flop house in Dunkirk, New York, on August 25, 1968.

When Elmer died, he had a joint checking account with Storey. Storey and Lydia later fought in probate court over the less than $2,000 balance. Lydia's lawyer claimed that her former husband had not been competent since his 1956 hospitalization. The feud generated more ugliness in a family that seemed somehow cursed.

In 1960 Jacob I. Brasser, a prominent Wayne County attorney and cousin to Elmer Kleasen, executed a will leaving Lydia Kleasen a seventy-five-acre farm, with a farm house, in the town of Williamson near the intersection of Bear Swamp and Brasser Roads. His will expressly left little to his own relatives and suggests his gift came with a recognition that his cousin Elmer was mentally ill.

The farm was just a few miles from Palmyra, where Mormon prophet Joseph Smith, Jr., grew up, and where the sacred grove and Hill Cumorah—sites revered by Mormons—are situated.

Under New York law, a will is not filed until the individual's death. Brasser died in 1968, the same year his cousin Elmer Kleasen passed away. Apparently, his relatives were ready to contest the will because Lydia ended up paying his estate $8,500 for what was set out as a gift. Lydia quickly transferred a joint tenancy interest with a right of survivorship to her son Bob for $1, recording the transaction in the Wayne County clerk's office. Kleasen was thirty-five and still married to his second wife at the time.

Wayne County, New York, is beautiful green farm land with rolling hills and thick woodlands, teeming with game. Kleasen loved it, especially for the hunting opportunities it afforded him. He frequently made the hour-and-a-half drive from Buffalo to stay at the farm.

Kleasen continued to take college courses during his second marriage, probably as an excuse to avoid a regular job. Then his second wife divorced him in a Buffalo court less than four years into the marriage.

A November 1970 family court intake report filed in the divorce said Laura Salazar-Artiedia was referred by the suicide crisis office and was under a doctor's care for "nerves." At the time Kleasen had not worked since leaving the Wilsolite Corporation in March 1970 after being employed there a year.

"The petitioner alleges she has been living with the respondent for the past year in a very threatening atmosphere, so she has had to support the respondent since March, 1970 and has been assaulted and threatened with her life," the report said. Kleasen was mostly living off his wife's $50 a week earnings as a seamstress and the school loans he had finagled. The report went on to say he "apparently has threatened to 'kill' her relatives and she is extremely fearful of him." All the guns he kept in the house gave her good reason to be afraid. The report went on to note that Kleasen was then under psychiatric out-patient care through Jewish Social Services of Buffalo. (In January 1966 he was hospitalized at the SUNY-Buffalo Infirmary following a car accident. He then began outpatient psychiatric treatment in 1966 through the SUNY-Buffalo Psychological Clinic.) Laura regarded Kleasen as "'dangerously sick,' because she had been told this by a priest and others who know him." She showed "considerable emotion as she relates her fears toward the respondent."

Kleasen was also seen by the family court intake office and denied everything, but agreed that a divorce was necessary. It was granted on January 21, 1971.

The fall semester of 1968 Kleasen had enrolled at the State University of New York at Buffalo, carrying over his 1962-66 credits from the Erie County Technical Institute. His transcripts show only an average student. He earned as many D's as B's and frequently failed to complete courses. Among the D's were courses in criminology, religion, economics, logic and scientific method, and foreign political systems. He did not take many demanding subjects. Only twice did he receive an "A" grade in a substantive course, once for United States History and once for the Psychological Development of the Child.

Kleasen would later claim to speak several languages fluently, but in college he took only two semesters of Spanish, receiving a "C" and a "D." This in spite of the fact he was twice married to native Spanish speakers.

On June 1, 1969, the State University of New York at Buffalo awarded him an associate of arts degree in general studies. The next year he received a bachelor's degree in sociology from SUNY-Buffalo. On September 1, 1971, he also received a New York teaching certificate in high school social studies good for five years.

Studies have suggested that graduating from a university of moderate difficulty requires an IQ around 115 to 120. Whatever Kleasen's mental problems in life, he was an intelligent man.

In September 1971 he began graduate work at Buffalo State, which he continued until May 1972 without receiving a degree. He told some associates his graduate study concerned pornography. He later told a Wayne County probation officer his doctoral thesis was titled "The Sexual Revolution in Scandinavia" and that he had traveled extensively in Scandinavia researching and gathering material, mainly pornographic films, pictures, and literature. His pornography stash was later noted by ATF agents who raided his house the fall of 1971. Most of it was in a safe in the basement of the Victoria Avenue home.

A later pre-sentence investigation report commented, "One investigator who viewed this material saw no evidence of orderliness in packaging these things and believed that Kleasen kept the goods only for his personal prurient pleasures. This Officer noted that Kleasen was unable to pronounce correctly several words pertaining to sexual deviations and thus this Officer doubts the defendant's efforts and ability toward a Doctorate Thesis."

His college transcripts do not reflect a final grade in any of the four graduate level courses he registered for in the fall 1971 term. Under each he is listed as having "Resigned officially." He did not register for any further course.

In late May 1969 Kleasen was on a hunting trip in the Texas Hill

Country with his friend Ivan Makuch. On May 30 they came across a female buffalo about 130 yards off Highway 281. This was on the Diamond X Ranch owned by A. W. Moursand, an intimate and financial confidant of former U.S. president Lyndon Johnson. After shooting the buffalo, they cut off its head and four legs and skinned it, then cut a hole in a fence to drag out their trophy.

The next day Kleasen showed up at Rathbone's Taxidermy Studio with the buffalo parts, saying the hide was still "hot." Rathbone, who later testified that he helped arrange an exotic animal hunt for Kleasen on the Diamond X Ranch, mounted the head and prepared the hide. The discarded carcass was discovered by ranch managers and reported to law enforcement on June 7, 1969.

Some weeks later Texas game officers showed up at the Taxidermy Studio, asking about animal parts Kleasen had left to be mounted. The buffalo head was mounted and hanging on Rathbone's wall at the time. He vigorously protested the seizure because Kleasen had never paid him for the work. Game officers took the buffalo head and two or three other trophies anyway. Kleasen was finally charged in Blanco County with the misdemeanor offense of "killing a game animal without a permit." The charge was filed in February 1970 in a Blanco County court.

At the request of Blanco County, the Erie County sheriff's department tracked Kleasen down in Buffalo to inform him of the charges. Since it was only an out-of-state misdemeanor, the sheriff did not take him into custody. Kleasen claimed he and Makuch were on an organized exotic game hunt and had paid $450 cash to a mysterious "Mr. Burns" for the right to shoot the animal. By March 3, 1971, the Erie County sheriff's department wrote Blanco County informing them that Kleasen's attorney would soon provide proof. Kleasen and Makuch later executed affidavits to this effect with an obviously faked receipt. They claimed to have met the mysterious "Mr. Burns" in a parking lot and provided no information as to his identity or whereabouts.

Because the offense was a misdemeanor, Kleasen was not extradited. Though the matter just sat, it would resurface to haunt him a few years later.

When Kleasen's second wife left him in January 1971, his depression became severe. He had been an outpatient of Buffalo's Jewish Family Services where his doctor persuaded him to voluntarily admit himself to the Buffalo State Hospital. (Kleasen listed himself as Jewish when he first came to the agency for treatment.) He was brought to the hospital by a friend the afternoon of January 20, 1971. Kleasen was then thirty-eight years old and described himself as a SUNY-Buffalo social science education graduate student.

He told admissions officers: "I feel I can't go on like this. I can't study; I cannot cook to feed myself; I have no one but my aged mother who is near 80 and cannot care for me." He was still living at his mother's home. An admitting physician noted a diagnostic impression of "Depressive Reaction in an Emotionally Unstable Personality."

Kleasen told admissions staff he had been an outpatient of the SUNY-Buffalo Psychological Clinic since 1966, but neglected to mention the year and a half he was in the Gowanda State Hospital. He said his Ecuadoran wife had recently moved out. She had filed for divorce and her attorney had scheduled a hearing for the day following this hospitalization.

But his stay at the hospital was short-lived. The following morning Kleasen was anxious to discharge himself. "On regaining his perspective the day after admission, patient asked for his release and discussed his realistic plans for the future," hospital records say. "He was anxious to get out of the hospital in time to register for his classes and to continue with his plans of completing his master's degree requirements by the end of the coming Summer." Another doctor observed that Kleasen was "rather adamant" about being discharged. This would have been just after the fall 1971 semester where Kleasen withdrew from his four graduate courses without receiving any grades.

So a compromise was struck. Kleasen was placed on convalescent care to attend a day program five days a week. He was prescribed Vivactil and Elavil, drugs used to control depression.

Two weeks later Kleasen again appeared at the hospital for a routine check-up. He had attended his day program faithfully and stayed with his medications, telling a doctor that he no longer was depressed but still worried about the unresolved Texas charges. Kleasen said he had just been served with a warrant which he did not understand but which he suspected had to do with his hunting. The doctor observed that Kleasen was "pleasant and appropriate."

Three weeks later, on February 24, 1971, Kleasen returned to the hospital feeling better still. He was now anxious to finalize his unresolved divorce so that he could bring a Swedish fiancé to the United States. This was apparently Anna Irene Fredriksson, whom Kleasen said he had met while traveling in Europe the year before. The doctor reduced the dosage of his medications.

A month later Kleasen returned to the clinic saying the Texas hunting charges had been dropped. He told his doctor he was still feeling lonely at home alone with his mother. The doctor recorded that "he intended to marry his girlfriend from Sweden and was saving some money so he could get her into the United States." The doctor was comfortable enough with Kleasen's condition to discharge him from convalescent care if he continued meeting with a social worker at Jewish Family Services.

During this same spring Kleasen became involved with Mormon missionaries who taught him about the LDS church. Apparently little teaching was required as Kleasen had been learning about Mormon beliefs for a number of years.

Kleasen expressed a desire to join, but church leaders hesitated, possibly because of the Texas charges or because more experienced Mormons found him odd. They would not authorize his baptism. The missionaries visited Kleasen's and his mother's home several times. Kleasen entertained them with stories of his exploits as a CIA operative and took them to the attic floor to show off his large gun collection. There was a lot of scientific-looking gear which Kleasen used to load his own ammunition and modify his many weapons. The missionaries thought the house looked like a zoo, filled with mounted animals Kleasen claimed were hunting trophies. They believed everything Kleasen told them about being a spy, big game hunter, Olympic marksman, and scholar.

Not surprisingly, Kleasen did not tell these missionaries about his interest in pornography.

On one of his frequent trips to Europe, Kleasen met and wooed Irene Fredriksson. Born in 1951, she was about nineteen when they met, while Kleasen was thirty-eight or thirty-nine. She worked for a Swedish pornography retailer Kleasen frequented. He had known Irene for about a year and a half. Kleasen told her of his heroic past, that he was a captain in the air force and was a fighter ace in the Korean War.

Irene came to the United States on May 25, 1971, and the two were married in Buffalo on July 1, 1971. The Mormon missionaries who attended the wedding thought she was a street-wise, hard-looking woman who spoke fair English. Kleasen toasted his new bride with champagne, which also surprised the missionaries. Given his professed belief in the LDS church, they had assumed Kleasen was living the Mormon Word of Wisdom which does not allow the use of alcohol, tobacco, and coffee.

ELEVEN

N MID-JUNE 1971 KLEASEN AND HIS NEW WIFE VISITED THE
Wayne County farm. Kleasen's friend Ivan Makuch, a Ukranian national, came with them.

They arrived about 2:00 in the afternoon. Kleasen mowed the
lawn while Fredriksson lay out in the sun, then Kleasen and Makuch
ran an errand in Rochester. By about 6:00 they were back at the farm.

Shortly afterwards Fredriksson and Kleasen heard three or four
gunshots. At first they thought it was Makuch who had just taken a .22
rifle to shoot woodchucks. Makuch returned to say two men had been
shooting in a field near the farm house. Kleasen became convinced
that bullets had passed close to Fredriksson and him and was furious.
He ordered her into the house, grabbed a .338 Magnum rifle, and
drove off in his Volkswagen to pursue the shooters. Makuch was in the
passenger seat.

The two roared down Brasser Road where they found two young
men walking, Dennie Lee DuBoise of Williamson and his friend Lynn
Warney. They had guns in their hands. The two pair did not know each
other.

"A bullet just missed my wife," Kleasen screamed, then threatened to "blow their brains out."

DuBoise claimed they'd been shooting frogs in a ditch. One of
them carried a .22 rifle, the other a .22 pistol, which Kleasen demanded. Makuch, looking more scared than DuBoise and his friend,
got out of the VW and collected the guns at Kleasen's order, throwing
them into the back seat.

"Get going," Kleasen then yelled at DuBoise and Warney. As the
two walked away, Kleasen shot DuBoise in the left foot with his .338
rifle with a scope. The man yelped and began limping quickly down

the road, bleeding.

Kleasen would later claim this was an accident, that he was just shooting into the dirt and that DuBoise was injured by flying pieces of pavement. In any event, DuBoise was hospitalized for nine days and on crutches for four weeks. He lost his middle toe as a result.

DuBoise was treated at Meyers Community Hospital in nearby Sodus and police were called. New York State criminal investigator Ernie Zanett took the complaint. Later that night Zanett and state trooper Melford Drake went to the farm house where he arrested Kleasen for assault.

The officer would later note that Kleasen did not turn himself in as he had claimed, dryly telling a 1978 federal jury, "It wasn't a surrender situation." Police seized the two firearms, and Kleasen was arrested for Assault 2, a class D felony in New York with a maximum sentence of seven years in prison.

Kleasen was held in jail for about a month. He wrote everyone he could think of for help, including a number of SUNY-Buffalo faculty members and his Texas taxidermist, Lem Rathbone. He urged Rathbone to secure him a defense attorney such as F. Lee Bailey who was then very visible. Rathbone did try to arrange bail for Kleasen.

A New York state police investigator went to the Buffalo State Hospital on June 18, 1971, wanting to know if Kleasen was considered competent to possess firearms. The patient had stayed there only a short time and firearms had never come up, the investigator was told. This was the first time his treatment team was made aware of Kleasen's earlier violence and confinement to the Gowanda State Hospital.

After an August 30 preliminary hearing, Kleasen was bound over for trial.

Then Kleasen's car was repossessed by the bank. Money that Kleasen had on him at the time he was jailed—he claimed it was to register for the next term of graduate work at SUNY-Buffalo—was impounded by police. It was turned over to the lawyer who had represented Kleasen in his recent divorce and at the preliminary hearing on the assault charge, but the lawyer refused to continue representing Kleasen unless he was paid an additional $2,500 owed him.

Kleasen was formally indicted by a Wayne County grand jury on September 20.

Things continued to deteriorate. On September 30, 1971, three New York State troopers showed up at Kleasen's Victoria Avenue home to serve a new arrest warrant on him. They brought along a search warrant and six ATF agents who were investigating Kleasen's use of a federal firearms dealer's license. He had failed to comply with the required paperwork, and the government doubted his was a legitimate business. The agents seized all the guns they found in the house.

The raid netted what the senior ATF agent first claimed to the press was $300,000 worth of weapons and ammunition. Official ATF paperwork from the raid would give the seized items a more modest value of $15,000. In a front page *Buffalo News* article, Agent Irving F. Pierce said they seized over 100 shotguns and rifles, three submachine guns, several automatic rifles and sawed-off shotguns, over 40,000 rounds of ammunition, 100 pounds of explosives, tear gas grenades, and a variety of firearms parts. There were also thirty-two handguns which under New York law required a license Kleasen did not have. The weapons were stored throughout the two-and-a-half-story house, but most were in the attic. Some of the guns were described as "museum quality antiques." Kleasen claimed the machine guns had been given to him to hold by a mysterious FBI agent. The entire collection was hauled off in a truck to the evidence locker in a downtown federal courthouse. Kleasen would never regain any of these items.

The agents were openly suspicious of how Kleasen, who had not worked in two years, found the money for such weapons. They also commented on the house being filled with mounted animals and birds, including a full-size standing black bear by the front door.

In an effort to control Irene, Kleasen had placed her passport in a basement safe where much of his pornography was stored. During the raid, Makuch took advantage of the commotion to help Irene open the safe and regain her passport.

The U.S. attorney declined to prosecute Kleasen on the federal weapons violations because of Kleasen's psychiatric history. He doubted Kleasen's sanity. However, federal prosecutors didn't object to the state district attorney prosecuting Kleasen under state law. Erie County prosecutors filed thirty-eight counts of state weapons law violations.

D.A. investigator Dick Murphy, who only a year earlier had moved over from the Buffalo police department, took over the investigation. Kleasen was charged with illegally possessing thirty-two semi-automatic and revolver handguns, a sawed-off shotgun, a Thompson submachine gun, two Schmeiser machine pistols, and other illegal weapons. After arraignment in an Erie County court, he was released on a personal bond. Kleasen never showed up for any further court dates on these charges.

It was after the ATF raid that Kleasen began calling the district attorney's office to complain that his former friend Ivan Makuch had stolen some of his most valuable pornography and rare bullet collection. His calls were routinely routed to Murphy who was more than a little amused. Murphy began building files on the strange man.

Kleasen was returned to the Wayne County Jail. For a time some wondered if he qualified for court-appointed counsel. SUNY-Buffalo had arranged for attorney Norman Effman to represent him during this period. The local public defender was appointed to investigate his finances but later told the court that Kleasen was a federally licensed gun dealer with too many assets to qualify as indigent. Apparently the problem was his gun collection and its supposed $300,000 value. It reportedly included valuable antiques, including items once owned by the Russian czars. After the raid on Kleasen's home, the trial court refused to believe he was indigent.

Establishing a pattern he would later repeat in Texas, Kleasen also complained bitterly to the judge that he was sick and was being mistreated in jail. He wrote a steady stream of letters to various people complaining about his plight and seeking representation. In a transparent example of selective memory, Kleasen assured the court, "I have never been in trouble before."

A series of September and October hearings about Kleasen's ability to hire counsel followed in the assault case. Lawyers appeared on his behalf and disappeared almost monthly. Finally his bond was lowered from $7,500 to $2,500 and he was released after assuring the judge, "I am not a flighty person." His mother put up their farm as security for the bond. Kleasen made at least five subsequent court appearances before trial was set for April 3, 1972, in Lyons, New York.

While Kleasen was back in the Wayne County Jail, Irene decided she had had enough and returned to Sweden. Kleasen would often say she left after witnessing AFT agents beat him while raiding his Buffalo home, terrified that such things could happen here. "She was afraid of the United States as a whole," he later claimed. "She considered you all [law enforcement] a bunch of gangsters, and she didn't want any part of it."

TWELVE

AFTER BONDING OUT OF THE WAYNE COUNTY JAIL, KLEASEN flew to Sweden on November 21, 1971, where he remained until the 27th, to try to patch things up with Irene. Now he was a different person, courteous and charming, promising to be better. He wanted Fredriksson to return to the U.S., and she foolishly relented, but this time a male cousin, Curth Ekgren, came with her. Irene had been staying with Curth and his family in Enköping. They left Sweden on December 26, 1971. Kleasen bought both their tickets on a TWA credit card.

But Kleasen had not changed. Only hours after meeting Fredriksson and Ekgren at the airport, he beat her again for refusing to have sex with him in the middle of the night. He had told her he could not sleep, that it was her obligation.

A few days later he beat her again for failing to prepare his lunch as quickly as he wanted. She would later tell police he didn't beat her often, and usually struck her in the face and head with his hands. Twice he'd threatened to kill her, and she was beaten often enough, once almost breaking her neck, she said; she took the threats very seriously.

Once Fredriksson witnessed Kleasen beating his mother, who was then nearly eighty. Lydia Kleasen turned up with a broken leg during the first week of December 1971; Dick Murphy was convinced Kleasen had done it.

Kleasen had run up substantial credit card debts, and creditors were constantly at the Victoria Avenue home trying to collect either the cards or some of the money. Kleasen would hide and force his mother to handle the collectors.

When he felt his mother had mishandled one encounter, he exploded. Kleasen grabbed a rifle he had intended to chase the bill collector with, but the man had already driven away. He came back inside the house, still carrying the rifle, and took Lydia by the throat with one hand. Kleasen didn't threaten to shoot his mother, but Fredriksson was afraid he was going to beat her with the rifle. Fredriksson was able to save the old woman from further harm.

From behind closed doors, she often heard Kleasen screaming at his mother and her crying. At other times she heard what she believed was Kleasen slapping and beating her.

After the fight over the slow lunch, Kleasen took Fredriksson's passport from her purse and said he would never let her leave him again. Kleasen threatened to kill Curth if he tried to help her. He also refused to allow the two to speak to each other in Swedish for fear he wouldn't understand what they said or planned.

Fredriksson contacted the Swedish Embassy in Washington, D.C., for help and somehow Kleasen's lawyer became aware of this, telling Kleasen. Ekgren had left for New York City to visit relatives. Irene was then alone with Kleasen and his frail mother.

Kleasen wanted to head off any threat to his domestic rule that might come from the Swedish Embassy. He drafted a letter in English for Fredriksson to rewrite in Swedish and mail to the embassy. Kleasen's draft said everything was all right and she did not need help. He wrote for her that they were newlyweds and she had just overreacted to a domestic spat. Fredriksson wasn't sure if Kleasen could read Swedish, so she copied his letter slowly trying to measure his understanding while he watched over her shoulder. After a few lines, she concluded he did not read Swedish. She began to insert information about the real situation. She wrote:

> I am writing this letter in order to take back what I said about my husband Robert Kleasen in my telephone conversation with the Swedish Consulate in New York. I regret this telephone conversation and what I said about him is not true. This letter is written under a threat. My husband and I have agreed to repair the damage to our marriage, which I caused through my actions. I, therefore, ask you to stop all your actions and my husband is innocent. Please help me I am in danger. I have been forced to write this letter. Please help me I am in great danger but be careful.

The Swedish Embassy routed the matter to their New York Consulate which immediately contacted the Buffalo Police Department. Within hours a squad of police and the district attorney's investigator, Dick Murphy, already aware of Kleasen's propensity for violence and love of guns, appeared at the house. A sheepish Kleasen let them in where they were able to ask Fredriksson if she wanted to leave. Without hesitation she said yes and gathered up her things. Again this group of officers was struck that the house looked like a zoo or museum with stuffed animals everywhere. Later that day Fredriksson gave a tape-recorded statement to police and prosecutors setting out her harrowing experiences as Kleasen's prisoner. Federal AFT and immigration agents were part of the debriefing.

Authorities could not get her on a plane back to Sweden that day, so Murphy and his wife volunteered to put her up. A flight had been booked for the following morning. Fredriksson kept talking to the investigator and his wife well into the night. Kleasen, she claimed, had shipped several crates of guns to Rathbone in Texas for "safekeeping" and planned to ship anything returned to him from the September ATF raid. She told them of the time she and Kleasen were at the Wayne County farm and she walked in on Kleasen in the bathroom. He was in the bathtub naked with a freshly killed deer carcass. He had gutted the deer and was smeared with its blood and entrails.

The next day Fredriksson was on a plane back home, determined to be forever rid of Kleasen. Buffalo authorities did not prosecute Kleasen on any matter relating to Fredriksson because doing so would have prevented her immediate return to Sweden. She quickly divorced him in the Swedish courts. The Swedish government had bought her a round-trip ticket, leaving her a return trip to the United States if she wanted it. Fredriksson mailed the unused ticket back to Murphy saying she never intended to get that close to Kleasen again.

Kleasen was furious.

The day after Fredriksson's extraction from his home, January 13, 1972, Kleasen wrote an angry letter to the Swedish Consulate complaining that "a great wrong has been done to me." All he would accept was "she has had some difficulty adjusting to the U.S.A., and it is true she is only 20 years old and I am 39." He flatly denied any suggestion he had abused his wife. He urged that Fredriksson be placed in psychiatric care and challenged them to put her on a polygraph to verify her claims he abused her. The Swedes ignored Kleasen but forwarded his letter to Buffalo law enforcement which had a growing file on him.

Erie County district attorney Michael Dillon wrote the Swedish Consulate in New York to report. After briefly describing Kleasen, Dillon wrote, "As you can see from his prior record, Robert Kleasen is unstable and anyone living with him could be in danger if they upset him in any way."

Now back in Sweden, Irene wrote Kleasen an angry letter on January 17, 1972. Her written English was rough, but her message was unmistakable. "I will tell you your damn stupid nut that from the day I left I am gonna live my own life. And you your illegal deer-hunter if you want to fuck four your damn deers. Women in not for a bastard like you," she wrote. She was angry about property and money she had lost as a result of their relationship. The letter closed with "You damn bastard can fuck and suck yourself now and the right place for you to be is in a nut-house damn bastard."

Kleasen saved her letter, only to have it seized by Austin police when he was arrested in 1974. He would later claim that Irene was subsequently killed in a Swedish auto accident.

With debts, legal fees and other financial pressures mounting, Kleasen pressured his mother to sell their Wayne County farm. On January 25, 1972, she got $12,500 for it. He apparently took most of the proceeds.

The assault charge continued to loom. One of his attorneys, Norman Effman of Buffalo, finally struck a deal and Kleasen pleaded guilty to reduced charges on December 15, 1971. Judge Reginald Oliver walked Kleasen through a routine series of questions to determine if the guilty plea was informed and voluntary. Kleasen also signed an acknowledgment of rights form indicating he had discussed the matter with his attorney and understood what he was doing. In an effort to present Kleasen to the sentencing court in a positive light, Effman arranged an evaluation by a Buffalo psychiatrist, Dr. Guyon Marsereau. His December 20, 1971, evaluation found Kleasen to be "a schizoid personality with a strong possibility of simple schizophrenia."

Meanwhile, David Williams, senior probation officer in Wayne County, was assigned the Pre-Sentence Investigation. Williams undertook a thorough investigation of his background. His dogged pursuit of Kleasen's real life turned into the defendant's worst nightmare. Williams did not interview Kleasen until he had done his background investigation, determining much of what was the truth. He later set out Kleasen's claims in the written report, finding many of them to be baseless. Among other things, Kleasen also claimed to have been a Mormon for the previous three years.

Williams spent two days in Buffalo combing through criminal and family court records, university transcripts, credit materials, and bad debt judgments, as well as interviewing local police. He received considerable help from Dick Murphy in the Erie County district attorney's office. Williams learned about Fredriksson's virtual imprisonment and secured the relevant Buffalo police reports. He reported that Kleasen was suspected by U.S. Customs officials of smuggling drugs into the country but "nothing ever came of that investigation." Under the heading "Special Problems," Williams listed "Psychopathic Personality."

Williams's seventeen-page report concluded Kleasen was a dangerous man, and strongly urged that Judge Oliver sentence him to four to seven years in prison, the maximum:

> Inasmuch as the defendant has shown a continual trend towards irrational behavior, since this is at least the second time that he has been in trouble due to gross negligence with firearms and since he appears to be an unstable and unpredictable person, who has not benefitted from community oriented psychiatric counseling this Officer believes that the Court has no alternative in this instance other than incarceration with the hope that adequate residential psychiatric care can benefit this individual.

The report was completed in January but not yet entered into the record. Effman pestered Williams by telephone to know his recommendation. The probation officer finally told Effman he was recommending prison time; the lawyer then apparently told Kleasen. Kleasen panicked.

At the scheduled sentencing on January 26, 1972, Kleasen once again fired his lawyer and tried to withdraw his plea. "Sir, I sincerely tell you that I am innocent," he insisted to the judge. "I have lost everything that I thought was important in my life through this case." He claimed he had lost his wife and all his friends "except the ones in the church."

Oliver at first would have none of it. "This has been going on, Mr. Kleasen, since October," he snapped back.

Kleasen persisted. Oliver finally relented and let Kleasen withdraw his guilty plea, but at the same time he revoked his bond and sent him back to jail.

The next Kleasen lawyer, Basil Tzetzo, filed a petition for habeas corpus and managed to get Kleasen released again shortly thereafter. He was at least the fourth defense lawyer brought into the case by Kleasen. The trial was set for April 3, 1972.

When that date arrived, Tzetzo appeared but told the court, "I have been unable to contact my client for the past week and a half." Kleasen had fled to Europe in March. Tzetzo told the court his client was in Denmark. "I contacted the American Embassy in Sweden and they contacted his wife," Tzetzo explained. "Defendant apparently was in Denmark and had contacted her through other people in Sweden and she didn't know his exact whereabouts." The embarrassed lawyer said, "It's my feeling that he's gone and not about to return."

Kleasen's bond was revoked and a bench warrant issued. Efforts to extradite him from Sweden did not meet with success. The FBI was contacted about a fugitive warrant. New York authorities would have to wait him out.

THIRTEEN

KLEASEN HAD NO INTENTION OF BEING CONVICTED OF OR SEN-tenced for the Wayne County shooting. He had a passport in his own name. But Kleasen had also obtained records on a dead cousin, John Townstead Williamson, and made a fake passport under that name. Williamson had died in 1951 and Kleasen had secured many of his identity papers. It would become his favorite alias.

Either as Kleasen or Williamson, he made his way to Europe. In April 1972 he surfaced in Copenhagen. He first tried to get into Sweden to get at his ex-wife Irene Frederiksson, but the Swedish government apparently spotted him and wanted no part of him on their soil.

Kleasen also began attending a Copenhagen branch of the LDS church. Mormon missionaries first arrived in Denmark in 1850 and thousands of converts immigrated to Utah in the next half century. Copenhagen had been the headquarters of the Denmark Mission of the LDS church since 1970, and in 1974 the Denmark Copenhagen Mission was organized as a separate district. When Kleasen arrived, there were about 4,300 Mormons in Denmark in two stakes.

As Williamson, Kleasen told the branch president he was already a baptized member ordained to the church's lay priesthood. He sometimes passed the sacrament of bread and water with other priesthood-bearing men. He liked to hang around the young missionaries who listened to and seemed to believe his fantastic stories of CIA spying and fighter pilot combat. In April 1972 one young missionary assigned to Copenhagen inscribed Kleasen's copy of the Book of Mormon: "It's been really really interesting getting to know you and hearing about your life!"

But the local branch could not secure membership records for a John T. Williamson from Salt Lake City. Mormons are meticulous records keepers and every baptized member can be found in centralized listings in Utah. These include birth and ordination dates, marriages and children, and previous congregations. When members move, their new congregation will secure those records from church headquarters.

Faced with this lack of records, Kleasen began telling friends he was really a member of a small Mormon splinter group but was never very clear on the details. At first he claimed to be a member of the "Reformed Mormon Group," then backed away from that story when LDS members took this to mean he was part of the Reorganized Church of Jesus Christ of Latter Day Saints. (When Joseph Smith Jr., founder of Mormonism, was murdered in 1844, his followers broke up into several groups, some of them gathering in the 1860s around his son Joseph Smith III as the Reorganized Church.)

As Kleasen rationalized in one letter to Mormon friends, his group of Mormons was "a growing group of men and women who because we can not support the existing Government of the United States can not be Baptized under the 'Articles of Faith.' We go to the same Church ... and we pay tith [sic] and participate in everything except 'priesthood' things within the Church." He claimed there was a formal church organization and he could call upon its leaders to verify his claims. In another letter Kleasen claimed his group was small and did not even exist in Denmark. He assured his Mormon friends that as soon as the Vietnam War was over, his little group of independent Mormons would merge into the regular church.

Trying to avoid returning to the United States, Kleasen had his Austin friend Lem Rathbone order some rubber stamps he used to alter his bogus passport. He wanted it to reflect permanent resident status in Denmark.

For a time Kleasen apparently stayed with an English-speaking Danish family from the LDS branch he had attended, Elise and Frederick Jensen (not their real names). He sometimes was their dinner guest and got to know their two young children.

Kleasen also had some sort of relationship with a young LDS woman named Christine Madsen (not her real name). She was an

English-speaking friend of the Jensens and may have been a university student in Copenhagen. Some of Kleasen's letters suggest she was from London.

At one point Kleasen wrote the Jensens, proudly announcing Christine and he were engaged and she was wearing his ring, but marriage had to wait. "Christine & I are now *officially* Engaged. She will be wearing the ring all the time now. We have not told her parents yet *must wait* on that 'proper length Engagement'—you know." Kleasen's letters hint that she later returned the ring and broke off the relationship, if a relationship ever truly existed.

While Christine was away for several days, apparently to England, he moved into her apartment, told people they were married, and began selling her clothes and belongings. When she returned and protested, they began to argue. Kleasen exploded. He choked her, pinning her on her bed by sitting on her chest and beating her in the face. She was a mess afterwards, her throat bruised from the choking and her face bloody from his fists.

Kleasen was arrested on August 20, 1972, jailed, and prosecuted. The local Mormon leadership assisted the police with their efforts in determining who John T. Williamson really was.

Within a month Danish prosecutors indicted "American Citizen Robert Elmer Kleasen" in the City of Copenhagen Court. The charges were for attempted forgery in trying to alter his passport; two counts of stealing motor-assisted bicycles in late July and August; and assault and battery of Christine. He told the Jensens that he bought the bicycles in good faith from a shady character whom he did not know was selling stolen goods.

The third count described the assault as by "pressing one hand against her throat and pushing her down on to a bed, where she came to lie on her back, whereupon he sat down on her chest and hit her several times in her head with the flat of his hand and with his fist, took stranglehold on her, and again hit her in the face, by which time the person assaulted contracted several marks from strangling on the front of her throat, spot hemorrhages in her eyes, and a wound at the left-hand corner of her mouth."

From jail Kleasen tried to write his "Dearest Darling Christine," but the letter was intercepted by censors and returned to him. Communication with the victim in such a crime was prohibited. He had written her that "the police are doing everything possible to prevent our meeting and talking things over," that they were spreading "damn lies," and that "I love you with all my heart and soul dearest and I will keep the vows I made to you and God and I expect you to do the same."

While Kleasen was in jail, he regularly wrote the Jensens in English, at first by hand and later on a typewriter. Apparently the couple at first gave his stories some credence, wrote him back, and sometimes visited him. Kleasen believed his letters were read by jailers so he was careful and was not allowed to discuss the details of his offense. He always wrote as John T. Williamson.

The letters are a mixture of self-righteousness, of self-pity, of obvious attempts to manipulate the Jensens, of inflated ego—he liked to compare his trials to those of Mormon prophets Joseph Smith and Brigham Young, writing in one letter "I feel very much as our Founders J.S. [sic] felt when he cried out from his cell"—and of a complete refusal to admit he had done anything wrong. They read like bad acting and are filled with the terrible spelling that is inconsistent with Kleasen's claims of graduate level education. "I am lost in a foreign world I don't even understand," he lamented in an August 24, 1972, letter. He often recited the number of days he had been in "solitary confinement"—the 11th, 32nd, 46th, 51st, 55th, or 62nd such day. He complained bitterly about his treatment by jailers and the poor food he was given, persuading the Jensens to bring him oranges when they visited.

Kleasen was jailed several times in his life and always complained about how he was being abused and starved. "I am caught in a *trap* & only truth can save me. I have done nothing I am ashamed of," he wrote in the next letter. He was certain that the members of the branch believed him and not Christine. "They all know & love me & I am sure they are 'sticking up' for *me*."

He always spoke of Christine as his wife whom he loved, but said she was making up the whole matter of his violence. He knew he was forbidden from contacting Christine, but in a September 22, 1972, letter, he pleaded with the Jensens to buy a "cheap" birthday card and mail it to her signed with "All my Love & XXXXXXX," even though "Christine does not deserve it." On October 5 he wrote, "I will of course try to save the marriage but that too is beyond my power."

At the same time he increasingly attacked her in his letters as dishonest and treacherous. At first he hinted that there were rumors about her—"You will remember the rumors as to Christine ... Well I thought they were lies—now I do not think so," he wrote on August 30, 1972. He wanted the Jensens to start investigating her. After Christine's testimony against Kleasen at an October 27, 1972, trial he dismissed her as mentally sick. "This was as I tried to explain in the split personality syndrome. I feel bad to see her this way," he wrote on October 28, 1972. Within a month of the trial, he began writing that Christine was really "a Call Girl" and a lesbian, and that she had recently had an abortion. A few years later Kleasen was claiming she often went to England to receive instructions from a "Whore Master" who was outraged that she could not "work" because of her relationship with him. The "Whore Master" beat her as retribution for her love of this noble man Robert Kleasen, he claimed.

Another recurring theme of Kleasen's life is played out in his letters, that of being an honest man railroaded and tormented by a corrupt system.

As his trial date approached, he wrote the Jensens that "they are now trying to ram-rod me thru court," that he would not get a jury trial which "*is absolutely shameful,*" and that his supposedly incompetent lawyer was "a gift from the police." On October 10, 1972, he wrote that the Danish courts, which he characterized as "a real Monster you have in your mist [sic] here in Denmark," had engaged in an "extremely serious violation of my Civil Rights ... In the U.S. as bad as conditions are [such things would never happen]."

After Kleasen had been in the Copenhagen jail for almost two months, he wrote to the president of the LDS mission in Denmark. On October 14, 1972, he wrote to "humbly ask that a bi-lingual representatives [sic] of the Church come [to his] trial and when it is over decide what Church Action should be taken." He also asked for a visit, insisting that he and Christine were married, that "We were *not* married in the church. But we did or at least I did solumnly [sic] take our vows before our Heavenly father." He said they lived together in her college apartment until his arrest. He stressed his innocence. "I have been falsly [sic] arrested for beating my Wife who is a member Baptized in the Kobenhavn Branch," he wrote. Kleasen signed the letter John T. Williamson.

The mission president, Grant R. Ipsen, was not persuaded and on October 18, 1972, wrote Kleasen a stinging one paragraph response. "At an earlier request of the Police Department, I wrote to our record section in Salt Lake City, Utah to see if you are, or have been a member of the Church of Jesus Christ of Latter Day [sic] Saints," Ipsen replied. "According to the records there, you have never been a member of the Church, and are not now a member. We believe in fully sustaining the laws of the land in which we are guests. Judicial systems are designed and established to bring about righteous judgments based upon the facts of the case. We are willing to assist and have been assisting in helping the police to establish any facts that they desire." Ipsen followed through, offering Danish authorities any help he could provide.

At Kleasen's urging, the Jensens did attend his court dates. Instead of being converted to his paranoid view, they began to see him as less than honest.

Kleasen's letters grew panicky. On October 20, with the trial a week away, he wrote that "no one can win in a trial like this" and "I want to prepare you for the worse [sic]. I am innocent but that does little when you face a situation like this." After the trial he tried to dismiss Christine's testimony as both a lie and the product of her "split personality syndrome." He wrote of the guilty verdict, "My heart is sad. I too must shoulder much of the moral blame but I did not lie or bare falsely [sic] and I hope Our Heavenly Father takes pitty [sic] on me."

The Jensens confronted him about his real identity, feeling betrayed. To that, Kleasen offered a "Cassus Clay" [sic] defense, writing on November 15 that having two "legal names" was "so common in the U.S.A. and in my case I explained in court how mine came to be." He claimed "most of my papers and diplomas are under the name Kleasen although my true name is Williamson. However, this is just a little thing."

In the same letter he wrote that he would soon leave Denmark for Lebanon, giving the Jensens an address for Robert E. Kleasen in Zahle, Lebanon. He was staying with the family of a Lebanese man he met in the Copenhagen jail. He said he would soon be teaching there and did not write again for some weeks. "I knew that direct return to the U.S. would be far worse," he later wrote the Jensens, without mentioning that it was a New York felony assault prosecution that he really feared.

Kleasen did go to Lebanon from Copenhagen but didn't stay long. He had convinced his Lebanese fellow prisoner that he could supply guns for him and his comrades. Once in Lebanon it became obvious that Kleasen was not a gun runner but an unstable con man.

The Lebanese quickly grew weary of him and dropped him off on the embassy doorstep. On November 24, 1972, he showed up at the United States Embassy in Beirut trying to get home. An embassy cable to the State Department said he was "completely without funds, apparently emotionally disturbed, and acted in uncooperative and occasionally truculent manner." He identified himself as Kleasen and carried a Boston issued passport under that name, but admitted traveling under a false passport as John T. Williamson. This was necessitated, he explained, by a "conspiracy on the part of federal agents involving the illegal possession of machine guns and other violations of federal firearms and tax regulations."

Admitting the obvious, Kleasen confessed he was suffering a nervous breakdown. In a rare confession he told embassy staff he was friendless "except for an ex-wife in Denmark who was definitely not inclined to assist him." The State Department tried to contact Kleasen's mother, who he said was senile and on welfare, to assist in his repatriation. Failing that, they tried to contact a Mormon bishop in Williamsville, New York, whom Kleasen said would help him. No one would accept his collect overseas calls. Finally the embassy loaned him $465 for a ticket home and $50 to live on until takeoff.

Kleasen later recalled that he landed in Washington, D.C., and immediately made his way to Lem Rathbone's place. "He told me he went over there to teach school or do something at one time or another," Rathbone would later testify.

Kleasen continued writing his letters. On Christmas Eve 1972 he wrote to a Mormon family from Calgary, Alberta, Canada. He signed the letter "Jack" but gave a return address for Robert E. Kleasen. Once again his 007 fantasies got the better of him. He explained that the teaching job he had been offered in Lebanon was "FAKE" and that he arrived only to find himself a captive of "Palastine-Bandits" who wanted him to fly drug runs into Greece in order to finance the war with Israel. He refused, and was held a prisoner for "22 days mostly without food." Kleasen wrote that he finally wrestled a pistol from one of his guards and forced his former captor at gunpoint to drive him to the U.S. Embassy in "Beirute." There he "received rather cool and shabby treatment from My Government as I had lost everything." He wrote that a doctor was finally secured to treat the illnesses he had endured during his captivity and that he convalesced in Beirut for some period. He then flew across Europe and finally to Washington, D.C., where he called his friend Rathbone. After a few days visiting Rathbone in Austin, he flew to Calgary because "I had a [teaching] position offered here and I thought I would look into it."

There was no "position" in Calgary, although Kleasen wrote the Jensens that he "lost" it when the Canadian government froze all work permits in an effort to protect the jobs of its own citizens. In a later letter Kleasen said he'd worked "illegally" as a "powder monkey" for $175 a week handling explosives for a remote timber company. This was at the Dominion Paper Company, located in Radium Hot Springs, British Columbia. He stayed a month until he was found to be working without the proper papers. He wrote that he "was very disappointed in Canada" but had saved enough money to return to Texas and buy a Honda motorcycle.

Kleasen closed the Christmas Eve letter by thanking the family "for sticking by me when all were against me," hoping to make them feel guilty about their obviously growing doubts about him.

His Christmas had been "a dismal one," he wrote in January 1973. "I did not send a single card to anyone I was so misserable [sic]." He said he was looking for a job and was thinking of getting a mobile home—"about a 50-75 foot long house on wheels." Kleasen also wrote that he was confident of securing a Texas teaching job by the fall of 1973.

Once again he pleaded with the family to write back. He said they could write to him either as Kleasen or Williamson at the Austin Taxidermist, 2708 South Lamar Boulevard, Austin, Texas. This was the original location of Lem Rathbone's taxidermy studio.

FOURTEEN

KLEASEN STAYED IN TEXAS, EITHER BECAUSE HE FELT MORE confident there or because he had simply lost the ability to move about as he had in the past.

He again wrote to the Jensens on January 28, 1973. Now he was "working for a Boat Company tempararily [sic] on the side so to speak." He talked about all the hunting available in the Hill Country, describing "deer right in the back yard [sic] every morning" and saying "over here hunting is a way of life and we enjoy it." He was getting around on a little Honda motorcycle but was looking for a car.

Former U.S. president Lyndon Johnson had died on January 22, 1973, at his ranch about thirty miles down the road from where Kleasen was staying. Kleasen complained of funeral traffic on the roads. "We Texas Hill People do not like things done that way and few of us attended," he groused. He told the Jensens he was living with the Rathbones "but that is a temporary arrangement." He wanted Mrs. Jensen to write back "giving me all and I mean *all* the news," hinting that he wanted to know about Christine.

Kleasen also mentioned in the letter that he thought his chances for international employment were over. "You have to stop and consider my age, I will more than likely not get another chance abroad." He was forty.

By this time the Jensens no longer believed anything Kleasen wrote. Mrs. Jensen had asked Christine for suggestions on how to stop the disturbing mail that continued to flow from Texas. Christine suggested she tell Kleasen they were not to have anything to do with apostates. "He is caught in his own lies," Christine wrote in a note to Mrs. Jensen. "He cannot admit that he is not at all a Mormon ... or that he must take the consequences for his actions."

In February 1973 the Danish family tersely rejected Kleasen. In a two-line letter they wrote, "We're not supposed to have contact with Apostates. Please don't ever contact us again." From that point forward, Kleasen was obsessed with regaining the respect of these people. At the same time his rage with the LDS church for, in his paranoid mind, having destroyed that relationship would contribute to the 1974 murders.

Kleasen responded to the Jensens within a week, this time writing as John T. Williamson. "All I can say to you is I am NOT a Apastate [sic] ... I'm not even sure of the meaning of the word," he insisted. "I have done nothing but disagree and refuse to endorse the carte-blanch [sic] attitude of the Mormon Church LDS in their agreement with the American Govt. (My own Govt.) in the War we have been involved [sic]." He vowed to become a member in good standing in the LDS church when the Vietnam War was over and "send you a photostate [sic] of my Membership and hope you will then understand."

Kleasen also wrote, "I humbly ask you to forgive my indiscressions [sic] with Christine. I am sorry I had to tell little Lies to keep you from knowing we were together. I truly wanted to tell you but Christine sealed my lips and I was in her control." This was complete fantasy. "Please do not desert me," he pleaded. Kleasen did not contact the Danish Mormon family again for the next six months.

Initially Lem Rathbone allowed Kleasen to sleep on a cot in an unused office area of his taxidermy studio. In 1972 he moved his business from its South Lamar Street location in south Austin to West Highway 290 in the Oak Hill community. He had a new 40-by-120-foot building with two front windows on the narrow side facing the highway and some large loading bays on the west side. Rathbone recalled that Kleasen arrived looking for a place to stay "right after deer season," one of the busiest times for his business. They struck a deal. In return, Kleasen was to clean up around the shop and act as a night watchman. Rathbone had been burglarized a few times and was happy to have his shop looked after. Kleasen was given keys to everything.

Also sometime in January 1973 Kleasen contacted a Mormon

bishop in Buffalo. He asked if the church would be willing to help his elderly mother, apparently still living in the Victoria Avenue home, with her utility bills.

On April 26, 1973, Odell Bowen's 22-foot camper trailer—a Twilight Bungalow—was stolen from Christian Mobile Homes in Oak Hill, not far from Rathbone's taxidermy studio. Someone hitched it up and drove away during the night. Bowen had purchased the trailer the previous November but found he didn't use it as much as he hoped, and friends at Christian Mobile Homes had agreed to try and sell it for him. James L. Chisum, the mobile home lot manager, called the sheriff that morning when he realized the trailer was missing. The All-State Insurance Company quickly paid Bowen's claim.

About that time Kleasen showed up with a 22-foot camper trailer, a Twilight Bungalow. Police would later match the serial numbers to those of the stolen Bowen trailer. Rathbone didn't object when Kleasen set up the trailer behind his shop without asking. Kleasen also began fixing the old out-buildings behind the studio and improvised a shooting range on a fence at the back of the property. He wrote in letters to friends that he was building a house.

Also in April Kleasen secured a post office box in south Austin, not far from Oak Hill. Post office box 3106 was rented to John T. Williamson who claimed to be a student at Southwest Texas State University in San Marcos, less than an hour south of Austin on I-35. He listed 2708 South Lamar Boulevard as his residence—the former location of the taxidermy studio and almost next to where the murdered missionaries' car was found.

Kleasen had returned to Texas carrying a Texas driver's license issued under his real name during an earlier visit. The address he gave on it was 2708 South Lamar Boulevard. But now he secured another Texas driver's license as Richard Raadt, born on October 11, 1931, listing his new John T. Williamson post office box as his address. He gave no street address.

Hunting, especially deer hunting in the Hill Country, is a passion for many Texans. Kleasen loved to hunt the area and didn't feel the least bit restrained by the requirements of seasons, licenses, or bag limits. He cruised the canyons and crags of the country constantly, shooting whatever he came across. He killed more than he could possibly eat and soon had freezers filled to bursting with deer meat. In the process he came to know the area's small roads and trails as well as a native. And he became known to just about every game officer assigned to the area. Texas game wardens in Burnet, Fredericksburg, Junction, Johnson City, Blanco, Marble Falls, and other small Hill Country towns came to know and be on the lookout for Bob Kleasen. He was one of the most persistent poachers they had to deal with.

In June 1973 Kleasen again begged the Danish family to restore their relationship. "You and your Family are the only family I really have," he pleaded in a letter to the wife, "I take all this very serious." He insisted that the Danish woman he had beaten lied at the trial. "I know I sinned [by living with the woman without being married]," he wrote, "but as you know Christine prevented this." He protested, "Don't you think I have been punished enough for this???? My gosh Elise I sat in that awful Jail for 90 days, I lost everything I had."

An almost religious love of firearms was still one of Kleasen's primary instincts. He hung out in McBride's Gun Shop of Austin so much that all the clerks came to recognize him. He longed for the time when his meager income would allow him to begin buying weapons once again.

On June 27, 1973, Kleasen bought a Colt revolver from the Montgomery Ward store in Austin. When filling out the federal disclosure forms, he indicated he had not been charged with or convicted of a felony, and that he had never been in a mental hospital. Less than two months later, he bought a Browning .22 rifle from McBride's Guns, again lying on the forms. The clerks there knew him but had no reason to doubt his honesty. Two weeks later, now in San Antonio on August 25, he bought a .22 Hornet rifle at Don's Gun Sales. This time he identified himself as Richard C. Raadt, but again gave the same false answers. He probably used his Texas driver's license as Raadt for identification.

For a time Kleasen drove an old pick-up truck. On July 17, 1974, he bought a 1964 American Motors Rambler for $100 from an Austin used car lot. He made the purchase as Raadt, apparently again using his newly acquired driver's license.

FIFTEEN

THAT SUMMER OF 1974 KLEASEN WROTE TO, AND PERSUADED, A young returned Mormon missionary from the west coast, Caleb West (not his real name), to visit him. They had met a year and a half earlier in Buffalo. West had never been to Texas and thought it would be fun. He also hoped the visit might complete Kleasen's conversion to the Mormon faith. So West hitched a ride with friends to San Antonio where Kleasen picked him up in a red pick-up truck.

However, the Bob Kleasen he found was more than he could deal with. They did talk a lot about Mormon beliefs and Kleasen asked thoughtful questions. But Kleasen talked constantly about his problems, at least as he saw them—his three unfaithful wives, his loneliness, the unfairness of the government, his persecution by the CIA, and his legal problems. He talked openly about his life as a poacher and his disregard for game laws. The returned missionary didn't see Kleasen as mentally ill, just "odd."

After a week or so, the young man had had enough. He was even too uncomfortable to tell Kleasen he was leaving. He waited until Kleasen was in town, then packed his things and hitchhiked out of Oak Hill. His family paid his way home from the San Antonio Airport about seventy-five miles south of Austin. Kleasen would later call the young man's father looking for him. After picking his son up at the airport, the father said West had done the right thing to get out of there. Later West counted his experience with Kleasen as evidence that some people don't tell the truth about themselves.

Kleasen persisted in his efforts to become a Mormon in good standing. Sometime in early 1973, he showed up at the Austin First Ward asking to be baptized. The local leadership, however, found him to be a problematic investigator.

Missionary Larry Doty, who served ten months in the Austin area, remembers the first time he saw Kleasen at church dressed in a white shirt with no tie. When Kleasen attended church, he often dressed in a clean white t-shirt and faded blue jeans. There is no enforced dress code among Mormons, but his dress still struck people as strange. Doty noticed the improvement when Kleasen began wearing an ironed white shirt in August 1973. There also were his stories about the CIA and other exotic matters which struck many older Mormons as bizarre. By July 1973 Doty was noting in his missionary journals when Kleasen showed up for services. On July 29 Kleasen appeared with a visiting Mormon friend from the West Coast, Caleb West.

Doty and others introduced Kleasen to single Mormons and encouraged him to attend their social functions. "Perhaps they all can get more acquainted in singles meetings," Doty wrote in his journal. This is probably where Kleasen met Mattie Cannon (not her real name).

Normally it is young missionaries who teach investigators, and at first Doty and his companion Blair Bell presented Kleasen the standardized instructions given to potential converts. On Monday, August 6, Doty was notified by the mission headquarters that he would be transferring to the Houston area. He packed his few belongings, then, with his missionary companion, drove to Oak Hill to say good-bye to Kleasen. It was apparently their first visit to the taxidermy studio.

"He says he gets lonely out there and was glad to see us," Doty wrote in his journal that night. "He lost two wives and is alone most of the time. He is industrious. Has a job and is building his own house and is a guard for the taxidermist place. He said he was just an unbaptized member of the church. He has had various contact with the church for several years in different parts of the world. He feels his CIA experience has marred his past. Bob is a good man and only needs love and attention," Doty continued. "We need to love him into the church. Brother Kleasen (and I say brother because I feel he will be a member of the church before long) also gave us a tour of the taxidermist building." Kleasen posed for Doty's pictures beside a mounted elk he claimed to have shot.

Kleasen again told them stories about his world travels as a sort of hired gun, claiming to have often contracted with the CIA. His obvious fondness for guns made Doty uneasy, but he left that day impressed that Kleasen was "a kind and thoughtful man." Not long after, Bell was transferred to San Antonio but continued to write Kleasen for the next year or so.

A few months later, Kleasen finally became a Mormon. After Doty and Bell left, he was taught by a local member, Boin Campbell. This was probably a reflection of the discomfort older Mormons felt about him. Finally Kleasen persuaded Texas Mormons to accept him and on September 20, 1973, was baptized. He asked Bruce Smith, bishop of the Austin Ward, to baptize him. Mormons baptize by full immersion, in this case in a font constructed for that purpose in their Parker Lane meeting hall.

Three days later Kleasen was ordained a priest in the church's Aaronic or lesser priesthood. Beginning in their early teens, males are ordained into lay priesthood offices of increasing responsibility. A priest is one of the lower of these callings and is a common beginning point for adult male converts.

As it worked out, Kleasen never did become an active Mormon. Almost as soon as he was baptized, he complained constantly and alienated most members who encountered him. This was especially true as the details of his past became known. No one recalls his bearing his testimony at monthly fast and testimony meetings, a ritual of faith in Mormon life.

Mormon congregations are organized by geographic boundaries with members being assigned to a "ward" or "branch" to attend. Soon Kleasen had become so angry with the leadership of the Austin First Ward that he tried to transfer to another one but was denied permission. He sometimes attended a small Marble Falls branch of the LDS church anyway.

In the summer and fall of 1973, congressional committees investigated Watergate and other abuses by President Richard Nixon. On November 21, the Senate Watergate Committee learned of a critical eighteen-minute gap in tapes of Oval Office conversations. Nixon and Kleasen had suspicious gaps in common, and just as Nixon's caught up with him, Kleasen's omissions began to unravel on him as well.

Within two weeks of his baptism, Kleasen had persuaded Bishop Smith to write the Jensens in Denmark confirming his baptism and enclosing a copy of his priesthood ordination certificate. "I consider Brother Kleasen to be a member of the Church in good standing and an asset to the Austin Ward," the bishop wrote. Kleasen had been less than candid about his past.

The next day, October 7, he wrote to the Danish family anticipating their having received the bishop's letter. He pleaded, "You are the only Family I have. I ask you to try and understand that I am not perfect, and that I have cut some corners so to speak. However that is in the past." But the family was not convinced and took the letter, as they had others they had received, to Danish Mission president Ipsen. Ipsen was familiar with Kleasen and regarded him as a predator. He wrote Vaughn Featherstone of the church's Presiding Bishopric in Salt Lake City. The Presiding Bishop's Office administers the physical needs of Mormon congregations, including security concerns.

"Robert Kleasen, who we know here in Denmark as John T. Williamson, caused us great problems," Ipsen wrote on October 27, 1973. Ipsen briefly set out Kleasen's conduct in Copenhagen, including that he "took advantage of a young lady in the Church here," and finally "beat her up terribly." Ipsen dismissed Kleasen as "a confidence man and one who would bear watching." He went on to write, "I hope and pray, as [Bishop Smith's] letter states, that he has made a full and complete repentance. But I write this letter as a caution so that more people in the Church may not fall into a trap and be hurt if this is his aim."

Salt Lake City thanked Ipsen for the warning and passed his letter on to Smith on November 12, 1973. "We are forwarding this letter to you so that you may make adequate judgment and act accordingly," the Presiding Bishopric wrote. "We trust that you will exercise caution in light of this past experience to see that all of the Church principles are followed by this brother." They encouraged Smith to report back.

At first, Kleasen was involved with his ward, receiving considerable attention as new converts often do. While some members expressed suspicion about his grandiose stories, others seemed drawn to him, creating divisions in the congregations. Kleasen even was invited to speak about his life—his fantasy life, as it turned out—at a fireside in Smith's home.

Despite his delusions, Kleasen recognized that things were not going well. "I am living now rather poorly compared to some periods in my life," he confessed in a November 6, 1973, letter to the Jensens. But almost from the beginning, Kleasen registered complaints and demands with local church leaders. As was his habit throughout his life, he wrote a steady stream of letters to local Mormon leaders complaining about how he had been abused. When Smith was replaced as bishop by Frank McCullough, who had previously served on the stake high counsel, Kleasen immediately caught his eye. The first time McCullough heard Kleasen introduce himself at a priesthood meeting, an introduction laced with complaints, the new bishop saw him as trouble.

Kleasen was regularly discussed in the ward's all-male elders' quorum presidency meetings where he was described as a needy convert. Eddie Davis, young secretary to the quorum presidency and a University of Texas student, was assigned to be Kleasen's home teacher and attempted to visit him several times at his trailer. (Home teachers are priesthood representatives who visit every member family each month to check on their spiritual and temporal welfare.)

Kleasen also met an attractive twenty-six-year-old Mormon woman, Mattie Cannon, and persuaded her to go out with him three or four times. By the time of Kleasen's arrest and her interview by police, she had turned hostile toward him. Cannon was a conservative, strict Mormon and quickly discovered that Kleasen was not. Their dates often became wrestling matches with Kleasen being all hands. "We talked many times on the church's moral code. To him it was to keep children out of trouble and it did not apply to adults," she later told investigators. Kleasen, she thought, "had a rather distorted view of many of the church's policies and standards." Kleasen told her he had master's degrees in both sociology and education, "but due to some weird problems, he could not get his transcripts down here so he could teach." He told Cannon he wanted to teach. "He *loved* young people because he could appear as a hero to them."

Kleasen liked to brag about his accomplishments and travels, showing off his passport. He again claimed to speak and read several languages, among them Danish. Once Cannon picked out a verse in Kleasen's Danish Book of Mormon and asked him to read it to her in English. "He tried to wiggle out of that but I discovered that he could not read or speak Danish," she later said. He would also talk about that "witch" he had been involved with in Denmark.

Kleasen's weapons were all around and Cannon didn't care for them either. "I wouldn't tolerate his playing around with guns when I was there because I hate guns." The couple sometimes would drive around the Texas Hill Country where Kleasen liked to poach deer; she realized he knew the region "like the back of his hand." He told Cannon he "believed that the deer were for anyone and he didn't believe in the hunting laws." She thought he "was quite depressed" and saw the naive missionaries "as a great ego boost. They fell `hook, line and sinker' for his stories." Different missionaries would often come to his trailer to target shoot with him.

By the late fall of 1973, Cannon was concerned about Kleasen's state of mind. "I knew he had problems and that he was unstable, but I was afraid in a self destructive way," she'd later tell police. "He seemed to feel that he was a failure at life and that the whole world was now, and always had been, against him; that due to circumstances he always got the 'shaft' but never because of his own doing." She also observed, "Bob is a clever man, and *many* (most) individuals that I have observed are suckered into where he wants them, and he is proud of this."

The last time Cannon saw Kleasen was October 28, the day of the murders. It was the day before her birthday.

SIXTEEN

KLEASEN'S STOLEN BUFFALO TROPHY FINALLY CAUGHT UP with him, and on December 7, 1973, he was back in jail. A. W. Moursand, owner of the Diamond X Ranch, was tenacious about the buffalo killed on his property in 1969. A private investigator had been hired to track down the poacher. The investigation had finally brought Texas game officer Larry Brock to the Austin Taxidermy Studio where Moursand's buffalo had been mounted and was hanging on the wall along with an Aoudad sheep, an Axis deer, and a black buck Kleasen had shot.

An arrest warrant was obtained for Kleasen, this time on felony theft charges. Officers now knew he was living in a trailer behind the taxidermy studio. Fredericksburg game officer Max Hartman and FBI agent Joe Butler were sent to arrest Kleasen, which they did the evening of December 7 after first spending a couple of days trying to locate him. The FBI got involved because it was now known that Kleasen had fled the New York felony assault charges.

At first, Kleasen was held in the little white 1894 limestone jail outside the Blanco County Courthouse in Johnson City, but within twenty-four hours he was moved to the Gillespie County Jail in Fredericksburg. In 1973 the jail was a squatty rooftop pillbox atop the county courthouse.

On December 10, 1973, Kleasen appeared in the Blanco County Courthouse in Johnson City where his bond was set at $2,000 and an attorney was appointed for him. What had first been a misdemeanor hunting charge was now prosecuted as a felony rustling offense. Extradition proceedings were also started to return him to New York for trial in the 1971 shooting of DuBoise. Kleasen secured a new lawyer, Randy Savage of Marble Falls, to help him fight both counts. He lingered in jail for months while this was being fought out.

In Fredericksburg Kleasen was housed with other inmates in a cell with a dozen beds arranged as bunks along one wall. Jail standards were pretty lax in Texas at the time, and the Gillespie County sheriff's wife prepared meals for the inmates. She ran a nearby rest home and twice a day cooked extra portions for Kleasen and the other inmates. It was usually brought up the three flights of stairs in syrup buckets by another game officer, Norm Henk, who was often detailed to help the sheriff. The sheriff was old and found the three flights of stairs too demanding, so he often asked Henk to "take care of our buffalo killer" and the others. The inmates also had a hot plate in the cell to cook their own food if they had any. Kleasen hated the food and complained about it constantly.

Henk soon learned to loath Kleasen. Not only was he constantly complaining about the food, the words "thank you" never passed his lips in spite of his regular insistence on personal favors from the jailers. He read steadily and checked out a whole series of books from the local library on World War II, the Nazis, military history, and political philosophy. Henk had to pull the books from the library and return them when Kleasen was done. Jailers recall that Kleasen never smiled.

Kleasen wasn't any more popular with the other inmates. They grew quickly tired of his complaining, his boasting about his espionage and hunting exploits, and his habit of staying up all night and sleeping during the day.

During this time Kleasen kept up a stream of complaints to local Mormon leaders. He asked Bishop Smith to post his bail and secure an attorney to represent him, but the bishop declined. LDS policy prohibits church leaders from getting involved in criminal cases in such a way, but Kleasen didn't want to hear this.

Smith did visit Kleasen in jail, often bringing his small son, but the convert's behavior became increasingly strange, and Smith decided to stop bringing his boy along. A local Mormon, rancher Frederick Grote, was also assigned by the church to visit Kleasen in Fredericksburg. He left food and small amounts of money for Kleasen, again without ever being thanked.

Also during Kleasen's time in Gillespie County, he became involved with members of the Pentecostal church. They came to the jail to preach. Jailers, who thought Kleasen was taking advantage of anyone who offered kindness or concern, could only watch his manipulations with disgust. From that point on, he spent as much time in Pentecostal churches as he did with the Mormons.

At some point district judge Jack Miller, after hearing another round of Kleasen's moaning about his jailers, decided to give everyone a break and transfer Kleasen to the Burnet County Jail. No one in Fredericksburg missed him.

Leaders of the Austin First Ward elders' quorum read Kleasen's complaints about jail food—Kleasen claimed jailers were deliberately starving him—and asked his home teacher, Eddie Davis, to investigate. Davis and his wife brought a large bag of groceries to the Burnet jail, selecting items Kleasen could prepare on the cell's hot plate. The jailers were friendly and allowed Davis to deliver the food. No doubt they hoped the food would reduce Kleasen's complaining. Kleasen never thanked Davis for the food. Instead he ranted against the courts, the government, and the Mormon church, never once looking Davis directly in the eye. As Kleasen rambled, he focused on a far ceiling corner of his cell. It was an unsettling encounter.

On February 18, 1974, a plea was worked out on time served for the misdemeanor buffalo shooting charge. The felony theft charge remained but was not pursued.

The New York charges were more difficult for him to resolve, but he temporarily accomplished this as well. After hard lobbying, Texas Secretary of State Mark White recommended that the New York request be denied. Kleasen was released from the Burnet County Jail on May 31. Five days later Texas governor Dolph Briscoe refused the New York request for extradition.

White later told reporters his office had looked at the entire record of the New York case and concluded that Kleasen "appeared to be foredoomed. It looked like a case of vengeance." White was especially concerned about Kleasen's having been denied counsel for some time based on his being able to afford a lawyer by virtue of his valuable gun collection, a collection that had been seized by ATF agents thus denying him its value. White saw a "catch 22 quality" to Kleasen's prosecution. At another time, White justified his decision to reporters with the observation, "The way New York treats people is a little different from Texas."

The situation caused enough concern that when Smith attended the church's general conference in April 1974 in Salt Lake City, he reported on Kleasen at length with Mormon security officials. With the earlier letter from Denmark Mission president Ipsen, large parts of Kleasen's erratic history were now known.

McCullough, who succeeded Smith as bishop in July 1974, continued to regard Kleasen as a divisive influence in the ward. (Smith, a University of Texas botany professor, had taken a similar position at Brigham Young University in Provo, Utah.) Kleasen had a way of turning members against each other, of constantly sowing friction. In light of this and Kleasen's lies about Denmark, the new bishop felt it was time to initiate excommunication proceedings against him. He felt Smith had bent over backwards to make the new convert feel welcome, but Kleasen was still filled with bitterness.

One of the Mormons who'd visited Kleasen's trailer was Blair Bell, the young missionary who'd introduced Darley to him. Bell was later transferred to San Antonio and Kleasen began to write. Kleasen had shown him the fake Raadt driver's license, saying he used it to buy things when he didn't want his identity known. Bell was with him at least once when he bought weapons as Raadt in San Antonio.

With Richard Nixon's resignation as president on August 9, 1974, Kleasen's paranoia blossomed. That August and September, his letters to Bell were angry and violent. He complained bitterly about his treatment by local church authorities, especially their questioning him about Denmark. Bell told mission president Loveland about the tensions and tried to mediate. On August 17 Kleasen replied to a recent letter from Bell, writing that he was surprised to learn Bell was trying to get Loveland to help resolve his personal conflicts in the Austin First Ward. He claimed he stood "accused of false things in Denmark" and that he'd asked Smith to clear this up "but he sat on his ass and nothing was accomplished."

Growing more indignant, Kleasen insisted, "I do not want a pat on the head and a paw shake, I want BLOOD. I want to go in and finish this mess one way or the other. Either some authority will get up on his two legs and vindicate me publically [sic], or they can excommunicate me." Complaining again about the lack of attention he felt he got in jail, he went on to write, "Few thought of me when I begged for help, now I listen to no one, I go for the Kill." He also stated he would not abide by game laws but would continue to shoot his food anytime he wanted because it was his right.

On September 6 Kleasen wrote Bell to report on his meeting with stake president Amos Wright. He was indignant that Wright had denied his request to be transferred to another ward. "Too many lies had preceided [sic] my meeting, he would not listen," Kleasen wrote. He ranted that Mormon leaders were unwilling to work with him, and hinted at revenge. "This is 1974 and you can't call a man out in a gun fight so I am going after all my oppressors with vengence [sic] using my brains, and training, and the pig. Perhaps you can see what has happened to me the running, the sellout, and the endless solitary confinement. I have learned to hate."

The next day Kleasen wrote again, this time complaining about other Mormons he insisted had stolen from him. "I will not mess around any longer, I am going for the 'kill.'" He also wrote that missionaries Darley and Jenkins had stopped by, apparently at Bell's urging. Kleasen had invited them back on a Monday night for a steak supper. "*Many Thanks*," Kleasen wrote Bell. "It will be nice to see another Mormon. But I will not return to the Austin Ward."

Then Kleasen wrote McCullough, demanding that the bishop visit him at his trailer, alone and without telling anyone they were to meet. McCullough sensed danger and refused. "I didn't come in on a turnip truck," he later quipped. The new bishop would meet with Kleasen in the ward meeting house, but not in some isolated setting.

One night McCullough took home Kleasen's bulky ward file of letters and materials. He found a private room where he could read every document in the file, then prayed to ask for guidance and direction in the matter. Immediately he felt inspired to warn the missionaries not to go to Kleasen's any more. He communicated this to ward leaders who worked with the missionaries, a lay priesthood body called seventies.

When the two missionaries expressed a desire to keep working with Kleasen, McCullough called them himself and urged them to avoid the man. They told the bishop they had a dinner appointment on the 28th and felt they would let Kleasen down if they didn't keep it. McCullough decided not to go over their heads and call mission president Loveland. Meanwhile, Kleasen continued to attend a Pentecostal church in Burnet, Texas, west of Austin.

Sometime in the fall of 1974 Kleasen's path crossed with a widowed Pentecostal woman named Linda Miller. Her husband, Charles, had been killed in an Alabama auto accident on Christmas Eve 1973. She moved with her five-year-old son to Longview, Texas, to start over. A devout member of the Pentecostal church, she began attending meetings in nearby Gladewater. Somehow Miller and Kleasen began exchanging letters.

By now Kleasen was too wedded to his fantasies to change them for Miller. His steady stream of letters boasted of his rapid rise in the CIA. "I was not a minor agent. I ranked fourth from the top at the last although I had a humble beginning as a pilot testing missiles at Alamogordo, N.M.," he wrote. After graduating from the National Police Academy and the FBI School at Quantico, Virginia, he continued, he was "exchanged" for a British agent. He spent the next part of his career in the British MI-6 school in Dundee, Scotland, and later went for additional training at Kastel, Germany. "Yes, Linda, I was headed for the top in that profession only I could not put God out of my life."

Again his letters boasted of intellectual accomplishments—speaking six languages, graduate degrees from universities in Sweden and Denmark, and world travel such as few men ever dream of. In one letter he boasted of his prowess as an outdoorsman. He acknowledged poaching all the deer he needed, filling his freezers with the meat. "Naturally I can butcher," he wrote, "and cut up all my own meat to my specifications."

SEVENTEEN

JACK PARIS, A MORMON, MET KLEASEN THE FIRST MONDAY IN
September 1974. Kleasen had invited Gary Darley and Rich
Jenkins to his Oak Hill trailer for a deer steak dinner. Paris and his
wife, Chris, drove the missionaries over, thereby saving them miles on
their car. The missionaries had another appointment at 6:30, so after
dinner Paris drove them and his wife back to Austin, but returned
about 9:00 with two other Mormon friends from Houston.

The four sat around and talked. Kleasen told his captive audience
about his experiences as a CIA agent, as a U2 pilot and fighter ace in
Korea, and about his defection from the CIA in response to "corruption." Among his stories were those about killing communist revolu-
tionary Che Guevara in South America, then cutting the man's fingers off to send to Fidel Castro. He also talked about how he had recently been harassed with a "trumped-up charge of rustling a head of
buffalo."

Kleasen talked bitterly about how for six months he'd been
dragged from jail to jail, humiliated, and ridiculed. He swore he'd
never go back under any conditions. He said if a policeman pulled up
in his driveway, he'd shoot him, cut him up, and spread him out so far
they'd never find the body. "Believe me, I have everything I need to do
it with right here," he said. Paris was discovering that Kleasen was a
colorful talker, fond of violent threats and dramatic language. He recalled that about half of Kleasen's conversation concerned his bitterness toward law enforcement. Afterwards Kleasen gave his guests a
tour of the taxidermy shop—he had all the keys. They left about 11:30
that night.

Paris, a son of stake patriarch Paul Paris, was a friendly young
Mormon anxious to fellowship a recent convert. He visited the trailer

five or six times after that. At least once he picked Kleasen up at his trailer and drove him to a Safeway to buy groceries. At first, he regarded Kleasen as violent but not dangerous to him. However, the longer Paris knew him, the more he came to fear him.

On one occasion, while telling Paris about his escape from the CIA, Kleasen said, "I know how I'll end up dying, but I don't know when. President Ford hasn't decided what to do about me and the other defected agents yet. The CIA will get me though. That's why I always carry a gun with me 'cause if they shoot and miss, I won't." Another time Kleasen held a loaded pistol to his head and said he didn't have any reason to keep on living, that sometimes he thought he should just kill himself. Paris said that scared him. And Paris believed everything Kleasen told him. "He seemed very serious," he'd later say. Paris passed some of these stories on to local church leaders.

Kleasen had shown Paris the renovations he was attempting in the rundown sheds around his trailer. Paris's apartment was next to a construction site and he sometimes helped Kleasen gather scrap lumber for his projects.

Kleasen invited Darley and Fischer to his trailer for their usual deer steak Monday night meal on October 21, but they canceled with a letter on the 19th. "We are running out of miles and we have a General Authority coming to speak to the missionaries," Darley wrote. Missionaries with church-issued cars—always American Motors vehicles, a result of Mormon George Romney's having run the company—had a strict limit on the number of miles they could drive each month and a round-trip to Kleasen's rural location ate into them badly. The missionaries wrote, "We'll plan on seeing you Mon. the 28th. See you then."

On Wednesday night, October 16, 1974, Paris and his wife had other church friends over to their modest apartment for dinner. Once a week they invited missionaries to dinner and on this night they asked Darley and his mission zone leader, Christopher Warnock. Darley's earlier companion, Elder Jenkins, had been released and had returned to his home in Utah. The Parises' home teachers, Eddie Davis and Greg Molineaux, were also invited. Paris had suggested to Kleasen that he stop by that night, promising to help him gather more lumber. In fact, Kleasen had asked to be invited for dinner.

Dinner was still spread on the table when there was a loud knock on the door. It was Kleasen. He stepped into the apartment and upon seeing Davis, who was also Kleasen's home teacher, launched into a verbal assault on the Mormon church and its local leaders. He looked only at Davis, his voice rising to a shout. Discomfort quickly became tension as Paris and Davis feared Kleasen would punch someone.

Kleasen claimed the church had done nothing for him when he was jailed, that no one had ever visited or sent a card. Davis tried to calm him down and reminded him of his jail visit with groceries. Kleasen gave him a hard look and insisted, "I've never seen you before in my life." Davis was stunned; it struck him that Kleasen believed what he said. Kleasen became so heated that Davis and his companion feared they might be assaulted so they excused themselves and left. Kleasen had terrified them.

Afterwards Paris was both embarrassed and furious. When the two were later alone, he chewed Kleasen out. "You had no right to speak to my guests, who are also my friends, that way," he told Kleasen. "He told me that the Austin First Ward had not treated him right and that he had reason to speak to Davis in that manner. And I told him I was a member of the Austin First Ward myself and I had always treated him right." Kleasen didn't disagree. Having made his point, Paris dropped the matter and went with Kleasen to the parking lot to load scrap lumber.

An hour had passed, but Paris spied his home teachers talking in another part of the parking lot. One of them also lived in the apartment complex. Paris excused himself from Kleasen and jogged to his friends. In the dark they only heard the footsteps and, thinking it might be Kleasen, started to run until Paris called to them.

Talking, they found they all were frightened of Kleasen and agreed it might be a good idea to stay with friends or relatives for a few days. Davis, who'd been around Kleasen off and on for some time now, sensed that something about Kleasen's anger was escalating. It frightened him. When Paris returned to where he'd left Kleasen, the man and his car were gone. This unnerved Paris all the more. That night he and his wife left to stay with relatives for a few days.

Late on October 27, a Sunday, Darley telephoned Paris. They talked about Kleasen for half an hour, about his outburst and the fact that Darley was to have dinner at the trailer the following Monday. Darley was uneasy. He said if Kleasen "gave them any trouble," they'd tell him they couldn't return. Darley felt that Kleasen was "crazy enough to shoot someone if he got upset with them." But Darley said he felt obligated to keep his commitments, including dinner with Kleasen.

EIGHTEEN

WITHIN HOURS OF KLEASEN'S ARREST, OFFICERS BEGAN delivering possible evidence to a lab for testing. The Texas Department of Public Safety ran the state crime lab in Austin which did most of the scientific work in the Kleasen case. Lab technicians gathered anything that looked interesting.

On November 6, 1974, Leslie Smith, a chemist with the lab, spent the better part of the day inspecting the missionaries' abandoned Hornet, then stored at the Reveile Body Shop. The car was dusted for prints; a few were found, but nothing from Kleasen. Police had also searched Kleasen's 1964 station wagon, impounded at the Austin Police Department quonset building, giving Smith things that might have some value as evidence.

From the Hornet, Smith collected what he thought was a very small amount of blood from the right front seat, an unknown powdery substance from the trunk, and the battery cables which someone had cut through. From Kleasen's station wagon, he was given an automobile jack, some bolt cutters and other tools, a pair of gloves, a green plastic bag, and blanket, hair, and more suspected blood stains.

The next day Ranger Spillar brought to the lab some clothing and a section of rope, plus two wheels with tires believed to be from the missionaries' stripped car. Over a month later Lt. Jordan would bring in three more matching wheels with tires. All the tires were collected from a shed near Kleasen's trailer. Police had also found the license plates from the missionaries' car in the shed.

Jordan brought four brake drums that had been removed from the victims' Hornet. He also brought concrete blocks found at the same location along with chips of suspected concrete collected from Kleasen's station wagon.

The next day another policeman brought in a metal plate from a band saw at the taxidermy studio. After reading the poaching manuscript seized in Kleasen's trailer, investigators feared the biological material caked on it might contain more than just animal remains.

Smith accompanied officers searching the taxidermy studio and grounds on November 11, and collected hair samples from the band saw. Later that day Spillar returned to the lab with head hair known to have come from both Darley and Fischer.

Still later Jordan came back with more material seized at the taxidermist's: a Seiko watch, Fischer's name tag, a hunting knife, a pair of rubber gloves, and another fatigue jacket. He also had mud, vegetation, and hair collected from the underside of Kleasen's impounded Rambler. And he brought in the fingernail scrapings he'd taken from Kleasen the night of his arrest. There was also a suspicious bone fragment Jordan found in the missionaries' Hornet. He wanted the crime lab to tell him if it was human or animal.

Every few days some officer would return to the crime lab with more materials he hoped would prove to be evidence against Kleasen. Hub caps found near his trailer, hair and suspected blood stains from the porch of the missionaries' Mary Street apartment, bits of trash from Kleasen's trailer with blood droplets on them, spent bullets, and more clothing. Then police brought in frozen meat found in the freezer near Kleasen's trailer. Anxious friends of Kleasen had also returned meat he had given them, sheepishly asking that it be tested. Everyone was relieved when it proved to be deer meat.

The taxidermy studio septic tank was pumped and four bags of material brought to the lab for testing. It was thought that the hair, bone fragments, and other biological materials might include something from the missionaries. Testing could not verify any human substances from that source. The lab was also given materials collected alongside rural roads during the November 9 search by volunteers. Nothing of value was found there either.

As testing unfolded, it became obvious the band saw was going to be important. It was a big, squat, gray, six-foot Rockwell. A large circular housing topped it, containing the long blade. It looked almost alien, like something from a low budget science fiction movie. Spillar had it loaded up from the taxidermy studio and delivered to the crime lab. Rathbone was not happy about having to give up his band saw during the busy season.

As the evidence gathering concluded, the crime lab had a variety of items. There were suspected human hair, blood, and tissue, along with other biological material. The band saw was part of this. There were automobile parts and tools collected from the two American Motors cars. And there was ballistics work to be done on the Fischer name tag and with firearms seized from Kleasen.

Two crime lab veterans, Fred Reymer and Smith, did most of the work. Smith had a degree in chemistry and had been with the DPS lab for seventeen years. He was its chief chemist and toxicologist. It was his job to analyze the composition of anything submitted to the lab. Reymer did the ballistics work.

In the lab Smith inspected a fatigue jacket and trousers collected by game officer Frank Henzy from a large metal can outside Kleasen's trailer. The chemist could see what he thought were very small blood stains, some hair fragments, and a substance that looked like tissue or possibly wood fibers. Testing verified that the stains were blood, both human and animal. He used what is called the antihuman precipitant test in which a sample of evidence is brought into contact with an antiserum. A chemical reaction indicates if the sample is human protein or not.

Such tests can be run for animal material as well as for human. Smith also tested for deer and bovine blood, finding both on Kleasen's clothing. There was not enough human blood to test for type so he couldn't say anything beyond its being human. The tissue substance also contained human protein or possibly more blood. The hair was human as well.

Known hair samples from both Fischer and Darley were then compared with the three individual strands found on Kleasen's fatigue jacket. Such hair comparisons are done under a low-power microscope first to determine if they are human or animal. Those found to be human are then mounted and examined on a high-power microscope for basic characteristics. Such inspections can differentiate between head, body, and pubic hair. It can be sorted by race. Coloring, both natural and artificial, and the condition of the hair also help in identification.

It's not a perfect system, but valuable. One critical factor for positive identification is the opportunity for hair from a victim to end up where they were found. Are there other indications the victim was where the samples were found, and when? Or a suspect's hair if they are gathered at a crime scene other than places where the suspect regularly visited. A suspect's hair on the body of a victim, such as on his clothing or under his fingernails, can be important. But this was for detectives to gather, the crime lab can't often address that. In Smith's opinion, two strands of the head hair found on the jacket came from Gary Darley and one from Mark Fischer.

The band saw was now in Smith's lab. He removed samples of biological material from inside the housing, on the rubber tension wheels, and from the blade channel area. Much of the material was sawdust and small wood chips. This caused lumps or wads with plenty of mass for collection and examination. Both animal, deer mostly, and human hair were found in every sample Smith took off the band saw. All the human hair matched Darley's or Fischer's. Smith didn't find any human hair which could not be attributed to one of the victims.

All the hair was in fragments; only two included root structures. The hair was broken and splintered as opposed to clean cuts. Smith concluded that the hair had been chopped up with a relatively blunt instrument like a band saw blade. He also felt that the object to which the hair was originally attached was held in the band saw rigidly enough for the blade to get a good bite on it. The hair could not have been thrown into the blade loose and left these kinds of cuts. Most of the hair Smith recovered came from the immediate area of the blade.

This was not body or finger hair. It was definitely head hair and could only come from the scalp. It was not the result of some non-fatal accident by someone working in the taxidermy shop.

When he ran tests to determine if there was human tissue or blood, he kept coming up positive, but again he could not get a specific blood type. Considering that the human material he was finding appeared to be muscle, fatty tissue, and bone, there should have been a lot more blood than appeared to be the case. Smith concluded that two entire bodies had not been dismembered on the band saw. Had that been the case, he would have found body and pubic hair, plus a lot more human tissue from large muscles and blood. Only the heads had been cut on the band saw.

The human body is, for the most part, tied together by muscles and tissue. It can be disassembled with a hunting knife by someone with minimal skill. Someone who knows how to break down an animal carcass can do the same with a human being. An experienced hunter who dresses his own kill would certainly know how. The one exception is the skull.

When Smith tested the metal plate removed from the band saw, he again found human blood stains and fragments of human head hair. The hair again matched that of Fischer and Darley. He also found a single cut hair fragment on the plate that apparently came from Kleasen. He compared under a microscope the tissue gathered from the band saw with that found on Kleasen's pants. It appeared to be the same material.

Smith later prepared samples of the hair and tissue from the band saw for an FBI crime lab outside Washington, D.C. Much later another set of samples was collected for Dr. Joseph Jachimczyk, the Harris County medical examiner in Houston.

The Seiko watch appeared to have faint flecks of blood on the band. When Smith looked at them under a microscope, he was positive. Testing again verified that it was human blood. The second watch, a Voumard, also had what looked like small amounts of blood on the back near where the wrist band was fastened. Again testing confirmed this.

Lab scientists also considered the non-biological materials gathered in the investigation. The white, granulated substance removed from the trunk of the Hornet was less obvious. It was of particular interest because it looked like the same substance on the car jack found in Kleasen's car. It turned out to be powdered laundry detergent. The same laundry soap was found on one of the five tires stored in a shed outside Kleasen's trailer which had apparently come from the missionaries' car. Smith could not make a positive match but was ready to testify that by all appearances the same substance had been found in all three locations.

Then Smith went to an Austin American Motors dealership and asked them about car jacks in new cars. He found that the factory issue jacks were essentially identical with that seized from Kleasen's car, right down to the unusual white grease that American Motors used to oil the shaft and threads. Most other automakers used a brown or black grease in their cars. This strongly suggested that the jack had been removed from the missionaries' year-old Hornet. Smith thought the jack also looked as though it had never been used.

Smith tried to match the four brake drums to the five wheels with tires. The size, mounting holes, and general configurations were consistent. There were also matching wear indentations. He concluded there was an exact match on four of the wheels to an individual brake drum. They had come from the missionaries' car.

In addition, soap powder was on one wheel, apparently the spare. It too had markings matching one of the wheel drums, indicating it had been mounted at some point. If it was the spare from the missionaries' trunk, laundry they had loaded in the trunk may have at some point spilled out onto both the tire and jack.

In order to get a more precise match on the recovered tires and the brake drums, Smith set up a photographic comparison. Crime lab photographers shot the wheels and brake drums at a 90-degree angle in a special "view box," then produced actual size negatives with x-ray film. When negatives of the wheels were laid over those of the brake drums, there was an exact match. Smith was already convinced the wheels and brake drums matched, but this experiment clinched it. There was no doubt the wheels in Kleasen's shed had come from the abandoned and tireless Hornet found in south Austin.

The bolt cutters proved interesting but not as conclusive as the wheels. The battery cables in the missionaries' car had been cut in two, but the battery was bolted down at the base so it could not be easily removed. The lab had both the severed cables removed by Smith from the car and the bolt cutters seized from Kleasen's car by police. The hope was that the cutting tool could be matched with marks on the cables.

The lab found almost pure copper fragments and a black rubber material in the jaws of the bolt cutters that were consistent with the battery cables. They used the bolt cutters to cut other sections of the recovered battery cables. They compared the cuts and removed the residue left on the blade to see if it matched what Smith had first discovered. The cuts seemed to match, but there were no imperfections or specific marks on the cutter blades he could refer to for a positive identification. The individual strands of wire that made up the battery cables were not large enough to hold the kind of microscopic markings needed for identification.

All the crime lab could conclude was that the general cut pattern on the cables was consistent with Kleasen's bolt cutters. No one could say the cutters had not been used to try to extract the battery. The residue on the cutters after the test cuts seemed to match, both in how it appeared after being mashed during the cutting and in composition. This was enough for Smith and Rymer. They were confident Kleasen's bolt cutters had been used to snip the battery cables in the missionaries' car.

Smith couldn't offer much help with the concrete block and chips he was given. He concluded they were of a slightly different type of manufacture—the density and color of the concrete and filler were not the same—but they still could have been made at the same plant during different runs. The fragments he was given were too small to allow any meaningful comparison with the single complete block.

The ballistics section was in the hands of supervisor Fred Rymer who had thirty-four years' experience in the lab. He was a recognized authority on the identification of firearms and bullets and testified up to forty times a year. He would need that experience because this time he was asked to perform a different kind of examination. Besides the Fischer name tag and firearms seized by police, Rymer also examined the bolt cutters and battery cables for a connection.

Rymer received the name tag in a November 6 batch of evidence and began by putting it under a microscope. The slightly elliptical hole had every appearance of having been made by a bullet. It appeared to be an entrance hole, but it was clean, there was no splintering or plug forced out of the back as the bullet passed through. There were carbonized deposits and what looked like little particles of lead on it, what he called a lead swipe or grease ring. Rymer thought he could almost pick up the land and groove impressions of a fired bullet.

Inside the hole he also saw what looked like two grains of nitrocellulose powder, what is commonly called smokeless powder. Rymer estimated these deposits would have been left if the name tag was fired at from a range of five to ten feet. This estimate was questionable given that Kleasen loaded his own ammunition and no one was sure how much powder he used. Rymer could see that the bullet had struck the name tag at some angle but exactly what he could not tell.

The lab then secured a dozen identical plastic name tags from assistant district attorney Spencer for test firing. They used a series of .22 rimfire cartridges hoping to match the apparent bullet hole in Fischer's tag. Rymer tested .22 shorts, a lower velocity round which contains less gunpowder, .22 longs, and .22 long rifles. All are generally considered lower velocity rounds. Not all .22s are exactly 22-hundredths of an inch in diameter. Depending on the type of round and manufacturer, they vary from .217 to .221.

Rymer also tested with .25- and .32-round ammunition. All were shot straight on or with 15- to 30-degree angles and from distances of twelve to eighteen inches. His firing angles were arbitrary. Rymer used commercial ammunition for his tests, even though Kleasen loaded his own. Rymer knew he couldn't reproduce the effect of a bullet striking the name tags on a human chest, he was simply trying to get an elliptical hole like the one on the Fischer name tag. None of the tests he conducted exactly duplicated the hole in the missionary's name tag. Finally, there are several different types of gunpowder, but Rymer made no attempt to test the tiny grains he discovered to see what kind they were.

Rymer first reported back to the Austin police department in a letter dated December 16, 1974. The lab's examination could not establish that the bolt cutters seized from Kleasen were used in the attempt to remove the battery from the missionaries' abandoned car. But the hole in Fischer's name tag was a different matter. "The hole in the name plate does have the appearance, in our opinion, of a possible bullet hole and if it be a bullet hole, it appears, in our opinion, to be closer to a .22 caliber than any other," he wrote. He would later receive two of the firearms seized from Kleasen. Agent Littleton gave him the .22 Hornet rifle and a .22 Ruger revolver on February 20 after the preliminary testing was complete. Rymer used both in more tests, including the high velocity .22s such as the Hornet.

Rymer considered all the test results and gave an educated guess based on his thirty-four years as a ballistics examiner. He was confident it was a bullet hole. It was closer to .22 caliber than anything else, and it likely came from a high velocity bullet. The holes left by low velocity bullets during his testing looked different, knocking out more of a plug from the back of the name tag. Kleasen's Ruger knocked out such a plug, leading Rymer to conclude it was not used on Fischer's name tag. That hole was much cleaner, the bullet cutting right through. But the hole left by the Hornet rifle came much closer to that in the recovered name tag.

Rymer believed the little grains of powder imbedded in the hole suggested a close shot, closer than ten feet and maybe five. Anything farther away wouldn't have produced powder residue like that, he thought. Rymer subsequently provided prosecutors with two sample name tags shot with .22 long rifle, low velocity weapons; one from a .32 revolver; another from a .25 automatic pistol; and two fired upon six times from the Hornet rifle.

The biological samples Smith had forwarded to the FBI were tested under a new cutting edge science called neutron activation analysis, or NAA, by FBI scientist Michael Hoffman. NAA was first used in the courts in the 1960s, and was an extremely precise and sensitive test to identify the composition of small samples, such as a single human hair. It did not use up the tested sample, a disadvantage with most other crime lab tests. Not only could it identify the substance, it could make a precise match with known samples. Its disadvantage was that it was very expensive, in part because it required a nuclear reactor. It could also be very complicated to explain just as DNA evidence often is today. NAA testimony ran the risk of confusing a jury, especially with an effective cross examination.

In NAA known and unknown samples are subjected to neutron bombardment in a nuclear reactor. This causes an atomic reaction which emits gamma rays. These gamma rays are then counted by means of gamma ray spectrometry and compared. Through this process, the unknown sample can be precisely identified and compared with known samples.

The FBI lab ran the known hair samples from the missionaries through this test together with samples removed from Kleasen's clothing and band saw. It was expensive work, but prosecutors hoped it would remove all doubt as to whom the unknown hair samples had come from.

NINETEEN

THERE ARE OVER 10 MILLION LATTER-DAY SAINTS IN THE WORLD today, with a majority outside the United States. Considering that there were just over 1 million Mormons in 1950, this is unprecedented growth. LDS membership has doubled roughly every ten or eleven years since then. Some 380 new church buildings were constructed in 1997. Non-Mormon demographers have projected 260 million members by 2080. This is due in large part to the high-powered missionary program. Volunteer missionaries have been a feature of LDS life since the church was founded in 1830.

About a third of all Mormon males between nineteen and twenty-five serve on such missions at their own expense. About 10 percent of young women also go on missions. Young men serve for two years, while young women are "called" to eighteen-month missions. LDS parents are urged to begin saving for a child's mission from birth. Many Mormon youngsters drop sticky pennies and dimes into a mission piggy bank. Sometimes their home congregations, called wards, contribute some or all expenses. No worthy young person is denied a mission call because he lacks the funds. Retired couples are also encouraged to go on missions, and many do. LDS temples and historic sites, such as those in Nauvoo, Illinois, are usually staffed by these retired couples.

Proselytizing missionaries seek out and teach prospective converts, called investigators, using standardized teaching materials prepared by church headquarters. Today over 56,000 missionaries are in the field seeking converts in 161 countries, far more than any other Christian denomination. In 1996 some 78,000 children of members and 330,000 new converts were baptized into the LDS church.

In 1974 elders Darley and Fischer were but two of 18,109 missionaries in the field, 9,811 of them set apart that year.

A mission "call" is extended by the young man or woman's home bishop, as local pastors are called. When an individual is accepted for such service, he is given a specific departure date and told the mission he will serve in. Just before a missionary leaves, his ward will hold a special "Missionary Farewell" meeting where he is often lavished with attention. While he serves, his picture is often displayed in his home chapel along with his mission address and a favorite scripture. Local members are encouraged to write, along with parents and sweethearts.

Missionary service is considered one of the most honorable responsibilities a young Mormon can undertake. "Where did you serve your mission?" is a very important question among church members getting to know each other. "RM's," as returned missionaries are often called, are considered prized mates in the Mormon world. A son's decision not to go on a mission can be especially difficult on many devoted parents.

In 1974 new missionaries began at the Mission Home (now demolished) near Temple Square in Salt Lake City. There they got accustomed to the regimented life of the missionary, and learned the standardized religious instruction the church employs. Volunteer mission presidents, usually successful businessmen accompanied by their wives and families, undergo a similar schooling before they enter the mission field.

The missionary's life is one of strict regulation. Virtually every hour must be accounted for to the mission president or to their missionary zone leaders, usually senior missionaries finishing up their service. They are told when to get up and when to retire. The church tries to limit the amount of money families send so that the missionary experience is the same without regard to personal wealth.

A few get cars they secure from the church, always with limits on how many miles they can drive. Many ride bikes. Wearing standard dark suits and white shirts with distinctive black-and-white breast pocket name tags, young male missionaries are easy to spot. Most religious teaching materials are produced by the church in Utah, but in the

1970s missionaries still had to purchase them.

Missionaries are assigned to specific geographic areas that can be anywhere in the world. In 1974 there were 113 such missions, today there are over 300. There a mission president, called for three years of voluntary service, acts as administrator and surrogate father to the young people in his mission.

Missionaries work, live, and travel in same-sex pairs as "companions." Companions rotate within the mission at regular intervals. These rotations often involve moving to another congregation or another city within the mission.

Missionaries are fully integrated into their local ward life. Members are encouraged to provide them with investigators ready to learn about the church, and local members often accompany them when teaching non-Mormons. They speak regularly in church meetings and become well known to local members.

Members are encouraged to invite missionaries into their homes for dinner. It is common in church meetings for sign-up sheets to circulate as members commit to feed the missionaries. It is not unusual for a released missionary to return to his former area to marry and make a life.

Gary Durley never doubted he would give such service to his faith, just as Kelle, his older brother, had before him. Like everyone in his large family, he had a testimony as to the truth of the Church of Jesus Christ of Latter-day Saints. Service in their Santa Susana Third Ward, located in Simi Valley, was expected. His father, David K., an engineer with Rockwell International, was a ward clerk. His mother, Jill, was a Sunday school teacher; and Gary was an assistant scoutmaster in the ward sponsored troop.

Gary was born on September 27, 1954. He turned twenty one month before he disappeared.

Kelle had already served in the Texas North Mission, later renamed the Texas Dallas Mission. He arrived at the Salt Lake City Mission Home in October 1971, then returned to California in November 1973, just a few months before Gary's departure. Kelle was twenty-two in 1974. Gary also had a twin sister, Gaye; a brother, Clark, seventeen; another brother, Todd, thirteen; a fourth brother, Bruce, nine; and a baby sister, Beverly, eight.

One of Gary's avid interests before his mission was a motorcycle, a Honda 350 with an *Easy Rider* extended fork and a sissy bar on the back. He used to ride it to work, earning extra money as a clerk at a drive-in dairy. However, he quit after his second armed robbery in two weeks.

One family story about Gary tells of a day when he was riding to school with a friend on his motorcycle. They were stopped by the police and a marijuana cigarette turned up on the friend. Gary hadn't known anything about it. The friend told the officer. "You leave him alone, he's a Mormon." The police let Gary go on his way.

Like many teenagers, he played bass guitar in a family garage band, joined by twin sister Gaye on lead guitar and younger brother Clark on drums.

In 1968 his mother, Jill, gave Kelle a watch with a distinctive band for Christmas. It was the same watch she gave her husband. Kelle wore it during his own two-year mission in Texas. There the humidity made the face of the watch turn green, so Kelle took it apart and tried to wipe the stain off. In the process he wiped off part of the words "17 jewels" on the face. Some of the green stayed near the remaining words.

Kelle returned from his mission in November 1973 and bought a new watch. When Gary left for his own Texas mission in March 1974, Kelle passed the old watch to him. He had it cleaned and tried to restore the damaged face at a local jeweler's, picking it up in January 1974, just in time for Gary's departure. Gary wore it throughout his mission, a kind of good luck charm and reminder of his brother's missionary service.

The gift was a natural thing as the two young men were close. When Kelle came back from Texas, he and Gary often double-dated to dances and movies. Gary took his Mormon girlfriend, seventeen-year-old Kerrie Lynn Hampton.

Kelle enrolled at Brigham Young University in Provo, Utah, in January 1974. BYU was a goal of many faithful, young Mormons and their parents, enrolling 25,000 students by the 1973-74 school year. Kelle and Gary planned to room together at the Y when Gary came home from his mission.

Gary wrote Kelle from Texas each week, often asking him for advice on various problems missionaries had to wrestle with.

During Kelle's first semester break, he visited Gary who was then serving in Cleveland, Texas. There Kelle met one of Gary's best friends in the mission field, Elder Conrad Hardcastle. They went out to dinner where they discussed missionary work, going to college in Provo, and future plans.

The big brother recalls being surprised at how muscled-up Gary had become on his mission, perhaps reflecting the regular regimen of exercise the new missionary put himself on each night and on his free Mondays. "You know, you have brothers and sisters, but you have friends, too. He wasn't only a brother, he was a friend," Kelle said of Gary.

Gary's hair was long when he got his mission call, and it fell to his mother to cut it in January 1974. Mormon missionaries always wear closely cropped hair. Major haircuts were often a last step before departing for the Mission Home. Gary's girlfriend, Kerrie, was there for this sacrifice and kept some of it as a keepsake. Kerrie saved mementos of their relationship and the small plastic bag of hair went with the other things. She wouldn't see it again for more than eight months.

His parents, bursting with pride, accompanied Gary to Salt Lake City to begin his mission. On March 2, 1974, they left him at the Missionary Home near the imposing Salt Lake temple, never dreaming of the final sacrifice his mission would require.

From that point on Gary was a missionary in every sense. He faithfully wrote his family every week. The letters were written on Monday, the missionaries' "free day," and arrived on Thursday. He wrote to Kerrie every week as well.

Once he wrote his nine-year-old sister with a drawing of the two of them together. He wrote, "I'll bet you're the prettiest girl in the class." Gary had tried to say things that made the rest of his family feel good about themselves.

A letter from Gary, dated Monday, October 21, 1974, arrived in the family mail box three days later. It was the last the Darleys would ever hear from their son.

Once in the mission field, Gary kept journals. He recorded his regular meals and camaraderie with Jack Paris, his close relationships with missionary companions, and his calls home. His last call came on his twentieth birthday, September 27, a month and a day before he was killed.

Missionary work was a growing experience for Gary, helping him make the journey from teenager to young man. His journals record his anxiousness about assignments of increasing responsibility and a growing spirituality. At the time of his murder, Gary was a district leader. On September 11 he recorded an intense discussion with his mission president which he described as "a very spiritual interview." President Loveland told Gary he would soon get "a brand new elder" as a companion, Mark Fischer.

In his journal for Friday, September 6, 1974, Gary wrote, "Drove out past Convict Hill to see an inactive member named Mr. Kleasen who Elder Bell wanted to see." On the 23rd Gary recorded that he and Clark had another steak dinner with Kleasen who "told us about all his problems again." Clark was transferred the next day, and on the 27th, Gary's birthday, Mark Fischer arrived. The next day they had lunch with Jack and Kris Paris.

Gary continued to visit Kleasen even though the man was beginning to wear on him. On Monday, September 23, he and Fischer had dinner at Kleasen's trailer which was probably Mark's first visit. Gary's journal records: "We came home and Jack and Chris Paris picked us up and took us to Bob Kleasen's. We had steaks and Bob told us his big story of what happened to him again. I've heard that story three times now. Kleasen really puts me in a spot by wanting us to stay longer and break the rules." Darley was referring to the rule that missionaries not stay in any home longer than an hour and a half.

Darley and Fischer returned for dinner on October 7. Two days later they were eating dinner at the Paris apartment when "Jack went out and got Kleasen which didn't please me a whole lot." Gary recalled the confrontation between Kleasen and his home teachers a week later. Once again Paris had invited the missionaries for dinner. "Bob Kleasen was there. Paris' home teachers came by and Kleasen gave them a hard time," Darley wrote. It was his last journal entry about Kleasen.

Mark James Fischer was born on August 12, 1955. His parents were James and Catherine Fischer of Milwaukee, Wisconsin. He was the oldest of five children, with three younger brothers and a sister. The Fischers were a close and loving family who were not reluctant to tell each other of their affection. And they were very religious.

The Fischers were converts to the LDS church, brought into the faith by young missionaries much like their son just a few years before. Mark was thirteen at the time of their baptism. Their testimonies of Mormon prophet Joseph Smith and the church he founded could not have been stronger. Other members of the Milwaukee First Ward came to see them as one of the most faithful families in the congregation. (The Milwaukee First Ward was one of the older outposts of the church outside the Rocky Mountain West. It was first organized in 1899 with just seven members. It became a ward in the newly organized Milwaukee Stake in 1963.)

From the beginning Mark shined. He was unusually mature as a youth and earned a reputation among adult Mormons as obedient and teachable, as dependable and willing to take charge. He took his lay priesthood ordinations seriously and threw himself into all the church activities he was offered. He looked forward to serving a mission himself. He worked and saved money for it. He learned the teaching discussions missionaries used with investigators. He was instrumental in converting his girlfriend, Barbara Bakewell, to the Mormon faith. In June 1973 Mark, then seventeen, graduated from Milwaukee Boys' Vocational and Technical School. He worked for the next year while awaiting a mission call.

Lance Chase was Mark's church seminary teacher through high school and also served as second counselor to Bishop Vogl. (Chase later taught history at Brigham Young University-Hawaii.) To him,

Mark was an exceptional young man. Mark believed fervently in his family's new faith, he was passionate and articulate when talking about it. There never was any doubt he would go on a mission. He had already served as president of the Mormon high school seminary and as an Explorer advisor in the church's Young Men's Mutual Improvement Association. This was consistent with the rest of his family. His father was a Sunday school officer, his mother was the Junior Sunday School Coordinator, his little sister Melissa was an officer in the young girls' organization Mormons call the Beehives, and his younger brother Michael was secretary of the Aaronic priesthood teachers quorum.

Four months and ten days before their son's murder, the Fischer family visited the Mormon temple in Salt Lake City and were sealed as an eternal family unit in a religious ordinance unique to Mormons. The missionary who had baptized the family in Wisconsin was living in Bountiful, Utah. He volunteered every Tuesday to work in the temple, but on this date felt compelled to work on Friday as well. Once there, he heard voices he recognized, those of the Fischer children who led him to Jim and Cathy. It was a happy and unexpected reunion for all. Mark told friends the sealing ordinance had been the high point of his life.

Fischer's mission call came on August 1, 1974, just weeks before his nineteenth birthday. Bishop Vogl extended the mission call on behalf of church leaders in Salt Lake City. Fischer would be one of eight young full-time missionaries serving from the Milwaukee Ward that year. Everyone in the family was excited about this opportunity. His decision to proselytize in the Texas San Antonio Mission made his parents proud, but he was already a model son in a family of outstanding children.

Church general authority Hartman Rector, Jr., himself a convert, came to Milwaukee to speak at a stake conference just days before Mark left. On August 25, 1974, Mark brought a blue wire-bound notebook to conference to record his thoughts. He wrote, "We have to love people in order to teach them. We have to love everyone like God loves us." On missionary work he wrote, "Sharing the Gospel requires living the Gospel." Rector went on to say, and Mark recorded, "we should be honest in all things. ... He asked why we should always go the second mile and then said because the second mile has all the blessings!"

As Mark prepared to leave, he talked to each of his younger brothers and sister, giving them family assignments. He told seventeen-year-old Matthew to wrestle with the younger children until he returned because it was something Mark had always done. Mark and Matthew were especially close. Mark told his brother Michael, who was fourteen, to watch out for his parents, to take care of them. He told his sister Melissa, twelve, and the youngest, eight-year-old Martin, to take care of his things while he was gone.

Mark's girlfriend wanted to give him something to take on his mission and settled on a Seiko watch from a J. C. Penney's store in Milwaukee. Mark had slender wrists, and Bakewell had to return twice to the store to have the band adjusted. She eventually had to have two links removed from the metal band. "I told him they were in case his wrist got bigger or something." Mark took the extra links with him on his mission.

Two days before Mark left, his cousin Susan Fischer came to his house to cut his hair. Mark scooped the trimmings up from the floor and put them into an envelope. That night he went to his girlfriend's for a spaghetti dinner. He jokingly gave Bakewell the envelope of his hair. She put it into a dresser drawer where she kept mementos of their relationship.

While Mark awaited his mission call, his mother, Cathy, was one day overcome with emotions about her oldest son leaving. She wished he could stay, but knew of his dedication and never said anything to him. She believed it was his duty to serve.

On September 18, 1974, the family, full of pride, took Mark to the airport to begin his mission. His father flew with him to Salt Lake City where he bought Mark a supply of basic black Bic pens at the University of Utah bookstore.

Finally Mark and his father, Jim, had to part. As with any parent, it was difficult to say good-bye and watch his son stride off into manhood. After a lingering farewell, Mark finally told his father, "Dad, I have to go now. I have a mission to serve." Jim never saw his son alive again.

That night Mark wrote in his notebook, "My first day away from home. Seems my prayers have been answered. I've been blessed not to miss home too much. ... I sure hope I can be a successful missionary."

Once in the Mission Home, Mark went through the intense training period with 257 other new missionaries who would disperse to fifty-eight separate missions. He recorded the instruction of various LDS leaders in his blue notebook. "We are personal ambassadors of Christ," he wrote the first day. "The next two years are the Lord's. Give him your best. We won't convert, the Holy Ghost converts." Also that first day: "Never leave your missionary companion. Your companion is your shield and protector." A few days later: "Procrastination is the thief of eternal life."

Church leaders urged Mark and the other new missionaries to "be yourself," to be positive, and to fellowship investigators. In particular they were urged to use Family Home Evenings as a missionary setting for investigators. Then church authority Hartman Rector addressed the missionaries, the second time for Mark in a couple of weeks. Rector followed general authority LeGrand Richards and was in turn followed by A. Theodore Tuttle. "Bear witness all the time," Rector urged. "Act like what you are, young men of God. Teach by how you live and act."

Just before Mark flew to Texas to begin his mission, LDS church president Spencer W. Kimball and counselors Marion G. Romney and N. Eldon Tanner addressed the new missionaries. Part of Kimball's message was especially appropriate. "Younger brothers, watch what you do," he said. "If you faithfully serve a mission so will your brothers. We build our lives by our attitudes. We are judged by the adversities we overcome. With privilege comes obligation." They were urged to eat right, to get adequate exercise, and to be conscious of their personal hygiene. They were instructed on how to handle their missionary cars, how to avoid accidents, and what to do if they had one. They were told that rank-and-file missionaries like Mark would be limited to 1,000 miles a month on the cars.

Mark later called his family three times after leaving Milwaukee, once each from Salt Lake City, San Antonio, and Austin.

After Mark and a new crop of fresh missionaries arrived in the field, they were again instructed by Texas Mission president Loveland. "Never misrepresent yourselves," he urged. "Teach with the spirit of truth. ... Make people sure you care about them." Loveland recognized Mark as one of the "best" young men under his service. "I will always remember my first interview with him the day he arrived. It was evident he had been planning to come on a mission for years," he recalled.

Once he settled, Mark wrote his family and girlfriend weekly. At first he was homesick and once wrote his parents asking for a family picture "so I can show these Texans what a real family looks like." He wrote how much he loved his family and how much he appreciated their supporting him.

For their parts, everyone in Mark's family wrote back steadily. One of their greatest heartbreaks came when their letters began to be returned as undeliverable after Mark and Gary disappeared.

Mark was quickly caught up in the spirit of missionary work. "Boy, I thought I was mature," he wrote in another letter. "I'm just beginning to catch the vision of the missionary program. Not only does it lay the spiritual foundations for the rest of my life, but it is teaching me to be responsible and in many ways preparing me for a family life. You know, I never thought I'd like a job where you work six days a week, 24 hours a day. But I sure love this one. Of course, I've got the best employer you can have."

His last letters were written Monday, October 28, and received by his family and Bakewell on Thursday, the 31st.

Both Mark and Gary had been serious, mature, and committed to their religion. Serving missions was the culmination of their personal ambition and family hopes.

TWENTY

WITHIN HOURS OF KLEASEN'S ARREST, IT WAS APPARENT HE was not rational. One police source told a reporter Kleasen was a "totally split personality." The U.S. magistrate who informed him of his rights concluded that Kleasen "may have been insane." He was moved to the Bexar County Jail in San Antonio for what was first described as medical problems, but was later disclosed as a preliminary mental evaluation.

Dr. Richard Coons, an Austin psychiatrist, was frequently called on to undertake competency evaluations for state and federal courts. Shortly after Kleasen's arrest, Coons was asked to do a preliminary screening of Kleasen. The psychiatrist was escorted to a room where he was left with Kleasen whom he knew almost nothing about. "He looked like someone who'd just crawled up out of the brush," he recalled. Not that he looked like he'd been roughed up by the police, he just seemed unkempt and surly. He looked big and muscular. And menacing. "His demeanor was frightening," Coons recalls. "He was scary." The doctor thought Kleasen was "somewhat paranoid" but didn't think there was any question he was competent to stand trial.

The first official action about Kleasen's mental illness came in federal court. On November 13, 1974, eight days after his arrest on the federal firearms charges, U.S. District Judge Jack Roberts ordered Kleasen committed to the Medical Center for Federal Prisoners in Springfield, Missouri. The hospital was given 90 days to evaluate Kleasen's competency to stand trial and sanity at the time of the federal offenses. District Attorney Smith lamented, "There's no way we can touch him," while Kleasen was in the federal facility. U.S. Attorney Jim Bock agreed that Texas officials could not contact Kleasen while he was hospitalized.

Crazy or not, Kleasen kept up a steady stream of letters. He continued to write his Pentecostal friend, Linda Miller, describing his cell and routine while still spinning yarns of espionage in the CIA and big game hunting. Two days after arriving at the Springfield facility, he wrote Miller describing the trip, and in one cryptic sentence added, "If you reread my first letters I told you this might happen in a round about way."

His almost daily letters described a 6-by-12-foot white solitary cell. He mentioned a cold draft through a window, complained about the flu, the intrusion of flashlight checks of his cell every thirty minutes, and talking to other prisoners by way of a radiator pipe. He told Miller about the one small window in his cell through which he watched traffic on a nearby highway, observed a flag snapping in the wind over a small post office, and airplanes approaching a nearby airport which he could not see.

As with his letters to the Jensen family in Copenhagen, he again complained about the weight of the passing days. "You can't let it get to you, you have to be calm and take each day one at a time and lick it. The main thing is to know in 84 days I will go some place," he wrote after his first week. "And so I cross off the days one at a time day by day. A calendar is a must for a prisoner or you lose perspective as to time passing as it is a world without calendars or clocks."

If Kleasen sounded rational in his letters, he was not viewed that way by the Springfield mental health experts who examined him, several of whom prepared written reports in December. They apparently had no knowledge of Kleasen's earlier psychiatric hospitalizations.

On December 11, 1974, Dr. Clifford Whipple, a forensic psychologist, described Kleasen as a paranoid. "He reports during the interview a history of being persecuted for his political views," and that "the CIA and FBI have been after him for years and any time he surfaces they are looking for something to charge him with."

Whipple administered a battery of standardized psychological tests. They showed Kleasen to be "quite guarded in his responses, somewhat evasive, and engaged in some degree of paranoid ideation." He went on to describe him as "somewhat depressed, and in general is rebellious and non-conforming." Kleasen would not take responsibility for his acts and saw "his difficulties as the result of other people persecuting him." The Rorschach test revealed him to be "quite constricted, somewhat explosive in nature, and [having] difficulty with interpersonal behavior." Other tests indicated Kleasen was "a person who has a very poor control of self and who is holding on to reality at the present time but with great deal of effort." In one likely important detail, Whipple wrote, "Especially significant on the House-Tree-Person [test] was a figure which was fairly well drawn with the exception of a grossly distorted left hand. One cannot help but speculate that there may be some guilt associated with behavior which the left hand has been engaging in."

As with anyone else who would listen, Kleasen made grandiose claims of post-graduate college education both in the United States and Europe. Whipple's WAIS testing revealed an IQ of 99, which, he wrote, was "not consistent" with Kleasen's claims. Nor was this consistent "with an organic disturbance," meaning a mental illness arising from a physically damaged brain. "They are consistent with an individual who has fairly high intellectual abilities but who is suffering from a psychotic reaction."

The psychologist noted that while Kleasen was "fairly cooperative," he seemed to have memory gaps and simply made up material to fill them. Kleasen reported "a history of blank periods" lasting "two or three days up to a week or more." Such blank spaces were frequently associated with his drinking, Kleasen reported, yet almost no one who knew him recalled his ever using alcoholic beverages. He could not recall what had happened during these lost days and weeks. Kleasen also "had difficulty in maintaining a coherent sentence and he frequently would forget what he was talking about."

Whipple diagnosed Kleasen as a paranoid schizophrenic with a possible psychomotor epileptic condition.

Dr. George S. Parlato, a consulting psychiatrist, reported that during his interview Kleasen said "he might have 'killed ... two men.'" His December 30, 1974, report describes Kleasen as paranoid with sudden mood swings. "He is quite tense and restless. ... At times he becomes very angry, talking about how he felt persecuted and then suddenly he becomes quite bland, staring vacantly past me, as if I wasn't sitting in front of him." Others who knew Kleasen would later recognize this description as similar to what they observed. Parlato felt Kleasen's grasp on reality was loose, his perceptions distorted.

Kleasen also expressed to Parlato a distorted personal identification with Joseph Smith:

> He indicates that he was having interpersonal difficulties in western New York, where "people didn't like me and mom", who were living on a Williamson, New York farm near Rochester. He states that "Joseph Smith" had lived in the area (founder of the Mormon church) and that "people avoided me", to which he made the association that Joseph Smith [was treated?] that way too and for that reason made his "exodus" to the west. Mr. Kleasen then tells that "I fled" the United States of America and went to Sweden and later to Europe, after the "pigs" raided his house, apparently looking for firearms. He states that he went to Sweden in order to contact his wife, a Swedish citizen, to testify on his behalf. Apparently he took his wife to "twenty-eight countries and Lebanon", and it was there that he and his wife were allegedly fired upon. Upon his return to the United States, Mr. Kleasen states that his mother "went (off) mentally" at a time when he was taken to jail in Lyons, New York.

The problem with this description is that no one in Wayne County recalls his mother ever being at the farm.

Parlato agreed with the diagnosis of paranoid schizophrenia. He concluded: "Mr. Kleasen gives every indication of being actively psychotic, and I doubt whether he could fully understand the nature of the charges against him and whether he could assist in his defense at this time."

Another report, dated December 16, 1974, recording the observations of psychiatric staff members, noted, "He has shown indications of a thought disorder through grandiose and paranoid ideation." Psychotropic medications were ordered for Kleasen "only if he became agitated." All reports agreed that because of his schizophrenic illness, Kleasen was incompetent to stand trial and probably insane at the time of the Federal Firearms Act violations.

The recognition and diagnosis of mental illness has never been an exact science. Some mental illnesses can be connected to what psychiatrists call impairment of brain tissue function—in other words, to something physical we know how to measure—but schizophrenia in general and especially paranoid schizophrenia are not among those. It must be diagnosed based on the behavior and apparent beliefs of the patient, and a subjective judgment as to whether those beliefs are grounded in reality.

In 1968 the American Psychiatric Association tried to bring order to chaos with its *Diagnostic and Statistical Manual of Mental Disorders*. The second edition, or *DSM II*, was published in 1968 and was the basis for the diagnosis offered by Kleasen's 1974 treatment team. The *DSM II* describes schizophrenia as "a group of disorders manifested by characteristic disturbances of thinking, mood and behavior. Disturbances in thinking are marked by alterations of concept formation which may lead to misinterpretation of reality and sometimes to delusions and hallucinations, which frequently appear psychologically self-protective." "Schizophrenia, paranoid type" is called a mental illness "characterized primarily by the presence of persecutory or grandiose delusions, often associated with hallucinations. Excessive religiosity is sometimes seen. The patient's attitude is frequently hostile and aggressive, and his behavior tends to be consistent with his delusions." That effectively described what nearly everyone observed in Kleasen as a patient, criminal defendant, and client.

Linda Miller had been saving Kleasen's letters. After his arrest for the murders, she agreed to talk to writers for *Texas Monthly* magazine. When their January 1975 issue hit newsstands, it carried the article "The Mormon Murders: Letters From The Accused." Above a picture of a grinning, rifle-wielding Kleasen, the article began, "Along with its resident legions of premier footballers and country western pickers, Austin seems to attract more than its share of vicious, brutal murderers." It went on to discuss Kleasen as such a killer, setting out the CIA, big game hunting, and paranoid fantasies contained in his letters to Miller.

Kleasen and the opinions of his Missouri treatment team were returned to Austin where a January 29, 1975, hearing was set regarding his competency. Faced with the evidence of Kleasen's mental illness, by January 15 the U.S. Attorney's Office had concluded they could not prosecute and notified Travis County prosecutors of their decision. Assistant U.S. attorney Jeremiah Handy agreed to an indefinite postponement of the federal charges. Kleasen's court appointed lawyers did not oppose the continuance. On January 29 Handy wrote District Attorney Smith that this was done "in order that the state murder trial may proceed in an orderly fashion to disposition." Kleasen was brought to the Travis County Jail that same day.

Kleasen was now in the Texas state courts. One federal official told a reporter he doubted that the Federal Firearms Act charges would ever be prosecuted now that Kleasen had been turned over to local authorities. Meanwhile a justice of the peace inquest and the Travis County grand jury took up the case of the two missing missionaries.

On January 23 Justice of the Peace Jim McMurtry heard two hours of testimony, while Kleasen sat impassively, scribbling notes on a yellow legal pad with a pencil. Detective Colon Jordan, Ranger Wallace Spillar, and Texas Department of Public Safety crime lab scientist Leslie Smith were the only witnesses. Spillar told McMurtry he believed the missionaries were dead based on five pieces of evidence: the two watches found with human blood on them in Kleasen's trailer, the human substances found on the band saw in the Austin Taxidermy Studio, Kleasen's clothing found with human blood on it, evidence that the missionaries' last known meeting was with Kleasen, and the five tires from the missionaries' car found near Kleasen's trailer. "All the people in connection with the missionaries from the Mormon Church have all been contacted; people that they had appointments with after the date that they were reported missing, hasn't [sic] shown up to any of their—no knowledge of their whereabouts," he said on the witness stand. He felt suicides would have been impossible given the evidence they found. What became of the bodies, McMurtry asked. They'd been dismembered, Spillar said, then "deposited in a dumpster, trash barrel type commercial garbage dumpster, or possibly put in a fishing hole in a burlap bag." McMurtry ruled that Darley and Fischer had died "at the hands of another," officially homicides. More importantly, he issued death certificates for both young men which would later cause Kleasen's defense considerable difficulty at his murder trial.

The grand jury heard evidence on January 21 and 22. In addition to witnesses who testified in the justice of the peace proceeding, the grand jury heard about the results of neutron activation analysis undertaken at the FBI lab in Washington, D.C. Investigators told reporters the tests had positively identified tissue samples found on the band saw as belonging to Mark Fischer.

"If the grand jury finds the evidence legally sufficient enough to indict," Smith told reporters, "we will place a hold on him and wait to see what happens on the federal charges and the mental competency hearing." Everyone still regarded Kleasen's competency to stand trial as an open question.

The grand jury did indict Kleasen on two counts of capital murder. A few days later, assistant U.S. attorney Handy asked that Kleasen be remanded to Travis County authorities. By January 29, Kleasen was in the Travis County Jail. That same day a justice of the peace formally notified him of the charges, informed him of his rights, and set bail at $100,000.

At a hearing the next day, Judge Tom Blackwell appointed two more psychiatrists, Drs. Stuart Nemir and Roger McCary, to examine Kleasen for competency. Prosecutors retained Dr. Coons to examine him as well. Coons was one of a small platoon of prosecution-oriented experts who testified often for Texas DAs on the controversial prediction of "future dangerousness" in capital trials. (Among others, the Nevada Supreme Court found this so strange it later commented in a published opinion that "an industry has developed supporting psychiatrists who specialize at this task" [*Redman v. State*, 108 Nev. 227, 828 P.2d 395].)

Armed with the federal mental health evaluations, Kleasen's lawyers began to develop a defense centered on his psychological illness. On February 4 they asked the 167th District Court for a trial to determine Kleasen's competency. By late February 1975, they filed pleadings to secure New York records of Kleasen's prior hospitalizations and to depose people who had treated him. Kleasen lawyer Glen Wilkerson described the federal proceedings in his motion to Judge Blackwell and attached the reports of the Missouri treatment team.

Mental illness exists on a long, fuzzy continuum. The majority of mentally ill people never see the inside of a hospital or significant treatment. Yet courts and lawyers look for that bright line dividing the legally competent from the incompetent, the legally sane from the insane. A defendant may be seriously mentally ill and difficult to represent without being considered to be incompetent and insane.

One important aspect of mental illness is that the sick person often refuses to acknowledge his illness. He considers his state normal; it is the rest of society who is somehow mentally off. Acknowledging that Kleasen was mentally ill neither cured nor controlled it, and in the absence of a judicial determination of his incompetence, he retained the right to direct many aspects of his case. No matter what was done, he would remain difficult to work with.

Texas law states that a defendant is incompetent to stand trial if he does not have sufficient ability to consult reasonably and rationally with counsel, or does not reasonably understand the proceedings against him. Every accused person is presumed to be competent, and if he raises the issue the burden is on the defendant to prove otherwise.

When a Texas defendant's competence is called into question, a jury is selected to hear evidence and render a verdict of sane or not sane. This is not the jury which will sit on the charged offense, and they are not supposed to know what crime is at issue. If the jury finds a defendant sane, he proceeds to trial before the next jury. If they find him to be insane, they can direct him to the state hospital in Rusk, Texas, for further treatment. Once a trial judge has reason to question the competence of a defendant, such a trial must be held, even if the accused insists he is okay.

While everyone around him questioned his sanity, Kleasen and his paranoia seethed and finally exploded. Realizing that his three attorneys were preparing an insanity defense and would attempt to establish that he was mentally ill, temporarily avoiding the actual murder trial, Kleasen rebelled. The result was that a workable attorney-client relationship no longer existed.

By March 13 Bob Gibbins filed a "Motion to Withdraw" on behalf of himself, co-counsel Sal Levatino, and Glen Wilkerson. The motion asked to be released "for the reason that irreconcilable conflicts have developed between the said attorneys and the Defendant ... as to the mode and manner of the defense ... making it impossible for said attorneys to continue to represent the defendant ..." In court that day Gibbins told Judge Blackwell, "I don't get along with Mr. Kleasen"—as if anyone could—"we've reached an impasse."

Kleasen did not want to undergo the competency trial, and by then was just as anxious to fire his lawyers as they were to quit. He and Gibbins began to argue in court, with Kleasen insisting he was sane and that their problems really had to do with his inability to pay their $30,000 fee. Kleasen continued to stress that he had wealth but "it's tied up in New York" as part of the harassment he experienced because of his anti-Vietnam War politics. "I have no hard feelings with my attorneys, but the amount of money ...," Kleasen said, letting the statement trail off.

During the hearing Kleasen kept referring to the judge as "Gen. Blackwell—the only general I see in the room." Blackwell was a general in the national guard. Some years later Kleasen would begin saying that Blackwell had been a general in Vietnam responsible for many atrocities, and that he rigged a conviction in order to silence Kleasen who knew about his activities through his CIA experiences.

The day after Kleasen fought with his attorney in court, he wrote a notarized letter to Blackwell which, in effect, fired his lawyers. "According to article six of the ten original ten amendments to the constitution I am entitled to the assistance of counsel in my jury trial," Kleasen wrote. "When the counsel I have—counsel who is *not* assisting me and/or my cause I ask they be discharged as my counsel and that I be allowed enough time to retain another." As this was not done at the previous day's hearing, he demanded that the capital murder charges be dismissed.

In a second notarized letter of the same date, which Kleasen called a writ of habeas corpus, he complained that he was not being given access to legal materials, "with any attorneys who may represent me in the future," and "only limited access to the courts" by his jailers. He again insisted that his charges be dismissed.

Also at the March 13 hearing, Kleasen asked to be appointed co-counsel in order to control every aspect of his defense. Blackwell "reluctantly" granted his request, then thought better of it by the following Monday after hearing Kleasen testify at a motion hearing. He withdrew the order.

But Blackwell wouldn't let Kleasen or his lawyers off the hook. "There's no problem in allowing you to withdraw on a trial on the merits, but not on a trial on the competency hearing. If I did, then we'll be in the same boat further down the line," he said. Blackwell felt bound by recent U.S. Supreme Court decisions requiring that competency questions be resolved. Blackwell likely could see for himself that Kleasen was functioning other than normally.

After the March 13 hearing, perhaps trying to placate his client, Gibbons said Kleasen "is one of the most interesting people I've ever been around. He's a brilliant man with an interesting background, riddled with tragedies—and some injustices." Gibbons told reporters he would like to try the case because the state's evidence seemed so weak, but that he just could not get along with Kleasen.

A nine man, three woman jury was selected and began to hear testimony on March 18. What they heard was one-sided as Kleasen had "instructed" his lawyers not to ask any questions or undertake any defense. In the hall Kleasen and Gibbins had another heated argument. "You're going to need that insanity defense," Gibbins said. "I understand that, but I also understand that I'm sane," Kleasen shot back. "What you're trying to do is wrong."

Drs. Nemir and McCary both testified that Kleasen was mentally ill. Nemir felt Kleasen was not competent for trial. Kleasen was "delusional and persecutorial," Nemir said. "He sees the charges against him as part of a conspiracy of larger governmental agencies to do him in. I think he gets confused," he told the jury. McCray also said Kleasen was not competent but could become so. Gibbins and his co-counsel did not ask any questions of these witnesses.

Dr. Coons, who had been retained by the district attorney, testified differently. "He has a personality disorder. He does not have a severe mental illness." Among these disorders is anti-social personality disorder, or, as it used to be called, sociopathic personality. These are not people who garner much sympathy from the public or the courts. Coons believed Kleasen could assist his lawyers in defending himself.

Gibbins did cross-examine Coons, telling the court, "I am pursuing cross-examination against the wishes of my client."

But Kleasen then insisted on taking the stand himself against the advice of his frustrated lawyers. Before he did so, Gibbins asked that the jury be excused and the courtroom cleared. "You want to be found competent so you can hurry on to trial and the electric chair, don't you?" Gibbons then said to Kleasen. "I'm anxious to face trial because I'm innocent," Kleasen shot back. "I know for a fact I didn't kill anybody. I don't even know if anybody has been murdered." Kleasen also said he wasn't afraid of any evidence the state may have, suggesting officers "planted" it at his trailer. When the jury returned, Kleasen was the most closely listened to witness of the proceeding.

District Attorney Smith asked Kleasen if he was the same man here charged with two murders. "If there were any murders, I guess that's a fair statement," Kleasen answered. Answering other questions, Kleasen told the jury who he was, where he was, why he was there, and insisted he was sane. He said he was anxious to stand trial and wanted a speedy one. He also testified that he had been denied access to law books in the Travis County Jail and began shooting questions at his lawyers. When Gibbins responded that he was the one who would ask the questions, Kleasen turned to Judge Blackwell and said, "Put him under oath or do something with him." Blackwell ordered the jailers to give Kleasen access to law books in the future.

Gibbins, again under orders from his client, did not make any closing argument to the jury, leaving the persuading to the district attorney. The jury was then instructed that they had to decide if Kleasen had "sufficient present ability to consult with his lawyer with a reasonable degree of rational understanding of the proceedings against him."

Kleasen and every other defendant is presumed to be competent unless the jury is persuaded otherwise "by a preponderance of the evidence," meaning 51-49, a considerably lower standard than "beyond reasonable doubt."

The jury, which no doubt had observed the bickering between Kleasen and his lawyers, deliberated for only five minutes before returning a verdict of "sane." Kleasen told reporters he was "pleased" with the result and anxious to get on with the trial. "I have nothing to hide," he said. "I want to be perfectly fair with the jury and the judge and the people of Texas." He was on stage again.

Gibbins told reporters, "I would like to have brought out that he's been in mental institutions ever since he was eighteen years old, has claimed CIA activities, and all these other weird things. He thinks this is part of a government effort to get him because he was a member of the CIA." "It is an intolerable burden to try a case when your hands are tied," he said, then left the case with his two co-counsel.

One ironic twist was that the movie *One Flew Over the Cuckoo's Nest*, a story of one man's attempt to prove his sanity in a mental hospital, had walked away with several Academy Awards shortly before the Austin jury ruled Kleasen was sane.

TWENTY-ONE

ROBERT O. SMITH WAS A CAREER PROSECUTOR, THE KIND OF man you didn't want drawing a bead on you in the courtroom. Stationed at the now closed Bergstrom Air Force Base outside Austin during World War II and the Korean War, he decided to stay in town. After his discharge, he attended the University of Texas, taking his B.B.A. in 1951 and his law degree in 1954. In addition to some private practice, he moved through a series of prosecutor positions with the county attorney, the district attorney (where he was a senior prosecutor), and the state attorney general. He was finally appointed to fill a vacancy as Travis County attorney.

In October 1968 District Attorney Tom Blackwell, who later presided over the Kleasen trial, was appointed to a vacancy on the 167th District Court bench by Governor John B. Connally. Smith had been a top assistant under Blackwell and was appointed by Connally as county attorney. Both then ran for and were elected to their offices in November 1968. Blackwell and Smith were not close personal friends but were much alike and had enormous respect for each other.

Smith served two four-year terms, gaining enough respect among his peers to be elected president of the Texas District and County Attorney Association in 1973. He gave up the District Attorney's Office to run unsuccessfully for district judge in 1976. The Kleasen trial came late in Smith's second term.

The district attorney was 6'3", a powerfully built man who worked on his ranch and built furniture as a pastime. He was never without a cigar bouncing up and down in his mouth under thick rimmed black glasses. To this day friends who tell Bob Smith stories pick up a pen and use it as the ever-present cigar in their tales. He was emotional and intense about the cases and defendants he prosecuted. That emotion was often close to the surface in the Kleasen case.

At the time of the Kleasen prosecution, there were nine or ten assistant district attorneys in Smith's office. His personal office was the first one you passed in the district attorney's suite. His door was always open where visitors would see him leaning back, feet on his desk, a big cigar in hand.

He was a teacher and mentor for his assistants. Charlie Craig was one of many former assistants who became fiercely loyal to Smith. Lawyers and judges came to rely on his almost encyclopedic knowledge of Texas criminal law. He knew everything that was going on in his office. Smith handled a lot of cases; it would be unusual for him not to be actively involved in a major prosecution. His personal prosecution of Kleasen was very much in character. And he was good in the courtroom, forceful and aggressive, a bulldog. He was not a glad hander, not a good politician. Smith said what was on his mind and could be gruff at times. He often prosecuted state legislators and other government officials for corruption. Smith didn't win many powerful friends that way.

Mormon bishop Frank McCullough, for one, could not have been more satisfied with how Smith handled the case. He felt Smith fought every effort by the defense to put the LDS church on trial. There were some real concerns about this, given the involvement of Mormon law enforcement officers, not to mention the investigation initiated by local church leaders while there was still hope of finding the missionaries alive.

In addition, defense lawyer David Bays called Smith, Craig, and David Spencer "the A team," the best the Travis County district attorney's office had to offer.

The Kleasen trial was unusual in almost all respects. It was watched closely by every district attorney and defense lawyer in Texas because it was one of the first to be tried under a radically new Texas death penalty statute. In the landmark 1972 decision *Furman v. Georgia,* the U.S. Supreme Court threw out every death penalty statute in the country. Among other things, the court found that the death penalty had been largely reserved for blacks and/or for the killers of whites. This occurred because juries were given unbridled discretion in sentencing those convicted of capital murder. They were given no guidance or direction to overcome the influences of race, class, and other prejudices. The problem was compounded by the routine exclusion of racial minorities from criminal juries.

In Texas 510 people had been sentenced to death between 1923, when the state adopted centralized execution by the electric chair, and the *Furman* decision. Some 378 of these people (74 percent) were sentenced for murder, another 118 (23 percent) for rape, and fourteen (3 percent) for armed robbery. Of the 510, only 361 (71 percent) had actually been executed, but of this number, two-thirds were black. Whites, Hispanics, and a single Native American comprised the remaining one-third. Approximately 80 percent of the victims in capital crimes had been white.

In the aftermath of *Furman*, most state legislatures raced to reenact their death penalty statutes, especially Southern States in what has come to be known as the "death belt." But the Supreme Court offered little guidance as to what kind of statute would be constitutional. Half a dozen different models emerged, ranging from mandatory death sentences in Louisiana and North Carolina to schemes that sought to balance lists of aggravating and mitigating factors. In Georgia punishment-phase juries balanced aggravation and mitigation then had to arrive at a unanimous recommendation of death. Florida had a similar system, but juries could recommend death by a majority vote.

The Texas legislature meets once every two years, so it was 1973 before they acted. The new law under which Kleasen was prosecuted took force June 14, 1973, and was unlike that adopted by any other state. First, it limited the death penalty to defendants seventeen years old and older who killed in the course of a list of specific felonies such as robbery, rape, burglary, or kidnapping. If the jury returned a verdict of guilty of capital murder, the trial moved into a punishment phase. There the jury heard additional testimony, then answered two, sometimes three, "special issues" about the defendant. Did the killer act deliberately in the death of the victim? Was the killer likely to be violent in the future? Did the victim do something to provoke or encourage the murder? "Yes" answers to the first two and "no" to the third brought a death sentence. Such verdicts had to be unanimous. Trial judges had no discretion in sentencing life imprisonment when faced with such unanimous "yes" verdicts. An appeal to the Texas Court of Criminal Appeals was mandatory under the new statute whether the condemned wanted one or not.

There was considerable speculation that the U.S. Supreme Court might throw out all these new statutes as well, and finally rule that the death penalty under any circumstance violated the Eighth Amendment's prohibition on cruel and unusual punishment. *Furman* had been a 5-4 decision, raising as many questions as it answered. It wasn't until *Gregg v. Georgia* in 1976, the year after Kleasen's trial, that the Supreme Court answered that question. It said that as long as certain guidelines were followed, the death penalty was constitutional. *Jurek v. Texas* was decided the same day as *Gregg* and the court expressly approved the Texas statute enacted after *Furman*.

Today the U.S. Supreme Court has more or less abandoned most of those guidelines and allowed states to drift back to death penalty practices that are nearly pre-*Furman*. Today the Texas death row is less than 40 percent white and more than 60 percent minority.

Executions did not begin nationally again until Gary Gilmore was shot to death in Utah in 1976. He was a "volunteer," stopping his appeals and asking to be executed. Florida executed John Spenkelink and Nevada executed another volunteer, Jesse Bishop, in 1979. Texas was the sixth state to begin executing again when Charlie Brooks became the first person ever to die by lethal injection in 1982.

But there remained many unanswered questions about the details of a death penalty trial under the Texas statute. How do you prove future dangerousness? Were you dangerous if you wrote bad checks or drank heavily? And dangerous to whom? Other inmates and prison guards? What kind of evidence would be permitted and what would be considered out of bounds? Future dangerousness was unlike any question other criminal juries were asked to answer so there was little past experience to consult. Defense lawyers had to weigh whether handicaps such as mental illness or retardation should even be presented to the jury because they would also lead to a yes answer on the critical questions.

As Kleasen's spring 1975 trial approached, no one was sure what the rules were. The Texas Court of Criminal Appeals hadn't even ruled on the new statute until just days before the Kleasen trial began. It was practicing death penalty law in the dark.

Kleasen's various defense lawyers filed several motions challenging the death penalty in general along with particular aspects of the new Texas statute. At a hearing six weeks before, trial judge Blackwell reminded the defense team that three cases involving the same challenges were pending in the Texas Court of Criminal Appeals. "We should expect a decision from them in the near future as to whether capital punishment is constitutional," he told the lawyers. "If they rule it is constitutional, your motions will be overruled. In the event they rule it's unconstitutional, then the motions will be granted." As it turned out, the Court of Criminal Appeals issued its decision in *Jurek v. State*, approving the new death penalty statute just before the trial.

One legal problem Smith and Craig had was specific to their case. They had charged Kleasen with murdering two young men but they didn't have bodies, at least not in the usual sense. A body not only convinces the jury that the victim is in fact dead, but it often provides evidentiary information on when the murder happened, how the killing took place, and often something about the killer. This investigation had produced no such evidence. Smith and Craig were confident that Kleasen had killed Fischer and Darley, but all they had to show for their deaths was perhaps a laboratory test tube full of human blood and biological material. Most of that they could not say with absolute certainty came from these two victims. All they had to speak to identity was a small amount of head hair found on the band saw and Kleasen's clothing, a common substance which in and of itself did not say a person was dead. There was enough circumstantial evidence to convince them they had the right man, but there was no smoking gun.

Until earlier in 1974, Texas law carried a statute, Article 1204, which required that a body, "or portions of it," be found before a murder conviction could be had. With a 1974 legislative rewrite of the criminal code, the statute was removed and death could now be proven with circumstantial evidence. Still, prosecutors fretted over whether they had enough of a body to convince both the jury and subsequent appellate courts that murders had taken place. And they had to prove it beyond, and to the exclusion of, all reasonable doubt. In fact, the Court of Criminal Appeals had held that in order to prove what criminal lawyers call the "corpus delicti," the prosecution had to establish that someone was dead and that the death was caused by the defendant. This takes more than a strong suspicion or an especially unsavory defendant like Kleasen.

The issue presented to past Texas appellate courts usually involved a body but ambiguous proof as to how the death came about. Only three cases from the Court of Criminal Appeals seemed to provide guidance for a "no body" case. In 1901 the court reversed the murder conviction of cowboy Gib Gay in the killing of his partner in a cattle venture. The partner just disappeared in the summer of 1897 with a lot of money in his possession. The normally poor Gay then turned up spending freely in town, bringing suspicion on himself. But the only proof of the "corpus delicti" was a small amount of what were believed to be human remains found at an old fire site on Gay's mother's ranch. The court ruled that human teeth, toe and hand bones, strands of hair, and pants buttons sifted from the ashes and never positively identified as belonging to the disappeared partner were not sufficient to prove a murder. Gay was set free.

In 1942 the court reversed the murder conviction and twenty-five-year sentence of Helen O'Keefe. She had been convicted of murdering her boss at a small loan company from which she had been embezzling money. O'Keefe had been trying to hire men to break her boss's legs but making it clear she did not want him killed. Then one day the boss's car was found engulfed in flames with what looked like a body in it. O'Keefe and her soldier boyfriend had been seen in the area. By the time the fire was put out, there were perhaps twenty-five pounds of human flesh and bones remaining. Several personal possessions belonging to her boss were found with the body, a single human tooth along with some false ones, and portions of hip and leg bones. The testimony of doctors and dentists as to whether these came from the disappeared man was sharply divided. Most telling for the Court of Criminal Appeals was testimony by morticians that it would take considerably more heat than this fire could have generated to consume all the human materials that were not present after the fire was put out. The court set O'Keefe free.

In a third case decided about the time of Kleasen's crime, the court affirmed the conviction and life sentence of Michael Lloyd Self in the murder of two girls. Skeletal parts, including a skull from which dental work was positively identified, along with a victim's necklace and crucifix wrapped around a jaw bone, were dredged up out of a bayou. However, that case was simplified considerably when Self confessed. His conviction was affirmed.

But with Kleasen there was no confession. Nevertheless, Smith and Craig believed their circumstantial evidence was so substantial that they would prevail. Plus they had the benefit of scientific testing that was not available in these older decisions.

The week before the Kleasen trial began, Craig traveled to Houston to sit in on jury selection in another death penalty case, that of Ronald Clark O'Bryan. Craig wanted to see how Harris County prosecutors handled *voir dire* before picking his jury in Travis County. O'Bryan had come to be known as the "Candy Man" for poisoning his eight-year-old son Timothy on Halloween 1974, just three days after the Mormon missionaries had disappeared. O'Bryan laced his son's Halloween candy with cyanide in an effort to collect insurance money. He was sentenced to death on June 4, 1975. One of O'Bryan's defense lawyers was Houston attorney Marvin O. Teague who would later come into the Kleasen case. By the time Craig returned from Houston for the final preparations, both he and Smith were as prepared and confident as they could be.

Travis County had not had a capital conviction since a man named Lee Belo Brooks was sentenced to death in 1970 for rape, and his sentence was commuted to life in the aftermath of *Furman*. The last actual execution on a Travis County conviction was another man sentenced to death for rape in 1959, Samuel M. Holmes. The prosecution team against Kleasen entered the courtroom confidently, but knew they had a lot to prove in the course of the trial.

TWENTY-TWO

KLEASEN WANTED NEW LAWYERS WHO WOULD NOT BRING UP embarrassing issues such as his mental fitness. He wanted a defense conducted on his terms.

One day, while Kleasen was visiting with Pentecostal friends in the Travis County Jail, the group encountered Austin lawyer R. Roscoe Haley. Haley was a flashy solo practitioner of no more than average legal talent. He was a gregarious, flamboyant character in his thirties. He enjoyed the limelight and public exposure, and the Kleasen case represented both. In many ways Haley and Kleasen seemed made for each other. Haley started talking to Kleasen's friends about his situation and volunteered, "It sounds like he needs a lawyer." Patrick Ganne, a "baby lawyer" just a year out of law school, was in the hallway and overheard the conversation. Soon Kleasen's friend Linda Miller was stopping regularly in Haley's office. On March 20 Kleasen wrote Haley: "I request your services as Attorney and Counselor of Record in the matter now pending before the 167th District Court ..." Haley agreed, and Kleasen's letter ended up in the court file.

Haley also appreciated that he would need help so he approached Judge Blackwell about assistance. Blackwell understood the situation and appointed Ganne and another recent law school graduate, David Bays, to assist. Bays had clerked for Haley recently. He was a graduate of the Naval Academy at Annapolis and had a master's degree in engineering, but little legal experience. Ganne was a University of Texas Law School graduate and at least had a year's experience prosecuting misdemeanors in New Mexico. He had done exactly one felony trial with the district attorney's office in Albuquerque.

While the penniless Kleasen initially promised a private retainer, Haley, Ganne, and Bays were eventually paid by Travis County.

Ganne and Bays worked on the case full time from that point through the end of the trial.

Haley was a competent lawyer but had a drinking problem. In the weeks leading up to the Kleasen trial, he could be found passing the afternoon in his office with clients and an open vodka bottle on the desk. It was the two young lawyers who undertook discovery and all the other preparation for trial.

The following week Kleasen was back before Judge Blackwell with Haley and Ganne. Gibbins, Wilkerson, and Levatino were now officially off the case.

On March 24 Judge Blackwell set the trial for May 19. At Kleasen's insistence, they scrapped the insanity defense planned by their predecessors and announced a defense of complete innocence. There were also rumors about Kleasen's having read several books from the Bastrop Public Library on mental illness right after his arrest, making his new lawyers nervous about how well an insanity defense would stand up. Kleasen felt he was now in a position to direct his lawyers rather than their directing him. He was an accomplished manipulator and quickly sensed how to get Haley to do his bidding.

Kleasen took advantage of his new leading role to grant a lengthy interview with Associated Press reporter Robert Heard which was published the following weekend. It was Kleasen who contacted the press, but Haley agreed to the 90-minute interview at the county jail and was present while Kleasen told his stories. Heard described Kleasen as looking tired but enjoying the attention. "He appears to be weary, believing himself to be the target through the years of incompetents and of evil men. But he somehow conveys the impression he has arrived at precisely the spot he has sought so long—the center ring."

Heard speculated on what sort of man Kleasen was. He probably came closer than any of the mental health experts when he wrote that Kleasen seemed like "a weak man with Walter Mitty dreams; a man with limited talent but a clever imagination; a man who has made exaggerated claims so long he has come to believe them." Kleasen insisted he was innocent: "I certainly haven't killed anybody and I certainly haven't seen anybody killed." He denied having seen the missionaries on October 28, 1974. "They sent me a letter stating that they were coming on that date. Well, I clean forgot about it." (At other times, he claimed he had prepared dinner but the expected missionaries hadn't shown up.) And he denied any motive for murder: "I certainly don't have any animosity towards these people. They were just two nice young men." But he also said he hardly knew them. "I knew these people very, very, very slightly. I knew them less than I know you."

Under instructions from his lawyer not to discuss the murdered missionaries, Kleasen would say, "I think they [ate] once" at his trailer, but he expressed plenty of bitterness toward the LDS church. He said he was baptized in Austin in 1972, ignoring his 1973 baptism by Austin bishop Bruce Smith. "My church did not support me in any way, shape or form during my trials. In fact, I never received even a Christmas card from any of them. In fact, any time they came they did everything they could to hurt me." This probably referred to the several months Kleasen was in Texas Hill Country jails for shooting the buffalo. He also complained that an unnamed Mormon lawyer refused to represent him in the case, probably Ed Guyon. He accused two other church members of going through his trailer while he was jailed and stealing "whatever they wanted."

As if to remove any doubt that he lived a life of fantasy, Kleasen insisted that this prosecution was really a CIA plot. He said he learned to fly by age fifteen and that his secret agent career began as a test pilot. In 1951, when he was only nineteen, he claimed he was sent to Korea by Bell Aircraft to test their air-to-air and ground-to-air missiles. When the reporter told Kleasen he could check Bell employment records, Kleasen backpedaled, saying he was not sure how they would list him. Kleasen went on to claim he was also a U2 pilot. Somehow, however, he had graduated from test pilot to spy. He claimed that with the CIA he helped plan the 1961 Cuban Bay of Pigs invasion, and knew the details of the assassination of South Vietnam president Ngo Dinh Diem in 1963. Later he was assigned to watch groups like the Students for a Democratic Society (SDS) and the Weathermen while at the State University of New York at Buffalo. His cover was that he was an ordinary college student. It was this assignment which brought him into contact with the Peace Movement and convinced him his CIA handlers were corrupt. Kleasen then decided to defect and save the world.

Admitting that he could not prove it, Kleasen said he quit the CIA in 1965 to join those opposed to the Vietnam War. He began to travel in Red China and North Vietnam on behalf of anti-war groups. With that act of conscience, Kleasen pronounced, the CIA became obsessed with silencing him. "I know too much. See, they don't know what I will divulge or what records I've taken or anything about it, so it's easier just to eliminate me." The agency was afraid of his "naming names, and embarrassing incidents," he boasted. After he quit the CIA, "they blew up my VW camper," he told AP. When asked if he still had CIA records in his possession, Kleasen laughed and asked the reporter, "You want to get me killed?" He then claimed his trailer was burglarized and ransacked after his December 1973 "fake" arrest on the buffalo rustling charge. "They took everything, including my dirty socks. How can I prove anything?" He recited dozens of misfortunes that had befallen him since leaving the CIA. Asked if he thought the CIA was responsible, he said, "I don't know, but how come all these things happen?"

After the interview, the reporter contacted the CIA and researched Associated Press files on the agency. There was no connection between Kleasen and the CIA. Bell Aircraft told the reporter Kleasen never worked for them either. Kleasen countered that the government had altered its records to remove him. He went on to claim he spoke several languages, that he was an expert marksman and designer of firearms, that he had two master's degrees and was just a few hours short of his Ph.D., and that he had an outstanding record as a sociology scholar. "You heard me speak at the sanity trial, and you know I am a highly educated, intelligent individual," Kleasen had boasted in a letter he had written to the Associated Press. At the conclusion of the interview, Kleasen told the reporter with a smile, "Sounds pretty wild, doesn't it?" He was basking in the attention.

The published interview did not just repeat the murder defendant's claims without challenge. Reporter Heard also interviewed

Kleasen's bishop, Frank McCullough, who was furious over the accusations of neglect by Mormons. "An outright lie," he said, noting that Kleasen "looses [sic] control easily." An indignant McCullough outlined for the AP the several jail visits to Kleasen by church representatives who left him fruit and other food stuffs.

Perhaps most galling to Kleasen's schizophrenia-fueled ego, Heard pointed out how badly he spelled. Kleasen's attorneys refused requests for further interviews.

Next Kleasen sought to make the courts a forum for his paranoid delusions. On April 22, a month before his trial was to begin, he persuaded Haley to sue the sheriff and chief jailer in a federal civil rights action. They sought $50,000 in damages. Kleasen claimed the sheriff and his chief jailer abused his rights by allowing him to be assaulted by other jail inmates, that they had denied him access to needed law books and access to his attorney at reasonable hours, that they were slowly starving him with inadequate food, and that they allowed a pattern of harassment and ridicule by other jailers. At the time the Travis County Jail was the subject of other suits about poor conditions, so Kleasen's claims were more plausible than most he made.

But his strangest allegation was that he had been deliberately fed a "centipede sandwich" by chief jailer Bill Mansell. The ever-creative Kleasen claimed the black insect—which he described as five inches long and an inch wide—was served to him between two slices of white bread alongside potatoes with cockroaches mixed in. The centipede was dead, Kleasen told reporters, because that was the only way it could be kept between the bread. Haley showed the press a dead centipede in a plastic bag at a press conference.

Kleasen insisted that Mansell had stood nearby watching "with a big grin on his face" while the meal was served. "I hope you enjoy your meal," he quoted Mansell as saying. Kleasen went on to insist that he had routinely been fed "cockroach tacos" in the jail. He said sometimes he was so hungry he would pick the insects out and eat the food, but at other times he could not bring himself to eat anything served him. In spite of this claim, Kleasen's lawyers noticed he had steadily gained weight in jail.

Sheriff Frank was indignant. He told an Austin newspaper he had "never seen a centipede in the county jail. We have a minor problem with cockroaches but the jail is not infested. Don't take my word for it," he challenged. "I invite the media to go up and inspect the jail."

No sooner had Austin newspapers published accounts of Kleasen's suit than another inmate, eighteen-year-old Renaldo Ramirez, came forward to say it was really he who had given Kleasen the dead insect. He told a reporter for the University of Texas student newspaper that he had obtained the insect from someone in the jail hospital tank. "I gave Kleasen that centipede. It was burned and put in a plastic bag, and I gave it to him to give to his lawyer," Ramirez told the reporter.

Kleasen had accused Ramirez of being one of two inmates who had assaulted him in the jail and implied he was a homosexual. He then went off on a discourse about homosexual liaisons among Travis County Jail inmates. He told the AP there were several homosexual couples in the jail and this caused considerable friction among inmates. Kleasen said these inmates fell into "he" or "she" personalities depending on their role in the relationship. He said he was in the habit, like other inmates, of referring to inmates as "him" or "her" based upon their persona. Kleasen took this opportunity to say again that any incriminating evidence found at his trailer had been planted there, including some pornographic homosexual materials. "I am not a homosexual," he defiantly added.

The civil rights suit, not surprisingly, was strictly theater. It was filed with the clerk of the federal court but was never served on the defendants nor was any other action taken. In January 1980 Judge Roberts dismissed it, noting it had languished without action since filing.

Surprisingly, the only other thing Kleasen demanded from his defense team was that they not rely on the hated insanity defense. Beyond that his approach was pretty much hands off through the preparation as well as during the May and June trial.

The newly reconstructed defense team met with Kleasen in jail two or three times a week. When talking to his lawyers, Kleasen did not blame the incriminating evidence found in and around his trailer on a CIA conspiracy. Instead he saw a Mormon plot to get him.

"Whenever you hear anything coming out of the Mormon church," he instructed his lawyers, "remember that Joseph Smith was hung as a horse thief in Missouri, and that's all you need to know about them." Kleasen always denied involvement with or knowledge of the disappearance of the two missionaries.

Ganne found Kleasen to be an arrogant blowhard and hard to like. An experienced Naval intelligence officer who once tracked Soviet nuclear submarines, Ganne was quick to see how ridiculous Kleasen's claims of an espionage career were. He never told Kleasen about his own background with the navy. Bays, also a navy man, found his client just as hard to believe.

In view of Haley being the lead chair, his unwillingness to investigate or prepare on the law was frustrating to both Ganne and Bays. "His idea of trial preparation was to buy more suits," Bays now says. Ganne and Bays looked to Haley for leadership, but it was well into jury selection before they reluctantly concluded it was not forthcoming.

Considering that the Kleasen trial was destined to be one of the first tests of the new Texas death penalty law and could have impacted the national death penalty picture, it is surprising that Haley, Ganne, and Bays were offered no help from outsiders. They were very much on their own representing an extremely unpopular client. The situation was further compounded by Haley's attitude and his increased drinking. There was no real division of labor, so Ganne and Bays did whatever preparation they could think of.

The new defense team had adopted the pretrial motions of the first group of lawyers, so they concentrated on the physical evidence. They spent a lot of time with assistant district attorneys Charlie Craig and David Spencer examining the evidence. When the possibility of neutron activation analysis testimony came up, Ganne began learning everything he could about the science, anticipating a technical cross-examination. Bays had also recently researched the subject, which he expected to combine with his engineering background.

One day Ganne and Bays were walking around the taxidermy studio grounds trying to get a feel for the place. Ganne suddenly felt a chill and the premonition that he knew exactly what had happened to the two missionaries, that Kleasen had used them for target practice. At the time Ganne did not know that other Mormons Kleasen had shot with would sometimes collect the targets down range then turn around to find Kleasen sighting down on them.

Ganne did most of the discovery, spending many days at the DPS crime lab or at the Austin Police Department looking over the evidence gathered by the huge state investigation and talking to expert witnesses. The band saw was still at the lab, looking sinister and ominous. He feared it could be devastating evidence at trial.

As the defense team came to appreciate the pile of circumstantial evidence accumulated against Kleasen, Ganne and Bays feared a guilty verdict was inevitable. Kleasen had no sane explanation to offer for all the victims' property found in and around his trailer. He would only say it was a Mormon plot. No defense strategy emerged from their preparations. They had no believable story consistent with innocence to offer to a jury. Ganne in particular started thinking in terms of preserving the record for their legal issues on appeal. "It was a loser from the word go," he thought, sensing nonetheless that the search warrant issue was worth pursuing.

TWENTY-THREE

JURY SELECTION BEGAN ON MONDAY, MAY 19, 1975. AFTER EAR-lier granting a defense motion to sequester the jury, Judge Blackwell surprised nearly everyone by reversing himself. Instead he imposed a gag order on the local press that prohibited journalists and reporters from naming or otherwise identifying individual jurors. The Austin media went to court to remove the order but lost. After this press accounts described jurors by occupation, age and gender, but no names or addresses. The judge saw this as preferable to "locking up" jurors in a local hotel for the duration of what everyone feared would be a long trial. The state's witness list of forty-eight didn't suggest a quick resolution. Initially 400 people were summoned as possible jurors, but their numbers were quickly reduced to 137 whom the lawyers would question.

Each side can make an unlimited number of challenges for cause when a candidate juror indicates a prejudice or bias about the defendant, the prosecution, or some aspect of the case which would prevent him or her from being impartial. A juror who said he would always believe the testimony of a police officer might be subject to challenge for cause. Jurors who could never vote for a death sentence or who would automatically vote for death once they decided to convict would be subject to such challenges. Jurors who had followed the case closely in the press and who had already formed an opinion as to a defendant's guilt or innocence would be excused for cause.

In addition, the prosecution and defense each had fifteen peremptory challenges to use. A peremptory challenge is the right to excuse a juror on what amounts to a hunch. Lawyers often enter a trial with a theory, a story they want to present. Part of that strategy is a decision about what kind of jurors they want to seat—that or a strong feeling about the kind of people they did not want on the jury.

Kleasen's lawyers no doubt would not have allowed a Mormon to sit on the jury no matter how unbiased she said she could be. By the same token, prosecutors likely would use peremptory challenges on persons who had a relative currently being prosecuted by their office but who claimed they could still be unbiased. Prospective jurors who might insist on seeing an actual body before they could be convinced that a murder had taken place certainly would have troubled the district attorney.

The 137 men and women who survived the initial cut were called into the courtroom one at a time—"individual sequestered *voir dire*" the process is called. One reason for the practice is to encourage candid answers. Examining potential jurors in groups runs the risk of their hearing the kind of answers that result in other jurors being seated or excused, thus coaching them on the "right" or "wrong" response. It's an effective procedure but it can be slow and, for the lawyers and trial court, mind numbing after a few days.

Prosecutors Robert Smith and Charlie Craig entered jury selection confidently. They didn't feel the need to ask detailed, intrusive questions because they felt their case was strong. If jurors were going to be offended by detailed personal questioning, prosecutors were going to let defense lawyers take the heat; they figured almost any jury could be brought to the verdicts they wanted. Both men felt the facts were so horrendous that if the jury convicted they would send Kleasen to the electric chair.

The defense apparently came to jury selection without a plan. Almost from the beginning, things began to fall apart for them. The junior members of the defense team came to jury selection thinking they were there mostly to observe, but very quickly it appeared that Haley was not functioning well as lead counsel. Increasingly Ganne and Bays had to fill the growing vacuum. Surprisingly, Kleasen did not try to control his defense team at this point and was not an active participant in jury selection.

The first day of jury selection concluded with only five jurors being examined. After the examination of each individual candidate, Judge Blackwell asked the lawyers if they would accept the him or her as a juror. If no objections were raised, he immediately swore the juror in, thus preventing either side from having a change of heart later on.

After less than an hour of questioning, the two sides had accepted the first prospective juror, Nancy Locker, a fifty-two-year-old housewife from Spicewood. After Locker, Kleasen's lawyers used three peremptories to excuse the son of a former district judge, a young University of Texas chemistry student, and a fifty-year-old architect. Prosecutors used one of their peremptories to excuse a University of Texas philosophy professor.

On the second day they agreed to four more jurors: a twenty-three-year-old female telephone company repairman, a forty-seven-year-old Texas Railroad Commission clerk, a thirty-six-year-old mother of several children who worked in a veterinarian's office. Richard G. Willis, a fifty-five-year-old retired Air Force colonel who once was part of the University of Texas ROTC program but now said he was looking for a job, was the third juror selected. The fifth juror, Mrs. Cynthia Bartlett, was asked about her current reading and reported a collection of short stories by Franz Kafka. His surreal book *The Trial* was not among them, she said.

Linda Miller, Kleasen's Pentecostal pen pal, sat through Tuesday's jury selection. Judge Blackwell allowed a brief visit between the two after court recessed for the day. The Austin newspaper described her as Kleasen's "girlfriend."

By Wednesday, after the examination of forty-one members of the jury pool, the panel reached nine members with the selection of a nineteen-year-old who would be the youngest member of the panel. A second Southwestern Bell telephone repairman, Kenneth Jones, fifty-six, was the eighth juror. A World War II veteran who'd flown B-17 bombers, Jones told the lawyers he'd read news coverage of the case. "They do a good job generally," he said, "but I wouldn't send anyone to the chair on what they put out."

The 50th candidate was a twenty-seven-year-old man who said he worked in the "intelligence business." During his examination, Kleasen, who still claimed to be a CIA veteran, was on the edge of his seat with uncharacteristic attention. The defense used their 15th peremptory challenge to excuse the man. They then asked for and were given an extra peremptory challenge which they never used.

On Thursday afternoon Karen Hood, a thirteen-year resident of Travis County, mother of two children, and wife of a Texas National Guardsman, was the last candidate questioned. With her selection as the twelfth juror, prosecution and defense now had a jury. Seven women and five men, all of them white, would decide Kleasen's fate.

TWENTY-FOUR

TESTIMONY WAS SET TO BEGIN ON FRIDAY, MAY 23, 1975. THE trial was moved to a fourth floor room in the back of the Travis County Courthouse on Guadalupe Street. Today it is District Court 261.

The room was large and sunny with high ceilings and two walls full of windows. Behind the lawyer's bar were fourteen rows of benches which were filled to overflowing for the biggest trial Austin had seen in more than a decade. Judge Blackwell would preside from an imposing raised bench, dwarfing the lawyers and witnesses in front of him. Two large counsel tables crowded the area between the bar and the judge's bench. The jury box was to Blackwell's right with two rows of six jurors each. Their backs were to the bank of oversized windows. Oak trees outside broke up the sunlight that spilled through the glass. The usual rule of sequestration had not been invoked for the Darley and Fischer families, so all were allowed to sit through the trial even though some were called as witnesses.

Just before trial, Haley refused to say if Kleasen would take the stand. He told reporters, "Defense attorneys don't put the defendant on the stand unless it's an exceptional case." Smith told the same reporters he would call forty or more witnesses and expected "five or six days" of testimony. Haley refused to say how many witnesses he might call for the defense.

One juror had somehow been identified and started receiving harassing telephone calls. She asked Judge Blackwell to sequester the jury for their protection. He again declined.

The trial was actually for the murder of Fischer. In Texas individual trials are usually conducted for each victim in cases of multiple homicides, but evidence of all the killings may be introduced.

The Fischer and Darley families were staying with the Mormon families who hosted them the previous fall. Austin Mormons didn't want to abandon them to a downtown motel. The Fischers again stayed with Bishop McCullough's family, the Darleys with FBI agent Bruce Yarborough and his wife.

District Attorney Smith made the opening argument for the prosecution. He was brief and to the point, telling the jury that the State's case was entirely circumstantial. Nonetheless, he told them they would be convinced beyond a reasonable doubt. "There are no witnesses to the crime except Kleasen," he said, and promised to prove that Kleasen had killed both young men and cut their heads up in the taxidermy shop's band saw. To the gallery's disappointment, Kleasen's lawyers reserved their opening argument until the conclusion of the State's evidence.

The first prosecution witness was Jack Paris, a Mormon "since I was eight years old." Paris, twenty-three, was boyish and blond-headed with a mustache. Charlie Craig used him to set the stage, to tell the jury who Kleasen was and about his threats of violence. Paris told the jury he first met Kleasen in September 1974, less than two months before the murders. He and his wife had been invited by two church missionaries to join them for a deer steak dinner at Kleasen's Oak Hill trailer. After driving the missionaries back to their apartment early in the evening, Paris had returned to Oak Hill with two more Mormon friends from Houston.

Paris described staying up late that night talking, listening really, as Kleasen spun yarns about his life of espionage, hunting, and persecutions. This, he told the jury, was when he heard Kleasen say he would shoot any policeman who pulled into his driveway, cut the body up, and spread the parts all over central Texas. He bragged that he had the skills to do that, Paris said. Kleasen also gave the three a tour of the taxidermy studio using keys he had on him.

Paris went on to describe as many as six other visits to Kleasen's trailer home and, finally, the tense confrontation at Paris's apartment on Wednesday, October 23, 1974. He identified pictures of the victims and of Kleasen's trailer. He also explained what a Mormon temple recommend was. Paris's own expired recommend was given to the jury as an example along with the photos.

David Bays cross-examined Paris but only seemed to bring out more damaging information. Paris described more of Kleasen's CIA fantasies and said he came to regard the man as a violent person. "Other things he said frightened me. Once he held a pistol to his head and said he didn't have much reason for living anymore and sometimes he thought he might shoot himself. That frightened me," Paris told Bays earnestly. "All the more with him saying that with a loaded gun pointed at his head right in front of me."

If Kleasen was such a scary guy, why did you keep visiting him? "I'm a member of the Mormon church. He is a member, and I was trying to fellowship him along with the missionaries."

Paris also explained how he told all this to local church authorities. "The Sunday after the missionaries had come up missing, I was called into the bishop's office at the chapel where I attend church. They asked me if I knew anything of the whereabouts of the missionaries. I said no. I told them I hadn't seen them since the previous Sunday at church. I also talked to them the previous Sunday night. The last thing they told me was that they were going out to Mr. Kleasen's house. Then I related the things Mr. Kleasen had told me to stake president Wright here in Austin and one of the bishop's counselors."

After Paris, prosecutors called David Owens of the National Weather Service to present records of Austin area rainfall from October 28 to 31. Presumably the 1.76 inches of rain would have washed away much of the blood and trace evidence that ordinarily should have been around the taxidermy studio. Owens provided charts of October's and November's rainfall which prosecutors introduced into evidence.

Owens was followed by Clay Rathbone who told the jury how he found the first missionary name tag along with other materials around the taxidermy studio grounds. He identified police photographs of and described for the jury the dilapidated out-buildings Kleasen had used for storage as well as his homemade shooting range. He told the jury he had known Kleasen for "several years."

Clay had worked in his father's business most of his life together with three brothers. He was familiar with guns and bullet holes. "I walked up to the property's fence line to look for deer tracks. It had been raining and the ground was soft, so you could usually find tracks and other signs. Anyway, I happened to see some stuff over in a corner. I noticed the name tag and a little prayer book laying back there in the grass. I remember Darley's name was on the name tag. The prayer book had a temple recommend in it, but I don't remember whose name was on it." The prayer book was actually a weekly planner with inspirational content. There was a bullet hole in the name tag as well as through the planner and the temple recommend. "The Temple Recommend hadn't expired yet. I figured somebody had lost it and would be looking for it, so I took the stuff to my father and showed it to him. I figured he would know what to do with it. He decided it wasn't of any value and threw it away." Clay's finds went into the trash which Kleasen burned every Sunday. "Robert has done that for us before, you know, on Sundays. He sometimes cleaned up the shop and burned the trash on weekends." When he heard about the missionaries being missing on November 5, Clay again looked for what he'd found but it was gone. He assumed it had already been burned. Under Ganne's cross-examination, Clay acknowledged that he hadn't seen any blood on the items or the ground around them, nor were there any powder burns.

Craig called Bill Buntzer next. He was the high school boy who worked in the taxidermy studio and found Fischer's name tag. He had known Kleasen for the past year and a half. After hearing about the missing missionaries and Clay's find a few days earlier, Buntzer also went looking—"out of curiosity." He told the jury how he found Fischer's black plastic name tag, also with a bullet hole in it. He took it to the taxidermy shop and the police were called. Craig showed Buntzer the name tag, which he identified. It was marked State's Exhibit eleven.

ATF agent Dale Littleton followed. He told the jury about their search of the trailer and Kleasen's arrest in Burnet. Littleton made a point of telling the jury about all the weapons stashed in Kleasen's

Rambler station wagon when he was taken into custody. "In the front seat right beside the defendant was a hunting knife about five or six inches long. Under his right leg sticking out from under the seat was a Colt .357 magnum pistol that was loaded. In the back seat within arm's reach was an open gun case with a Walther .22 Hornet rifle with scope."

The last witness of the day was Lem Rathbone. He had owned the Austin Taxidermy Studio since 1937 and very recently had moved the business from a South Lamar Street location to Oak Hill. Craig walked him through a description of how Kleasen came to live at the Austin Taxidermy Studio and what duties he had. He went on to the point of how after the missionaries disappeared his band saw had become fouled from misuse. "One morning I came to work and they told me they were having trouble with the band saw. It just wouldn't work. I went back there and saw the adjustments were all out of whack on it. Somebody had fooled with it that didn't know what they was doing. Nobody would take responsibility for it." They had to change several parts, including the blade, to get it working again. He thought this was October 28 or 29. The band saw had been in the shop ten years or more.

Craig showed Rathbone police photographs of the taxidermy shop and grounds, asking him to describe for the jury what they were looking at. This again included the out-buildings where Kleasen used to store some of his belongings. Rathbone also testified that Kleasen was a hunter who knew how to butcher and mount animals. Craig brought out the fact that Kleasen had keys and access to the shop at any time.

Haley cross-examined Rathbone, first about how game trophies were mounted, then about the ten years he had known Kleasen. "He would come to Texas about once a year to hunt, generally in the summer, and always left his trophies with us to mount," Rathbone explained. Sometimes Kleasen wanted Rathbone to arrange exotic game hunts for confined animals not normally native to Texas. He testified that on at least one occasion he set up an exotic hunt for Kleasen at the Diamond X Ranch, site of the buffalo kill that led to Kleasen's being jailed for several months. "I made the arrangements for him and took him out there. I don't remember exactly what he killed, but I think it was an Aoudad Sheep, an Axis Deer, and a Black Buck. He killed his animals, and we came back to the shop. And he was always writing me letters. He is a note writer."

Rathbone recalled that it was during the 1972 deer season—the second Saturday in November through the end of the year—that Kleasen showed up looking for a place to live. Other records suggest it was probably early 1973 when Kleasen returned. This was always a busy time for Rathbone's business, often demanding seven-day work weeks from all of his employees.

Haley asked Rathbone to tell the jury of the jobs he knew Kleasen had taken while living at the taxidermy studio. "He had a lot of different jobs, I don't even know about them all. He worked for the Texas Explosives Company for a while. He had several construction jobs. I believe he worked at a boat place for a while."

What was the band saw used for? To cut white pine for mounts and for the horns on some animals.

How about Kleasen's visitors? "I wouldn't say he had many, just a few. They were either church people or from the construction jobs that he worked on. I saw some church people there a number of times and met them. He would bring them into the shop and introduce them. There was a preacher from Burnet. And I think he had a boy down there with him one time from church." The boy was probably Caleb West.

Haley brought the questioning around to gutting and mounting animals. Rathbone said most of his customers gutted their kills in the field. His business did not dress the meat but would wrap it in brown paper so customers could take it elsewhere to be processed. He thought it usually took less than ten minutes to skin a deer.

Rathbone was the last witness called that first week. Judge Blackwell recessed the court for the extended Memorial Holiday weekend, until Tuesday morning. Jurors went home to their families.

The prosecution picked up on Tuesday morning with a series of witnesses describing the theft of the trailer Kleasen was living in and how police found some of the missionaries' teaching materials in it.

James Jenkins, a Mormon from Nephi, Utah, next took the stand. Nephi is the name of an ancient prophet in the Book of Mormon and is one of a number of distinctly Mormon names that dot the map in areas pioneered by the church more than 150 years ago. Jenkins had completed his church service, but in 1974 had been Darley's missionary companion in Austin for three months. He and Darley had sometimes visited Kleasen at the trailer.

About two weeks before being released from his mission, Jenkins had given Darley two religious instructional filmstrips and accompanying audio cassettes—*Man's Search for Happiness* and *Meet the Mormons*. This was about the time of Darley's birthday, around September 29 or 30, Jenkins thought. (Darley had actually turned twenty on September 27, 1974.) Jenkins recognized the materials found in Kleasen's trailer as the ones he had given Darley because his initials—JRJ—were still on them. These were missionary materials, not something given to a new convert like Kleasen.

Next the jury heard from Texas Parks and Wildlife lieutenant Frank Henzy on how he found the blood spattered fatigue pants and jacket in front of Kleasen's trailer. He was followed by sheriff's sergeant Robert Nestorff who testified about his identification of the trailer as having been stolen from Christian Mobile Homes in Oak Hill.

Conrad Hardcastle, a Mormon missionary then in his twenty-second month of church service, next told the jury about spending the day with Darley and Fischer on October 28. He recalled Darley telling him about their dinner appointment with Kleasen and inviting Hardcastle and his companion to come along. "We wanted to go with them, but before we left we realized that we had an appointment and couldn't come." He then described the frantic search for the missing young men that first week of November. Craig had him identify several of the paper items connected with the missionaries which were collected from the taxidermy grounds.

Each Mormon missionary carries a ministerial certificate signed by the church president. In 1974 the president was Spencer W. Kimball. At the top of this certificate was printed "The Church of

Jesus Christ of Latter-day Saints" in a unique type style. While crawling through the grass, Hardcastle had found a burned paper fragment with the word "The" on it in that distinct type style. He had a deputy bag and mark the discovery which he now identified for the jury. He also identified a burned page from Darley's weekly missionary planner found in the grass. Hardcastle had received so many letters from Darley he immediately recognized his handwriting on the page.

Ganne cross-examined Hardcastle. They had talked briefly in the courthouse hallway moments before, the only time Ganne had a chance to prepare for this witness. Hardcastle told Ganne and the jury that Darley explained their regular meals with Kleasen as "not just eating with him, but fellowshipping the man as well, trying to help him out."

Homicide investigator Albert Riley took the stand briefly to list the items he had inventoried from Kleasen's trailer during the search. These included fake identity papers, the letter from Darley and Fischer confirming the October 28 dinner commitment, blood-flecked watches that belonged to the victims, Hardcastle's filmstrips, keys that started the victims' car and opened their apartment, and what would become State's Exhibit 26, a typed manuscript entitled "My Thousand Whitetail Deer," by John T. Williamson.

Later Tuesday the jury heard the brief but dramatic testimony of Jill Darley. She told of meeting Kleasen in the jail when he lectured her for suspecting that her son was already dead. She squeezed a handkerchief tightly between her hands as she testified. Her voice broke several times. She would drop her head and pause long enough to regain her composure. She explained her son Gary's regular and predictable letter writing home. The last time she spoke with her son was on his twentieth birthday, September 27, 1974—"a month and a day before he was, uh, killed." Prosecutors asked if she had had any communication from her missing son since October 28. "I only wish I had," she replied, choking back her emotions.

She was followed by her husband, David, and the missing missionaries' eighteen-year-old girlfriend, Kerrie Hampton, who also lived in Simi Valley, California. She told the jury how she saved "quite a bit" of Darley's hair after his mother gave him a pre-mission haircut in the family kitchen. A reporter covering the trial wrote of Hampton's "own blond hair gently curling against her flushed cheeks" while she testified. Hampton had sealed the hair in a plastic bag which she kept with other keepsakes until Gary was reported missing. It was this hair that was given to Texas criminologists to match with samples gathered at the crime scene.

Hampton was followed by Gary's father, David. Charlie Craig asked him to briefly describe their family and missing son. "The last time I saw Gary was in Salt Lake City when we left him at the Mission Home," he said. "I think that was on March 2, 1974." He noted the regular correspondence with Gary throughout his son's time in Texas. "I would receive a letter almost weekly from him. Usually on Mondays he would write a letter to me. Monday was their free day to write home and take care of personal things." He went on to identify his son's watch, State's Exhibit 28, which was found in Kleasen's trailer. "Kelle wore this watch for several years, and then he gave it to Gary just before Gary left to go on his mission." Finally, Craig had Darley explain how he collected dental and medical records, as well as the haircut clippings from Kerrie, for investigators in Texas.

On cross-examination Pat Ganne asked about Gary's motorcycle. "Well, he was certainly interested in motorcycles and had one of his own before he left for the mission field," David replied, "but I would not say that that was his primary interest."

After Kerrie Hampton and the Darleys testified, Smith picked up the manuscript typed on yellow paper. State's Exhibit 26 had been seized by Investigator Riley during the search of Kleasen's trailer. "Your honor, I'd like to read to the jury some of what was written by the defendant here in his 'My Thousand Whitetails, a Poacher's Notebook.' It's by John T. Williamson whom we now know is really the defendant."

Haley and Ganne jumped to their feet to object but Blackwell denied the objection.

Smith began by reading a section of the twenty-page manuscript where Kleasen boasted of slaughtering deer at a creek where they came to drink. The courtroom crowd was hushed and leaning forward as Smith's booming voice began to read aloud.

> I just kept firing until it was too dark to shoot. I lost count of how many I killed, but I knew they were all laying within thirty feet of the creek which stretched out for about 200 yards. When I finished I loaded twenty-eight deer in my pick-up truck. And when I counted my empties I had 28 empty cases so I thought I did OK.
>
> The beauty was that at that range the sound of the Wasp rifle was so little that the deer did not sense the danger. I killed with each shot thus none of the animals gave an alarming cry.

Smith paused here for emphasis, then moved to the section he believed answered the question of what Kleasen had done with the remains of Darley and Fischer.

> One may say Wow, 28 deer, where did he put all the meat. The meat you get from these small deer is about 35-40 pounds each if you weigh the bones. This can be reduced even more with boning. The whole deer can really be cut up to fit a very small space. And as I like some parts better than others I give some to my dog and whatever is left away as fast as I shoot them. I assure the reader that nothing worth while is wasted. Even the guts are used in potato sacks in baiting for catfish. This is sown with large rocks and sent to the bottom of a near lake by the sack full. And the very best fishing is to be had over my "dumping ground" ...

Afterwards Haley stood again to renew his objection. "I wish the jury would be reminded that there is no evidence that this was written by Mr. Kleasen." It wasn't so much an objection as a comment for the jury.

With that Blackwell recessed the trial for the day. He now recalls that it was this manuscript which convinced him of Kleasen's guilt. "It was a confession," he observes.

Charlie Craig began Wednesday's testimony with Kelle Darley, Gary's older brother who had also served a Mormon mission in Texas and now ran a small motel in Santaquin, Utah, while attending Brigham Young University. Kelle was extremely nervous. Craig showed him State's Exhibit 28, Gary Darley's watch which was found in Kleasen's trailer. The Voumard watch was a family Christmas present given to Kelle in 1968. Kelle testified it had been damaged during an auto accident in 1969 and had been taken to a jeweler to be repaired. Then he'd worn the watch on his mission, where the humidity had caused a green growth to appear on the watch face. He explained that he had tried to wipe the growth off but had accidentally removed part of the words "17 Jewel" as well. The jury could see that the watch found in Kleasen's trailer reflected all of this unique history.

Ganne cross-examined Kelle on the day-to-day life of a missionary but made no attempt to challenge the history of the watch.

Bob Smith presented the next witness, crime lab technician Fred Rymer. He explained at length the ballistics testing on the missionary name tags. Smith moved the tested tags into evidence and they were passed down the jury box during Rymer's explanations. He displayed for the jury Fischer's recovered name tag which had been marked as State's Exhibit 11.

After a brief argument over whether Rymer would be required to turn over his written report to the defense, Pat Ganne began a lengthy cross-examination. He got the ballistics expert to acknowledge that he could not say for sure what kind of firearm had produced the hole in the Fischer name tag. "I had no basis for that," Rymer conceded.

On redirect examination Smith brought Rymer back to that point. "The purpose of my examination was not to match a specific weapon with the bullet hole in the name tag. My idea was just to get some idea on what we are dealing with." It would not be possible to match the bullet hole with a specific weapon or brand of firearm, Rymer explained.

Ganne tried again on recross examination: "So the only thing that you've told us is that maybe a .22 poked a hole in that particular name tag?" "Well, as I said in my testimony, it was closer to a .22 than any other," Rymer answered. Both men continued to duel for the remainder of Rymer's testimony on just what he said about the hole, whether it was definitely a bullet hole or merely looked like one but was perhaps something else.

Jim and Cathy Fischer, Mark's parents, testified next. Craig examined both. They presented for the jury a picture of a deeply religious, loving family. "We aren't embarrassed by telling each other how much we love each other," his mother said. They also testified to their missing son's regular communications which stopped on October 28.

Catherine Fischer's visit with Kleasen at the jail only came out in Bay's cross-examination. "Didn't you visit Mr. Kleasen at the jail?" he asked. He probably regretted giving her the opening. "We talked. He cried for a good part of the time that I was there," she told the jury. "He said he didn't think the boys were alive. And he told me if it was any comfort that he would be dead too." She also recounted Kleasen's boasting about what a good shot he was. He offered the explanation that the bullet hole in her son's name tag could have come from someone just horsing around and shooting it on a flat surface.

"At any time during the conversation did you give him a Book of Mormon?" Bays asked. (Mormons embrace both the Bible and the Book of Mormon as scripture.) "Yes," she answered, explaining how she had left her name and address in it so the two could correspond. "I also had bought him some banana bread and cookies from one of the Relief Society sisters, but I wasn't allowed to bring them to him."

If anything, the cross-examination generated even more sympathy for the Fischer family.

After Mark's parents, prosecutors presented his cousin Susan Fischer. She told the jury about the pre-mission haircut she had given Mark two days before he left Milwaukee for Salt Lake City. His girlfriend Barbara Bakewell followed, telling how she saved the cuttings as mementoes of their romance. She talked about the Seiko watch she'd purchased for Mark as a farewell gift when he departed for his mission. She'd bought it at a Milwaukee area J. C. Penney store and still had the receipt. She identified State's Exhibit 27 as her gift, one of the blood-flecked watches taken from Kleasen's trailer. She recognized it because Mark's wrists were so small she had had to have some extra links removed from the metal wristband. The seized watch had the same number of links removed.

After the family members' testimonies, Craig presented police sergeant A. P. Lamme to explain how he'd stumbled across the missionaries' car while on drug surveillance at the Inwood Apartments. Ganne's cross-examination brought out more details regarding the find, but nothing relating to how the American Motors Hornet ended up on cinder blocks in a south Austin apartment complex parking lot.

Jim Fischer, Mark's father, followed Lamme to testify for the second time. Craig asked him to describe taking his son to Salt Lake City at the beginning of his mission. There they bought a ten-pack of common black Bic pens at the University of Utah book store. "Mark said they preferred black in the mission home," his father told the jury. Craig then showed him State's Exhibit 19, the shattered Bic pen found in the grass of the taxidermy grounds near the recovered papers and name tag. The prosecution placed the pen into evidence and it was passed down the jury box.

Mormon FBI agent Bruce Yarborough followed several brief chain-of-custody witnesses. Craig walked him through his own investigation, including responding to Lamme finding the car and his visit with Ed Guyon to Kleasen's trailer. Yarborough told the jury he'd shown Kleasen his FBI credentials when they first met.

On cross-examination Ganne asked if Yarborough had authority from his superiors to work a routine missing persons case or was he a Mormon trying to use his FBI status to look into a church problem? The agent replied that he had been directed by his bosses "to determine if the FBI had jurisdiction in the disappearance." Yarborough acknowledged that he didn't have a search warrant but that Kleasen had never asked for one. In answer to Ganne's questions, he described asking Kleasen if he could look in the trailer but was only allowed to look in the windows. "He went in and got something out of a shelf first and stuck it under his carpenter's apron, then he came back out." Kleasen then talked to Guyon about church business while Yarborough looked through the glass. He didn't see anything helpful. The two left after about fifteen minutes.

Craig introduced mission president Loveland as his next witness. Loveland described himself as a "licensed journeyman plumber and fitter" serving in a voluntary church calling. "I preside over the two hundred-plus missionaries in South Texas," he explained. He went on to tell the jury about church ownership of the automobiles driven by missionaries and how they were used. "The vehicles are assigned depending on the size of the area they are to cover as missionaries. This particular area is quite large so a car was assigned." He explained the mileage limits imposed on missionaries with cars. "A zone leader has a mileage limit of 1,500 miles a month; a district leader 1,250; and a regular missionary 1,000. Elder Darley was a district leader so he had 1,250 per month allowed for his car." Those limits were what Fischer and Darley meant when they wrote to Kleasen on October 19 that "we are running short of miles," then confirmed their October 28 dinner commitment.

Under cross-examination by Haley, Loveland explained the young men's service in a mission area that "roughly covers from Brownsville, Texas, westward to the Mexican border just south of the Big Bend Country, eastward to the Louisiana border and south to Mexico." His missionaries worked full time "contacting people about the Gospel, sometimes door to door." He went on to say that missionaries were instructed not to stay more than an hour to an hour and a half when dining with members. "That is a rule imposed by Salt Lake City," he testified. Haley seemed surprised when Loveland said he'd never met Kleasen before. The mission president saw him for the first time that day in court.

After Loveland, prosecutors moved through a series of Austin police officers describing their investigation and the gathering of evidence. Harold Bilberry and Colon Jordan described how they had seized a key ring from Kleasen's trailer and how those keys had fit the recovered car, the missionaries' apartment, and a bicycle lock. They described searching the taxidermy shop grounds on November 6, 1974, and the recovery of the tires and license plates.

Judge Blackwell recessed for the night before Bays was able to get far into his cross-examination of Jordan. Bays briefly returned to his cross-examination the next morning. One point he tried to drive home was that fingerprints could have been lifted from the watches and other evidence found at the trailer but were not. Such prints, he complained, could have been clues as to who planted the items in Kleasen's trailer.

The prosecution presented more law enforcement witnesses on the recovery of evidence and establishing a chain of custody, setting the stage for crime lab testimony. Austin police officers Ruben Fuentes and Patrick Roth, Texas Ranger Wallace Spillar who had seized the band saw, and Travis County deputy sheriff John Barton, who first questioned Kleasen about the disappearances, all testified. It was Spiller who identified the missionaries' automobile license plates as State's Exhibit 50, Darley's blood-flecked Voumard watch as State's Exhibit 28, samples from the missionaries' haircuts, and other physical evidence.

During a pause Smith moved a number of written items into evidence. First was the grand jury indictment of Kleasen for capital murder, then death certificates for both Darley and Fischer. The death certificates were issued by Justice of the Peace Jim McMurtry after Kleasen's January inquest. The certificates listed the deaths as occurring on October 28, 1974, as the results of "unknown" injury.

Haley objected to the death certificates as hearsay. The defense had reason to fear their admission because they contended there was no proof the young men were even dead. The lawyers argued over their admission, and finally Haley agreed that Judge Blackwell should read the jury a state statute on the authenticity of such documents. State's Exhibits 53 and 54 then went to the jury. Charlie Craig thought Haley had just been snookered, that armed with the death certificates the jury would be satisfied the two missing men were dead.

That brought the prosecution to their most sensational scientific evidence, beginning with seventeen-year Department of Public Safety Crime Lab veteran Leslie Smith. He described himself as a "chemist and toxicologist," but in fact had done just about every kind of scientific investigation during his long career. Craig confidently walked him through his testing of the battery cables, the car tires and brake drums, the car jack, the tires and laundry soap, Kleasen's blood-stained clothing, and his analysis of the hair samples taken from the taxidermy shop and compared to those from the missionaries' haircuts. Smith matter-of-factly identified State's Exhibits 62A, 62B, and 62C as packets "containing material that was removed from the band saw at the taxidermists [sic] shop and carried back to the laboratory for analysis." Some of that material was what remained of Gary Darley and Mark Fischer.

The most damaging exhibit of all was the band saw. It was over five feet tall, gray and slightly rusted, squat and menacing. There was a large circular housing on the top of a thin neck for the blade. Bailiffs had set it directly in front of the jury box where it seemed to glower at the witness in the box an arm's reach away. The front row of jurors could have touched the circular housing by leaning forward in their chairs. A small circular white paper tag hung from tiny strings on the base identifying it as State's Exhibit 64. Worst of all was the encrusted substances that could be seen around the blade and housing, substances that Smith would soon identify.

Sitting at counsel's table, Pat Ganne knew that the band saw's physical presence was having a far greater effect on the jury than any words coming from the mouths of witnesses. He watched the jurors' troubled glances at the band saw and feared what they were thinking.

Craig asked Smith about the tests he conducted on hair removed from the band saw. "There was some animal hair on the saw. So the first test was to separate the hair as to either human or animal. I didn't try to identify what kind of animal hair there was but I recognized some from deer," Smith began. "The human hair was then separated out and compared to the known hair samples of human hair submitted by Mr. Darley and Mr. Fischer." This was from the pre-mission haircuts. "There was a number of hair that had all the characteristics of Mr. Darley's hair and a number that had all the characteristics of Mr. Fischer's hair." In Smith's opinion, it was the victims' head hairs on the band saw. "No human hair was found inside the saw that was not consistent with either Mr. Darley or Mr. Fischer."

Smith went on to explain that these were all "fragments of hair. None of the hair I compared had a root structure on them. Most of it was cut. At least one end of almost all the hair had a broken or splintered appearance rather than a clean cut." (In 1975 DNA evidence had not yet been used in court, but such testing of hair would not have been possible without the root or bulb.) "They appeared to have been cut or broken by a rather blunt type of instrument," he continued. "The distribution of the hair was completely around the full circumference of the blade area of the saw. I would have to assume that this hair was held rigidly enough for the saw to get a good bite in it to carry it that far around."

Craig asked where Smith had found the hair on the band saw. "Not from the actual blade. I collected it from the wheels which transport the blade and from the areas through which the blade pass."

About this time Cathy Fischer left the room. She could not bear to listen to any more testimony about her son.

Asked how the hair could have been splattered around the housing, Smith explained, "It would have to be attached to something rather than simply having a handful of loose hair thrown in the saw blade."

Smith testified that there was relatively little human blood on the band saw. Craig asked for an explanation. "In the first place, the type of hair would not have come from a finger." There are physical differences between head, body, and pubic hair which can be determined on close examination. "The amount of blood I found was consistent with the muscle and fatty tissue I found in the saw." Smith believed that the only body parts cut in the band saw were the victims' heads. "There just didn't seem to be that much tissue to allow for cutting through large muscles. That and the fact the only hair I found was head hair, not body or pubic."

At this point Craig asked Smith how a human body was held together, whether it could be disassembled without the use of the band saw. Ganne jumped up to object that the question was well outside Smith's area of expertise. Blackwell sustained the objection.

Craig circled back and asked Smith about his training and if any of it concerned human anatomy. Smith replied that he had audited physical anthropology courses at the University of Texas to help him identify skeletal remains. Craig again asked about human anatomy, Ganne again objected, but this time Blackwell allowed the testimony. "The bone assembly of the human body is such that when the connecting tissues are removed the bones can be separated from each other. All except the plates of the skull could be pulled apart from each other."

Craig finished by asking Smith if the human materials found on the band saw and Kleasen's clothing were of common origin and of the same type of material. Smith said they were. Craig returned to the prosecution's table, and Ganne stood to cross-examine.

Ganne wanted to know about the tests used to identify the blood. "Determining whether or not a specimen is human or not is based on chemical tests for blood tissue," Smith explained. "This is called a precipitant test, here using an anti-human precipitant serum in which a saline extract of the protein sample is tested. If there is a reaction where they come into contact this indicates the protein which the test is designed to detect. A positive result on this test means the material is human. The same test is available for various animals." Ganne then asked about the blood on Kleasen's clothing and was told "there are several spots of both human blood and deer blood, but the human blood spots are a little larger." Ganne's cross-examination probably cleared up a few questions, but it didn't undermine the State's case.

The last prosecution witness was chief Harris County medical examiner Joseph A. Jachimczyk. His questioning, though relatively brief, was devastating to Kleasen. Jachimczyk, who had as much experience testifying for the prosecution as Smith had prosecuting, had been in the Harris County medical examiner's office since 1957. He was a University of Tennessee Medical School graduate, had a law degree from Boston College, was a member of the Texas bar, had attended and was a teaching fellow at Harvard, and had extensive experience as a forensic pathologist, including as an assistant state medical examiner in Maryland and as a Massachusetts state pathologist. He was certified by the American Board of Pathologists in pathologic anatomy, clinical pathology, and forensic pathology. Equally important was Jachimczyk's forceful, authoritative manner.

On May 9, 1975, Travis County assistant district attorney Bobby Williams had traveled to Houston and delivered to Jachimczyk four cylinders for testing. They contained hair samples from Kleasen, Fischer, and Darley. The fourth was labeled "sample from band saw" and contained what the medical examiner described for the jury as "a crumbly tan-gray material" filling about three-quarters of an inch of the tube. The sample also contained short bits of hair.

Jachimczyk had arrived for court early enough to inspect the band saw. He had observed on the wheels and housing material similar to what he had tested, including visible hair. Jachimczyk began his testimony by telling the jury that a forensic pathologist was "one who concerns himself primarily with the problem involving death and death causation." He testified that after mounting the band saw substances onto slides, he performed an anti-human precipitant test which confirmed the presence of human proteins. Such a test would have responded to blood, muscle, or any other human tissue present in sufficient quantities, he said, even if it were blood soaked into sawdust. He then examined the substances under a microscope "for the histologic appearance; that is, the microscopic anatomy appearance of whatever this material or tissue might be. It turned out that they were portions of bone, of cartilage, of muscle, of hair follicles, of sweat glands, and fat tissue." After some description, he told the jury, "This was human tissue."

Over an objection from Ganne, Jachimczyk testified that in his opinion the human or humans these samples had come from were dead. As to the hair, he testified that he compared it with samples from himself, Kleasen, Darley, Fischer, and his own cat. He concluded that hair found in his sample was only similar to Gary Darley's. He did not find Fischer's head hair in his sample.

On cross-examination, Ganne brought out that Jachimczyk found no brain matter present which the medical examiner had seemed to expect. "The average brain of a male will weigh around 1,400 grams, and volume-wise that would occupy most of the cranial cavity," he explained. This was not especially troubling as brain matter was "one of the more rapidly deteriorating tissues in the body," quickly becoming unidentifiable. Brain matter begins to break down twenty-four to forty-eight hours after death at room temperature, more quickly in heat and humidity, he told the jury. "Wc had a study in Baltimore a number of years back where we took a fresh brain and placed it on the rooftop of the morgue as an experimental procedure. After approximately ten days there was no recognizable tissue there," he said, "it was just mush." Jachimczyk also noted that the average nineteen- or twenty- year-old male's head would be "somewhere between six and seven inches in various diameters depending on which way the head is positioned."

With Jachimczyk's testimony, the prosecution abruptly rested after calling forty-five of the forty-eight witnesses it had under subpoena. They elected not to call FBI expert Michael Hoffman but turned his written report over to the defense. The expert was held in reserve by the State as a possible rebuttal witness. Prosecutors had concluded not to call Hoffman earlier in their trial preparation, but left him sitting in the witness area with his notes and exhibits as a decoy. They wanted thc defense thinking they would have a lengthy cross-examination of the expert before they could begin putting on their case. The stratcgy worked perfectly, no one was more surprised by the State's resting than those at the defense table who had anticipated having to deal with Hoffman's neutron activation testimony and only then begin presenting their case.

A satisfied Smith told reporters during a break, "You quit when you've got enough. When you strike oil you quit drilling." Assistant district attorney David Spencer said, "We just didn't need Hoffman." He felt the State had solid testimony from its other witnesses and the jury could have no doubt that the remains found on the band saw were all that was left of the two victims.

"I don't know why they didn't call Hoffman," a stunned Ganne told the same reporters. "We talked to Hoffman and his testimony was solid for the State." There was no time for the defense to regroup. Haley, Ganne, and Bays had to scramble to begin their case.

TWENTY-FIVE

PAT GANNE, PUSHED TO THE FRONT OF THE DEFENSE TEAM, gave Kleasen's opening argument after the State rested. He promised the defense would undermine the State's case, leaving jurors with more than a reasonable doubt as to Kleasen's guilt. "The evidence we're going to present is going to make you uncomfortable, it's going to really shake the foundation of the State's case and raise serious questions with you," the young lawyer promised. "First of all, we will show you that the band saw was changed, was altered, the day before Mr. Kleasen was arrested. The State's physical evidence has been focused on October 28th, but what they are relying on didn't come into existence until a week later."

The State's case, Ganne argued, depended on Kleasen's having a reliable vehicle on October 28 to haul back to the taxidermy shop the tires from where the missionaries' car was found stripped. He promised testimony to the effect that Kleasen didn't have such transportation. "But most important of all, you will hear from a totally disinterested party, a young lady who did know Kleasen and was not a Mormon, that she talked to the missionaries about 8:30 on the evening of the 28th," Ganne continued. "This is going to bother you because it just does not fit." With that promise, he called Lem Rathbone back to the witness box.

Rathbone testified briefly that he changed the plate on the band saw after October 28, replacing the metal plate with a wooden one a week or so after the murders. The implication was that the plate tested by the State crime lab was not the one on the band saw after the murder. Rathbone went on to say they kept "probably thirty or forty band saw blades out there." When the police asked for the blade that was on the saw around October 28, he said "it was impossible to tell which blade it was." When they finally did find a blade to test, Rathbone said he wasn't told, so didn't know which one they'd actually taken.

Rathbone also testified that the teenaged Bill Buntzer was always cutting himself with a knife and bleeding. All his employees worked on the band saw, including Buntzer and his bleeding fingers. "We teased him about cutting himself all the time," Rathbone laughed. Since the State could not type the human blood found on the saw blade, Ganne hoped to convince the jury it was really Buntzer's, or another employee's, and not the missing missionaries'.

Rathbone went on to say that the chicken coop where the tires had been found under a sheet of plastic was poorly maintained and easily accessible. Ganne invited the conclusion that the tires were planted there by someone other than Kleasen. People were everywhere, Rathbone told the jury. There were perhaps 125 people milling around the property the day the tires were "found." "They took me down there and asked me if I had seen them tires before. They weren't my tires and I had never seen them before," Rathbone said. Finally, Rathbone told the jury that all current employees had keys to the taxidermy shop, along with another dozen former employees he'd had over the years.

During his cross-examination, Craig got Rathbone to admit one more time that Kleasen also had a set of those keys.

Ganne recalled Clay Rathbone to testify that it was Monday, October 28, or Monday, November 4, when he first noticed that the band saw was "out of adjustment." He thought it was the Monday after an FBI agent first came to talk to him about the two missing boys. Clay was then asked how large an object could be cut with the band saw. He thought about seven inches but hadn't measured it. Ganne also got him to say that all the out buildings near Kleasen's trailer were in poor condition, and thus easy to get into. Rathbone also stated that his brother Jimmy Byrd often repaired Kleasen's broken-down cars.

The third defense witness, called by Bays, was W. C. Roney, a Pentecostal church member from Lampassas. He had known Kleasen for some time and had often allowed him to stay in his home. Roney frequently volunteered to work on Kleasen's constantly disabled car.

He told the jury the car was broken most of October, including the last week when "the motor was laid out on the sidewalk." When asked if Kleasen could fix it himself, Roney laughed and said, "He didn't know which end was up on it, I don't think."

Under cross-examination by Craig, Roney admitted that Kleasen's car was working on November 5, the day he drove it to Burnet church services where he would be arrested that evening. He also conceded Kleasen was constantly looking for car parts to keep his vehicle operating.

With Roney's testimony, the trial adjourned early Friday afternoon. The final defense witness, Mrs. Claudia Farmer, was too sick to testify that day, Kleasen's attorneys said.

When they reconvened Monday morning, June 2, Farmer would be the first and last witness. Under direct examination from Bays, she said she was not Mormon but knew Elder Darley well enough to recognize his voice on the telephone. She lived in Austin and worked at the Bureau of Economic Geology, University of Texas. She said Darley had frequently visited her and her husband because of their mutual interest in motorcycles. Her husband was also a motorcycle enthusiast.

Farmer recalled that on October 28 her husband was in San Marcos. She was certain Darley had called several times that evening trying to reach him and wanting to come over to visit. She thought this was between 8:00 and 9:00 in the evening, probably around 8:30. She promptly called the investigators with this information, giving them a statement. "I don't remember the exact date I went to the police station," she told the jury, "but it was after I had heard on television that the missionaries were missing."

Confident the jury would conclude Farmer was simply mistaken, Smith decided not to cross-examine her. With that the defense rested and Smith announced the State would not call any witnesses in rebuttal.

After a brief conference, Judge Blackwell reconvened the trial for final arguments. The courtroom seemed even fuller than earlier. Not an inch of bench or a patch of wall was unoccupied by spectators, press, local Mormons, law enforcement, and courthouse gawkers. The crowd spilled into the hall, with more hoping at least to hear what they could not see.

Charlie Craig rose first to address the jury. He began by going through the jury instructions on circumstantial evidence. He then emphasized just how reliable the victims were. "These are not a couple of irresponsible teenagers who might just up and run off," he said. "These were very responsible, religious young men who had given up two years of their lives to serve their faith. They were devoted to their calling. They were close to their families and their friends. They stayed in close communication with those they were close to. But that predictably regular communication just stopped on October 28th, 1974." Craig then summarized the testimony establishing that Darley and Fischer were heading to Kleasen's trailer when last seen. "Both Gary Darley and Mark Fischer are dead," he assured the jury, then confidently ticked off the circumstantial evidence that their lives had simply stopped on October 28, 1974.

"Leslie Smith of the State Crime Lab found the material in State's Exhibit number 64, the band saw," Craig continued, pointing to the hulking gray machine positioned inches away from the jury box. "He examined a great deal of that material and he found human tissue, cartilage, and the head hair of the victims." "Dr. Jachimczyk also examined that material," he went on. "He found human tissue, hair follicles, sweat glands, and head hair that belonged to Gary Darley." And if that were not sufficiently convincing, there was the human blood and the victims' hair found on Kleasen's clothing.

"Kleasen has told us what happened in his own words," the young prosecutor said, moving to the defendant's statements and writings. There were Kleasen's jail meetings with the mothers of the missing missionaries, his statements that they were not alive, and that he would probably be dead soon too. Craig went on to recount Kleasen's threats to Jack Paris about killing and dismembering law enforcement. And there was the poacher's manuscript found in Kleasen's trailer. "Even if you don't believe he wrote it, he certainly read it. Certainly there is the idea of how to dispose of bodies, how to get rid of them without getting caught," Craig said. "Where do you put them? You spread them around. You don't put everything in one place. You put them in the dirty clothes, you put them in the trash, you place them in a number of packages, you saw the long bones if you have to. The rest you can just cut up with a knife." The courtroom was silent, its attention rapt.

Craig concluded by listing all the victims' property found in and around Kleasen's residence. The car parts and tires, the license plates, the missionary materials, the watches, none of which had been explained by the defense. He finally sat down after telling the jury there was only one reasonable interpretation of the evidence, that the missionaries had been killed and that Robert Kleasen had killed them.

Without a pause, young Pat Ganne stood. The air was hot and stale but no one moved. By this point, Ganne, at least, appreciated that a conviction was inevitable. The defense had not, could not, rebut the State's evidence. If there was hope for his client, it was for the jury to convict him of simple murder where the death sentence was not a possibility. That meant arguing these were simply homicides, not murders committed in the course of a robbery.

"Ladies and gentlemen of the jury, I have sort of mixed emotions as I stand here addressing you. I'm tired. I'm exhausted. This really has been trial by ordeal. I don't know how else to describe it and it really has got me down. But what really bothers me is that there has been a certain amount of intellectual dishonesty applied to you as this trial has progressed," Ganne said. He then attacked the State's theory that this was a murder in the course of a robbery, while also saying they don't know how the murders took place. "You can't have it both ways. Either you have a death that occurs during the course of a robbery, or you have a death by means unknown. They want you to believe that a murder was committed for two used watches and four used tires. That's ridiculous. It's unbelievable. It doesn't make sense," he challenged. "What they are trying to do is stampede your mind. They're trying to show you that if the murder—if it occurred, it was too gruesome—can you conceive of a person being run through a band saw? The gruesomeness of it. And it is gruesome. And they are trying to tell you: Well, we think that's what happened. That's why they found hairs on the band saw. Therefore, if a murder occurred, it's not good enough. He must have been stealing tires and hubcaps and—tires during the course of the murder." And where were the fingerprints? If Kleasen had handled all this property with so little concern for concealment, why weren't his fingerprints on the license plate, the tires, the watches, or any of the other recovered property?

After reading the jury charge on simple murder, he told them, "Now, reasonable doubt is not defined for you, but I believe that all of you are reasonable. A reasonable doubt is a doubt that you can articulate. It's a doubt that nags you. It bothers you, it's something that sticks in your craw." Ganne then sat down and turned the argument over to Haley whose role in the defense had seemed to diminish day by day. Kleasen had silently fumed during Ganne's argument, recognizing it as an admission that he was guilty of murder but not capital murder. He pointedly refused to speak to the young lawyer once Ganne sat down at counsel's table. In contrast, Haley gave the argument Kleasen wanted to hear.

Haley challenged Paris's testimony, asking the jury to wonder why he kept returning to Kleasen's trailer if he found him such a threatening man. "Robert Elmer Kleasen from the testimony of even Mr. Paris was opening up his heart, was opening his mind, and was telling the missionaries and this church how much he needed their help. ... This is a church-going man," he went on. "When his car doesn't work, he walks to church." You must conclude that Kleasen simply didn't do it, he told the jury. When Haley sat down, Bob Smith made the final arguments for the State.

The seven-woman, five-man jury was out less than two hours before returning a guilty verdict. When the foreman signaled the verdict with a knock on the jury room door at 3:44 p.m., a resigned Ganne sighed and told Bays, "Nothing good comes quick." Kleasen reacted emotionally. His face was still flushed red with the excitement of the day's testimony. When the verdict was read, his face blanched and he dropped his head into his hands. He sobbed softly, "But I didn't do it, I didn't do it," while Haley stroked his arm in consolation. With the verdict read, the jury was escorted to a downtown hotel to spend the night.

The punishment phase of their deliberations would begin the following morning.

Out on the courthouse steps, Haley told the assembled reporters, "We were all shocked by the rapidity of justice here." The Darleys also spoke to reporters. Gary's father, David, said, "Justice is done." His wife, Jill, found it "an empty victory."

Mark Fischer and his girlfriend, Barbara Bakewell, at a high school dance before his mission. Bakewell testified at the murder trial about how she came to have samples of Mark's hair which matched those found on the band saw. (*Courtesy Jim and Cathy Fischer.*)

Mark Fischer just before his mission. (*Courtesy Jim and Cathy Fischer.*)

Gary Darley on his mission to Texas. (*Courtesy David K. Darley.*)

Bob Kleasen posing in the Austin Taxidermy Studio in 1974 for a Mormon missionary. (*Courtesy Larry Doty.*)

Frank McCullough, a University of Texas professor, served as bishop of the Austin, Texas, Ward of the LDS church at the time of the murders of Mark Fischer and Gary Darley. (*Courtesy Frank McCullough.*)

Dick Murphy, a Buffalo, New York, police officer and investigator with Buffalo's district attorney's office, followed Kleasen's activities for years. (*Courtesy Dick Murphy.*)

Kleasen talks with girlfriend Linda Miller during his 1975 trial. (*AS-75-90284-8, Austin History Center, Austin Public Library.*)

Kleasen answers questions during a break in his 1975 trial. Note the bandsaw in the foreground. (*AS-75-90284-30, Austin History Center, Austin Public Library.*)

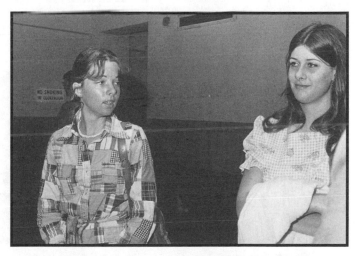

Karrie Lynn Hampton (left), Gary Darley's girlfriend, and Barbara Bakewell (right), Mark Fischer's girlfriend, during a break in Kleasen's trial. (*AAS 90261, #11, Austin History Center, Austin Public Library.*)

Kleasen in handcuffs, with two court officers, before his 1975 hearing for a new trial. (*AS-75-90892-14, Austin History Center, Austin Public Library.*)

Kleasen (center, in handcuffs) heading into the Austin, Texas, federal courthouse during his 1978 trial for federal firearms charges. (*AS-78-98955-3, Austin History Center, Austin Public Library.*)

Kleasen's booking photo on Texas's death row.

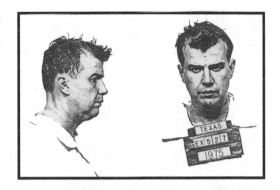

Marie Longley and Bob Kleasen at the time of their marriage in England in early 1991. Note the medals Kleasen is wearing, including his "Congressional Medal of Honor" at his neck. (*Courtesy Marie Longley.*)

Marie Longley's eighteenth-century home in Barton-upon-Humber, North Lincolnshire, England, where Kleasen resided beginning in 1990. (*Courtesy Marie Longley.*)

Fischer family after Mark's death. (Left to right:) Martin, Michael, Cathy
(mother), Jim (father), Matthew, and Melissa. (*Courtesy Jim and Cathy Fischer.*)

TWENTY-SIX

THE PUNISHMENT PHASE OF THE CASE CONSISTED OF NINETEEN witnesses testifying in less than an hour. Prosecutors were confident; the facts were so horrific, they would have to do little to secure a death sentence from this jury. They were also concerned about precisely where the new legal boundaries lay in death penalty trials. As of June 1975, the U.S. Supreme Court had not ruled on any state's new death penalty statute enacted after the 1972 decision in *Furman v. Georgia*. It wasn't until 1976 that the Court approved the new Texas law in *Jurek v. Texas*.

First, Craig lead eighteen witnesses through brief testimony on Kleasen's reputation in the community. All said virtually the same thing, mouthing the legal buzz words that translated into Kleasen's bad reputation for breaking the law. None went into his or her personal exposure to or opinion of Kleasen unless asked on cross-examination.

For instance, prosecutors called O. B. McKowan, Jr., who lived near the Austin Taxidermy Studio and Kleasen's stolen camper. He did not know Kleasen but, when asked about his reputation, said, "It's bad, sir." There were no questions from the defense. A rancher and Blanco County precinct commissioner, E. "Sonny" Bergman, was next. He testified that he knew Kleasen and that Kleasen had a bad reputation. Again the defense did not question him. Then Earl Dunagan, a Bureau of Alcohol, Tobacco, and Firearms agent and Littleton's supervisor, took the stand. Dunagan, a former Garland, Texas, police officer, also testified that he knew Kleasen and again said he had a bad reputation. This time Ganne cross-examined him, but his questions brought out damaging information that the jury had not heard before. Without going into details, Dunagan testified about Kleasen's earlier firearms violations in New York, saying Kleasen had been in mental hospitals and indicted for armed assault. "We talked with our New York office, and they furnished us with information that he was under indictment for an assault to murder in that state and that he had at one time been in a mental institution there," the former policeman said. In fact, Kleasen was charged with a New York assault, but not with an intent to murder. Ganne tried to recover by asking Dunagan about Texas authorities' refusal to extradite Kleasen to New York on those charges. Dunagan claimed he knew nothing about that. On redirect, Craig brought out details of Kleasen's New York problems with ATF. "There were 160- some-odd firearms seized eventually as the result of that investigation, some of which were automatic or machine-gun type weapons which were not registered as required by law," Dunagan testified.

The State pressed on with Texas Highway patrolmen Michael Pitcock and Leonard Vaughn; Texas State game wardens Robert W. Johnson, Max Hartman (who had arrested Kleasen on the buffalo shooting charge), Larry Brock (who had investigated the buffalo matter), Warren Guthrie, Larry Sodek, Norman Henk (who had come to loath Kleasen in the Fredericksburg jail), Roger Ensley, and Grover Simpson; Johnson City Justice of the Peace Albe E. Mayfield; Fredericksburg police officer Paul Oestreich; Gillespie County deputy sheriff David Nair; twenty-two-year veteran FBI agent Joseph G. Butler; and finally Travis County commissioner Johnny Voudouris, a close neighbor of the taxidermy studio. Only Hartman and Dunagan were briefly cross-examined by Ganne.

Then Smith called psychiatrist Richard Coons as the final prosecution witness. In addition to his University of Texas-Galveston medical degree, Coons's 1964 law degree from the University of Texas at Austin gave him added credibility with the jury. Coons testified that he first met Kleasen on November 13, 1974, during a competency evaluation. He met with Kleasen five more times in February and March 1975 when he administered a few tests. He also claimed to have consulted with three Springfield, Missouri, psychiatrists who had evaluated Kleasen at the federal facility there. "My opinion is that there is a probability that the defendant would commit acts of violence which would endanger society," he testified. Coons was, in effect, answering the most important special questions before the jury.

The brief remainder of Coons's testimony concerned the extent the three Springfield psychiatrists agreed with his conclusions. He admitted on cross-examination they did not share his diagnosis. On redirect, Coons said they didn't discuss future dangerousness in so many words, but "discussion of violence, fear, dangerousness did arise, and they, in fact, shared my opinions." With that, the State rested its case.

Before proceeding farther, the lawyers and judge huddled without a court reporter. After they broke, Haley turned and spoke to the courtroom. "Would you let the record reflect that we have instructed Judge Blackwell that Robert Kleasen is taking the stand on his own volition and against the advice of all three of his counsel." Kleasen's lawyers had entered the punishment phase hoping that even with a guilty verdict there was a possibility some jurors had doubts. A jury may convict someone of capital murder but still be unwilling to award a death sentence—what death penalty lawyers call "residual doubt."

The jury's verdict of conviction may well have been reached against a backdrop of such doubt. There was no confession, there were no bodies, some witnesses suggested the victims were still alive, and the evidence was all circumstantial. Pat Ganne, for one, entered the penalty phase reasonably optimistic. He felt the jury might still harbor some residual doubt about guilt, enough to make them uncomfortable about sending his client to the electric chair. The defense felt that Kleasen could do himself nothing but harm by testifying and tried to discourage him. Smith brought years of experience to his cross-examination.

To Ganne, Kleasen was "too arrogant to be coached." There was no telling what he might say, and no way to get him to appreciate how badly he could come across. No attempt was made to prepare him for his cross-examination because Kleasen had no intention of taking direction from anyone. The reality was that he would sit in the witness box virtually defenseless against Smith's aggressive approach.

There was more damning evidence the jury had not yet heard, evidence which would only come to light through cross-examination if

Kleasen testified. Kleasen's lawyers appreciated this and must have known how self-destructive their client could be. To a man they urged him not to testify. When he insisted, they tried to prepare him for what they knew could be a damaging cross-examination. Kleasen refused to accept any preparation. So now for the first time the jury would hear from the man who had been demonized for the past week. The courtroom was packed with spectators.

Roscoe Haley, whom Kleasen had first approached after firing his initial battery of lawyers, lead him through a brief direct examination. Kleasen prefaced his testimony by saying, "I realize this is the first time I've had to speak to the jury." Asked about his education, Kleasen said he had a 1970 bachelor's degree in sociology from the State University of New York at Buffalo, had done graduate work there and at Berkeley, and had master's degrees from the University of Stockholm and the University of Copenhagen. He explained that only a shortage of funds kept him from securing a doctorate at Copenhagen. Haley then asked about his work history. Kleasen said coyly his "work background varied considerably," that he had worked for "various companies, various lengths and periods of time." He added, "The last teaching job I had was in the town of Sale [Zahle] in Lebanon and I worked there as a teacher until it was destroyed by an Israeli attack. I was the only survivor."

Haley asked Kleasen to explain the 1969 buffalo rustling charge. Kleasen insisted it was all legal, that he had a bill of sale authorizing him to shoot the buffalo. Someone else had failed to get the required federal permit for an exotic game hunt, he claimed. Then he complained about being "paraded around in chains and ridiculed" for the entertainment of the game wardens. He said the game officers' earlier testimonies regarding his bad reputation related to this incident and to one other where he was hunting with a returned Mormon missionary who neglected to tag his kill properly. These, he said, "were the only convictions I've ever had."

Kleasen flatly denied having killed the missionaries, or even seeing them the day they went missing. "I want to say flatly, bluntly that I did not see or kill any human being, including Mr. Darley or Mr.

Fischer." He knew them "only very slightly," he said. Addressing the jury, Kleasen said, "I know you have all thought the thing over and convicted me of murder, and I'll probably die for it, but I didn't do it." The missionaries had never shown up for dinner on October 28, he claimed. "When 4:30, quarter to five came around and they had not shown up, I started my own supper, cooked a short meal and went out dove hunting until dark." When he returned, he claimed his trailer had been entered. "Nothing was taken but I noticed things had been rearranged. I thought the elders had stopped by or something, but there was no note."

Haley asked Kleasen to explain his living in a stolen trailer. He simply denied knowing it was stolen when he bought it. Then addressing the question of Kleasen's possible future dangerousness, Haley asked him if he thought he was a threat to society. "I don't think so. I haven't been in the past," Kleasen said innocently.

As Haley concluded his brief direct examination, Kleasen broke down and cried. "I know that Mr. Smith is waiting with his hatchet to chop me to pieces, and he probably will. I know that everything I've said will not make the least little bit of difference as far as the verdict goes. I have no doubts that I will die. But I will die for a crime that I didn't commit, so help me God," he told the jury through tears. With that Haley ended his direct examination. Kleasen seemed startled, not yet ready to face Smith. "I'd like to make one more statement if I may. I'd like to make some kind of a statement about the so-called evidence that was found and so forth and so on," he protested. "All right, I'll do it on redirect," Haley said on his way to the defense table.

Now Smith stood, armed with Kleasen's long history of conflicts with the law and his fabricated life. Smith had sized the man up and figured he didn't need to do too much damage on his own. Kleasen would destroy himself once Smith started pushing the right buttons in his twisted psyche. First, Kleasen denied having ever been arrested for game violations. Smith asked if he'd been kicked out of Denmark for assaulting a woman. "No," Kleasen denied, "I overstayed my visa." How about the New York assault charges, Smith asked. Kleasen launched into a long account of how someone had been shooting at his wife and how he had merely come to her defense and disarmed careless hunters. The man was never actually shot, Kleasen claimed, but was injured by stones when Kleasen fired into the ground. The only reason there was trouble was because the victim was "a local boy," he explained. Then Smith brought up the New York firearms charges. All a misunderstanding, Kleasen claimed; the offending machine guns had been left in his care by an FBI agent.

How about the time he went into a Buffalo hospital emergency room and shot up the place, Smith asked next. Kleasen told his story about having injured his foot while hunting, getting lost in a blizzard for three days, then waking up in a hospital room with no memory of the offending events. He claimed he was never prosecuted. When Smith told him and the jury that he'd been placed in a mental institution as a result, all Kleasen would say was, "Oh, they checked me over, sure." Kleasen said he couldn't remember if he'd been held in the hospital for the next year. The jury was wide-eyed. They were hearing all this for the first time.

Smith then asked Kleasen to explain why his Swedish wife, Irene Fredriksson, claimed he'd beaten her. She never made such a claim, he said flatly. She just got scared when she witnessed ATF agents beating him during their raid of his home, and that scared her so much she went back to Europe. Smith asked about Fredriksson's having seen him naked in a bath tub dressing a deer. Never happened, Kleasen said. Did Kleasen ever break his elderly mother's leg, Smith asked. No, never.

Smith next turned to Kleasen's use of false identities. At first Kleasen denied ever using any names other than his own, but when Smith confronted him with the evidence seized from the trailer Kleasen launched into his CIA agent fantasies. He used these names while working for the CIA, he said, and his handlers had provided him with the identities. "When you desire to become a different person, you have to assume a complete identity," he explained, and that was why he had been provided with birth certificates and drivers' licenses. "And were you many persons under many circumstances?" Smith asked innocently. "That was part of my job in the agency," Kleasen said, now warming to the part. He explained that the CIA was upset by his defection to the peace movement. "I happened to be trained as a field agent. They cared very much when I left because I had access to certain information which they did not want the general public to know."

Knowing Kleasen could not resist playing the role, Smith asked him to explain his CIA career. "It half started when I was working for Bell Aircraft in about 1951," Kleasen began. He would have been eighteen or nineteen. "After I had been under observation, checked out," he explained. There was a man in the courtroom who would testify to this part of his spy career, he claimed. "Point him out if you don't mind," Smith asked. "I can't see him at the moment, sir," Kleasen quickly backpedaled. "He was here every day since the trial began." Continue telling us about after you left the CIA, Smith encouraged.

Kleasen explained he thought he could lie low and continue his education in Buffalo, "but they weren't satisfied with that. And eventually I was more or less forced to leave the United States. And, of course, I did some work for the various peace organizations with their base in Stockholm, Sweden, sponsored by the Swedish government." He claimed he traveled between Europe and the United States thirteen or fourteen times during this period. The CIA was always after him. He had to travel under "many different visas."

Smith brought Kleasen back to Denmark, challenging him with his 1972 deportation. Now Kleasen brought NATO into the conspiracy, claiming the United States got the treaty organization to discredit him in Denmark. But the Danish government knew of Kleasen's vital role in the peace movement and was sympathetic, so when he was deported they arranged for his escape to Lebanon where he would be beyond the reach of the CIA. The Danish government and the police were in on it. "They had to get rid of me because it made them look rather bad."

Smith asked about his November arrest for making false statements while buying firearms. Kleasen claimed he'd never really been in a mental institution, that his answers had been truthful. As to the New York assault charge, Kleasen claimed Texas's refusal to extradite him represented a kind of amnesty.

And what about the gun purchased using the name Richard Raadt? "You can order a gun under any name you want as far as I know," he insisted.

Smith returned to the CIA and Kleasen's multiple identities. How many names did he use as an agent? "I have no idea. I went under so many. There were so many different passports, so many different countries from time to time that I have no recollection of how many names I have been under." So why return to the United States if the CIA was after him? "Because I love the United States. The United States is my home."

Unprompted, Kleasen then launched into a discourse on Southeast Asia. "The war was over with 'Nam. Thank God our troops were pulled out. At least most of them. The official ones were, although the unofficial ones were left. We were out of Cambodia. We were out of Laos. And I was sick to death of the whole thing. And I wanted to come home and I wanted to have some peace and quiet," he rambled. Smith leaned against counsel's table and let him talk.

As Kleasen wound down, Smith asked, But didn't you think buying guns as Robert Kleasen would tip off the CIA? No, there were too many government forms in existence. "The chances of me being run down through that were very slim." Yet he decided not to teach because he didn't want the CIA to hear of his whereabouts through his students. Smith didn't ask Kleasen if his earlier Associated Press interview might not tip off the CIA to his being held in the Travis County jail.

But Kleasen tried to explain the murder charges as a CIA plot. "You see, all your law enforcement agencies work hand in hand together. One scratches the other's back. I'm sure that the jury and everyone here is aware of that. You're arrested for a firearms violation and end up in a murder investigation. While the CIA does not like to expose itself in the open, it would have one of its agencies make the arrest for one violation or another," Kleasen explained. "And a good case of that is the buffalo shooting incident."

What about the Rambler jack found in his car, Smith asked. I got it in an auto junk yard, Kleasen claimed, then anticipating Smith's next question said he must have spilled his own laundry detergent on it while taking his clothes to the wash. He couldn't explain how the soap powder also turned up on one of the recovered tires. Asked in which junk yard he found the jack, Kleasen said evasively, "I haven't the foggiest idea." He also claimed he had the suspicious bolt cutters to work on cars.

Over an objection from Haley, Smith began to ask about how Kleasen secured and paid his lawyers. Kleasen claimed he didn't have the money to pay his first group of lawyers and fired them because they didn't follow his views about the case. Then Smith came to Kleasen's interview with Associated Press reporter Robert Heard. "I talked to Mr. Heard, yes I did," Kleasen acknowledged.

Smith next took up the license plates from the missionaries' car which were recovered from a shack near his trailer. "What moron would take the license plates off the car of a person who could be identified directly to them and put them in a chicken coop twelve feet from their house?" Kleasen asked rhetorically. "I don't think it's a very smart person. I think a person would have to be out of their ever-loving mind. What good would two license plates off a stolen car be to anybody except to point towards that person to make him look guilty. ... After you find the car and the car supposedly had two dead people in it, you wouldn't be running around with their license plates because any law enforcement agency would certainly be aware of that number. You certainly wouldn't take them home with you," he went on.

What about the five tires also found near your trailer? "I was in jail when all that stuff was found. It was pretty well strewn around the landscape," he said, but went on to imply that it was planted there by police. "Practically every law enforcement agency in the United States was represented and prowling around. We have people going through these places and not seeing these things, and then suddenly they appear. That's very strange to me."

The questioning then drifted back to October 28 and the time when Kleasen claimed to have returned from his dove hunt to find that his trailer had been entered. "I saw that someone had entered the trailer and things were not in the order that they were," Kleasen said. He didn't notice the victim's missionary materials or their watches, which he claimed were plants. "I didn't see anything missing. I just noticed that somebody had entered and somebody had left and I don't know who. This had happened before." He claimed "small things" had been stolen previously.

The D.A. returned to how Kleasen had acquired the trailer. He claimed to have bought it from a mysterious "Mr. Adams," a CIA acquaintance whom he knew "slightly" and who "was on his way to Cambodia last time I knew." He gave Adams $1,200 down and was to pay the remainder "bit by bit." Kleasen wouldn't get title to the trailer until he had paid for it in full. "I did not have any idea the trailer was stolen." How could you run into a CIA man when you were hiding from the CIA? "I maintained certain contacts here and there," Kleasen said, now completely consumed by his spy persona. "This fellow wanted to get out and he looked me up more than I looked him up. He had had enough. He was supposed to be part of Operation Phoenix which was an extermination program of the United States government against people not considered to be reliable, who were not considered pro United States, pro Saigon, pro puppet government. And Adams was sent over to head up one of those assassination teams. He wanted out of the CIA. He wanted to know what connections I had. He wanted to know if I could give him a contact. He wanted to disappear." Smith couldn't believe what he was hearing. Craig was so pleased he had to conceal his face at counsel's table.

"I assume the trailer had Oklahoma tags because Adams was living there at the time." Kleasen trusted Adams because they had worked together on at least two CIA missions. They didn't haggle over the price, Adams wanted to escape and Kleasen "wanted to get out of the taxidermy studio and out of the stinking smell." He'd been living in an unused office of the business at the time.

Next Smith asked about the human tissue found on the band saw. "I doubt very much if you could cut a human head on that saw," Kleasen responded dismissively as he gestured toward the band saw which still stood before the jury. "I don't know what advantage it would be to cut a human head on it anyway." He talked about how the saw was used in the taxidermy business. "I don't know if those are animal hairs, human hairs or any other kind of hairs. It's the normal practice to saw bones, tissue, skin, cartilage and so forth on that saw." Nor would he let himself be goaded into saying the CIA had planted the evidence.

At this point the court recessed for lunch. Smith and Craig could hardly believe their good fortune: Kleasen was destroying himself on the stand with his fantasies and patently unbelievable answers. Smith could hardly wait for the recess to be over. There was gloom among the defense lawyers.

The jury had barely settled in for the afternoon session when Smith went right for Kleasen's John T. Williamson identity. Kleasen would only admit that he may have used the alias in Denmark. After being shown an envelope addressed to him as Williamson, he acknowledged using it, adding, "I used several other names too." He couldn't remember if he'd used it before leaving the CIA in 1965. He also denied writing the Williamson deer poaching manuscript found by police in his trailer.

Smith shifted the questioning to Kleasen's return to Texas in late 1972. The witness denied ever telling anyone he was a student at Southwest Texas State University in San Marcos. Smith confronted him with his post office box application where he reported being a student there. Now Kleasen claimed he had planned to enroll there, "but I never completed it." Smith further pointed out that Kleasen had listed the former South Lamar Street location of the Austin Taxidermy Studio as his home. "At the time I was in transit," Kleasen replied.

Next Smith asked about Jack Paris's testimony. Kleasen claimed Paris was mistaken, he'd never said he'd killed anyone, including Che Guevara. "I told Mr. Paris that while I was in South America I was asked to secure proof of his death. My superiors told me that I should bring back his fingers because they had records of Che Guevara's fingerprints. I did not take the fingers. I was not there when they were taken. They were brought to me in a bottle and I transported them back to the United States."

Asked if Paris had misunderstood Kleasen's story, he replied "Deliberately or otherwise, yes, sir."

"And he's just like all the Mormons, as far as you're concerned?"

"I don't categorize people as all anything," Kleasen snapped.

"Well, you had a general animosity toward the Mormon church, did you not?"

"No, I didn't. I never had an animosity toward the Mormon church. I am a Mormon today," Kleasen shot back. "There were some people I liked better than others." Given the opportunity to explain himself, Kleasen went on: "I didn't have any trouble with the fact that the church, when I was in desperate need and had no family, that they could have done more than they did." He promised to produce the letter from Bishop Bruce Smith attesting to his being "a member in good standing." He denied having any enemies in the church: "I have no brothers and sisters, the church is my family." He claimed extensive correspondence with church leaders, including Apostle and later President Howard W. Hunter. Unknowingly, Kleasen had walked right into a trap set for him by Smith.

"Do you know a person by the name of Blair Bell who lives in San Antonio?" Bell was the Mormon missionary who had corresponded with Kleasen and apparently asked the two murder victims to fellowship him.

"Well, he lived in many places. He was an elder and a teacher. He taught me and I knew him very well," Kleasen said. "I carried out, I would say, a weekly correspondence that you're probably aware of because I guess you've got every paper that I've got." He had to have some idea of what was coming.

Smith then had four Kleasen letters to Bell marked as State's Exhibits 71, 72, 73, and 74. Shown the letters, Kleasen reluctantly acknowledged they were his.

Without making further use of the correspondence, Smith ended his questioning. Now it was Haley's turn to try to repair some of the damage. He began by asking Kleasen to explain the September 30, 1971, ATF raid on his Buffalo home.

He was outside on a stepladder painting the house, Kleasen said, when "one of them pointed a submachine gun at me and told me to get off the ladder and handcuffed me behind my back. They threw me to the ground, roughly searched me, kicked me in the ribs, then dragged me up the stairs." Agents cursed and insulted him. His young Swedish wife witnessed all this. "She couldn't understand this type of treatment. She had never seen anything like this." His elderly mother also saw this "and she went completely to pieces."

Haley then asked Kleasen about his Lebanon period. He claimed the American Embassy treated him badly in spite of the fact he had just barely escaped with his life after Israel had bombed the school where he was teaching. He implied he'd also been a PLO captive for some time. After a week of recovery, the embassy returned him to the United States where, he claimed, the buffalo shooting charges were almost immediately dropped on him.

Asked to account for the New York assault charge, Kleasen explained it in terms of local hostility towards Mormons like himself. "My farm was within about two miles of the Hill Cumorah, and as Mormons well know, it is not exactly friendly territory for us." He went on to explain how the shooting victim was hunting illegally on the farm and he was merely protecting everyone from their stray bullets. He claimed the two men would not give up their weapons when he confronted them. "I did the only logical thing that I could think of doing, and that was to fire at the roadbed next to his feet showering him with rocks and debris. Then he dropped the pistol." This was completely contrary to the established facts of the incident. When New York then tried to extradite him from Texas, an investigation was undertaken. "The State of Texas found that in no way could I receive a fair trial and that they would not extradite me under any circumstances to the State of New York," he claimed. "I'm sure Secretary of State Mark White has the transcripts of all that."

Haley turned to Kleasen's four bombastic letters to Elder Bell. They were written in August and September 1974, just weeks before the murders. The writings were filled with violent language directed toward individual Mormons and self-righteous posturing on the part of Kleasen. Knowing the jury would soon see them, Haley had his client read the letters and add a commentary as to what he really meant. He dismissed the more violent language as literary flourish, adding,

"The language is a little rough, but that's me."

In the August 17 letter, Kleasen had written of local Mormon leaders who questioned him about his conduct in Denmark: "I want their heads." Given the band saw evidence the jury had just heard, the phrase was chilling, but Kleasen dismissed it: "I'm not speaking literally. I mean I want to get this matter straightened out." The courtroom rustled with disbelieving reaction.

When he wrote in his September 7 letter, "I'm going in for the kill," he really meant: "I'm going for a lawyer. I'm going all the way this time. I'm through playing with this man," referring to Bishop Frank McCullough. No one in the jury box looked convinced.

After going through the individual letters and sensing Kleasen's explanations had not moved anyone on the jury, Haley asked him to explain the exchange with Bell. "It was a fight to stay within the Mormon church," he said. "I was having trouble in the ward that I was in and I wanted to transfer to another. I was having trouble getting my property back after it was taken from my trailer by Mormons when I was in jail. No one came out. No one visited. No home teachers showed up. In the Mormon church we have what we call a once a month Family Home Evening where we get together, and if you don't have a family generally there's some kind of arrangement where you have a group to meet with." He complained that none of these activities happened for him.

With that Haley sat down and Smith had one last crack at Kleasen. It was mercifully brief, with Kleasen saying the missionary materials found in his trailer would not have been of any value to him personally. "It has no intrinsic value to anyone who is Mormon and has already gone through the instruction and read the Book of Mormon." Then Smith turned him loose. At this point, the defense rested. Kleasen had been on the stand for nearly four hours.

The prosecution was not yet ready to let go and brought Lem Rathbone back as a brief rebuttal witness on Kleasen receiving mail as Williamson and on the use of the band saw. This time the defense did not cross-examine him. That ended the testimony.

The jury was read their brief instructions and set out the special questions they would be required to answer. Then Charlie Craig stood up to argue for the prosecution. "The people of this state, the people sitting in the jury box have got rights to be protected," he began, telling them those rights would only be protected with a death verdict. "He's a professional poacher," Craig said of Kleasen, "That's all he does." He then read from Kleasen's violent letters to Bell. "You know how deliberate he was—he put it on paper," he noted in reference to the deliberateness special question. There's no doubt John T. Williamson is Robert Kleasen. "Over two thousand deer he's slaughtered," Craig said, holding up the poaching manuscript. "Killing means nothing to the man. It means nothing."

Then the young prosecutor turned to Kleasen's future dangerousness. "It is established very clearly that he lives by criminal acts of violence. About all we can do to predict the future is look at the past, and this defendant has in the past done nothing but commit criminal acts of violence."

At this point Craig turned the floor over to the defense. Pat Ganne, hardly a year out of law school, was the only lawyer to plead for Kleasen's life. He began by telling the jury how as a child he was scared by memories of Julius and Ethel Rosenberg walking to the electric chair. "It scared me then. It scares me now. In spite of the fact that you found Mr. Kleasen did a horrible thing, are we, as human beings, going to reduce ourselves to his level? Are we that inhuman ourselves? What has been done has been done. Nothing can change that. Are we now going to lower ourselves to Mr. Kleasen's level?" He reminded jurors that being a poacher did not make Kleasen a threat to society. "Are we to crush whatever life he has out of him? He acts peculiar. You heard him. I have no doubt that Mr. Kleasen believes everything that he told you. Are we going to snuff the life out of him? Are we going to kill him? I hate to be so brutal with you, but that's what we're talking about. We're talking about legally killing another person. It's a hard thing to talk about. It's a hard thing to consider. But morally, can you do it? Can you look Mr. Kleasen in the eye and tell him: You are worthless. You're never going to amount to anything ever. Nothing you can do, nothing anybody can do for you will ever amount to anything. You are to die now. Can we right this wrong by killing another man?" Ganne argued that life in prison would be worse than death: "Is there a fate worse than death? There probably is when a person can no longer see the sun; can no longer see the grass; when a person is locked up like a dog for the rest of his life."

The last to argue to the jury was Smith and he went straight to Ganne's argument. "We have been challenged by Mr. Ganne on the idea that we don't have the moral right to do this. You hear people say all the time: I don't believe in capital punishment. But everybody does. There is not a person that you can think of that when you get right down to it doesn't believe in capital punishment. In Texas we have a frontier tradition of exercising our right to self-defense. Everybody you can think of probably believes in the right to self-defense, and that's what we're talking about today. The right of the community to exercise a basic right of self defense against a domestic enemy that is threatening society. It's just that basic." Kleasen can't be deterred, Smith argued. "He's been in mental hospitals, and they didn't keep him. He's been in jails, and they didn't keep him." He was beyond redemption.

Smith then attacked Kleasen's performance on the witness stand. "Do you remember the little man in the Little Abner [sic] comic strip? He walks around under the dark cloud and always has the hard luck. That's what Bob Kleasen acts like. Everybody's down on him. Everybody's been against him. He has so much hostility that you can feel it if you're ten feet away. He has never been treated properly by the authorities in the United States, by the authorities in Denmark, by the CIA, by NATO, by people in the Mormon church, and I wonder what he thinks about the treatment he got yesterday from your verdict." The jury then retired to a private jury room. Few people left, anticipating a quick verdict.

Jill Darley, who had sat through the whole trial, could no longer contain herself. She walked up to the defense table where only a low wall, "the bar," separated her from Kleasen. "Why did you kill my son?" she demanded.

"I didn't kill your son," Kleasen insisted.

The seven women and five men of the jury were out only twenty-one minutes before returning their verdict: death. His testimony had destroyed whatever chance he had for a life sentence. He'd scared them to death.

Smith was pleased. It was the first death sentence in Travis County in five years. He later told reporters, "The verdict was in the interest of justice." Asked if he was willing to pull the switch to the electric chair himself, he said, "I wouldn't ask anyone to do something I wouldn't do myself."

Kleasen was brought back to the 167th District Court for formal sentencing at 9:00 a.m. on Wednesday, June 4, 1975. Before court began, he chastised Ganne for "pleading" for his life during the previous day's closing arguments. "If you're going to die, you don't die like a dog," he scolded the young lawyer.

When Judge Blackwell appeared on the bench, Kleasen was more subdued. He stood up from the defense table and advanced to the judge's bench. He then rested his hands on the ornate wooden bench, surrounded by his three attorneys. Judge Blackwell asked Kleasen if he had anything to say before sentence was passed. "Yes sir, I'm innocent," he said quietly. "I did not kill Mark Fischer and I did not kill Gary Darley. I truly and honestly say this, so help me God."

Under Texas law, Judge Blackwell could not have sentenced Kleasen to life even if he had wanted to. "[I]t is therefore the order of this Court that the defendant is sentenced to death" were among the last things Kleasen heard in court that day. He was then taken away by Travis County deputy sheriffs. A pack of reporters stopped them in the hall to interview the condemned man. "All I can say is, I'm innocent, I've been convicted of a crime I didn't do," he said. Asked if he had any hope for an appeal, he answered, "Yes sir, I think God will help us." With that Kleasen was immediately driven the 200 miles to death row at Huntsville.

About six weeks after the verdict, Haley sheepishly approached Judge Blackwell with a "Motion To Be Appointed Counsel." Ganne and Bays also signed the motion. When Haley had agreed to represent Kleasen, he believed his client's representations about having plenty of money to pay his attorney fees. He now told Blackwell in his motion, "During the course of the trial, and with no lack of diligence and care or neglect on the part of Movant, it became known that the defendant had no such assets of any kind, and that the defendant was penniless and in destitute straits." Blackwell appointed the three luckless lawyers as Kleasen's representation and authorized a modest fee. A single check was issued to Haley. Ganne and Bays were concerned they might not get their fair share, so they accompanied Haley to a bank where they divided up the cash. After that, Haley was out of the case; Ganne and Bays kept looking for a way for their client to avoid execution.

TWENTY-SEVEN

BY AUGUST 1975 HALEY WAS NO LONGER PART OF THE DEFENSE team; Ganne and Bays kept pushing ahead. Almost out of the blue, they had received a telephone call from a sixty-nine-year-old retired eccentric named Earl M. Albrecht. He lived near Dripping Springs in the western end of Travis County and owned a large chunk of land that bordered Hayes County. He had lived in Travis County for eight years, moving there after working in Houston, Midland, and Abilene. More importantly, he had a sister who was an active Mormon and through her claimed to have known Darley for about three weeks, and Fischer only slightly. Albrecht insisted both missionaries had come by his property the morning of October 28 asking to fish in a lake there. They liked to visit his property to see all the deer, he recalled. He saw them two or three times during the day, relaxing at the lake as late as 3:00 p.m. This contradicted testimony from the trial.

The next day, October 29, he said, they were at an Exxon service station on Bee Caves Road in west Austin. This was critical because the state claimed the boys were both dead and dismembered by this point. It was about 1:30 p.m., Albrecht claimed, when he drove by the station and saw the missionaries tanking up. He slowed down, and when he was about 100 feet from them, he honked his horn and waved. "I blew my horn and they waved back, and that's the last time I ever saw them," he said. Albrecht was absolutely certain of the dates because he kept a kind of personal log in which he "kept daily notes of people's goings and comings."

Mormon FBI agent Bruce Yarborough had interviewed Albrecht in November 1974 after the missionaries first disappeared. Somehow the defense was never told of his story even though prosecutors are required to notify the defense of all exculpatory evidence they are aware of. The agent claimed Albrecht never said he had seen the missing boys. He had dismissed the old man as an "eccentric" with information that was "interesting, but not pertinent to the case." He told other investigators what Albrecht had to say was "either erroneous or irrelevant."

After meeting with Albrecht in early August and getting his sworn statement, Ganne and Bays filed a "Motion for New Trial" with the 167th District Court. They argued that Kleasen's conviction was unfair in light of this new evidence. They were well past the ten-day Texas deadline for filing such motions, and Bob Smith fought it on those grounds, but wanting to be abundantly cautious, Judge Blackwell scheduled a hearing for August 28.

The press jumped on this new twist with headlines suggesting Kleasen might soon be out from under his death sentence. Travis County deputies gathered Kleasen from his death row cell at the Ellis One Unit and drove him back for the hearing. He wore heavy belly chains; his hands were cuffed in front of him. The metal clanged as he walked. Never hesitant to talk to reporters, Kleasen told them in a voice choked with emotion, "I thank God" that Albrecht came forward. He said the two did not know each other. Reporters thought Kleasen was heavily sedated.

David Bays immediately put Albrecht on the stand to tell his story. He described how he knew the missionaries, describing Darley and Fischer as "real nice boys, always nice and friendly and they was dressed neat and clean and they spoke so well." He produced his personal notes which were supposedly proof of the dates. "I know that was the date I saw them last. I'll die believing that," Albrecht insisted of his October 29 sighting. He went on to describe taking some horns to be mounted to Rathbone's taxidermy shop on the 30th. Kleasen was there telling Albrecht and his wife about how taxidermy was done. That was the last time Albrecht said he saw Kleasen. Albrecht claimed to have called everyone he could think of with this information after hearing about the missing boys in the news, but no one took him seriously. It was weeks before Yarborough interviewed him.

It was pretty much down hill for the defense after that. Smith cross-examined the old man, asking why Albrecht had claimed to his neighbors that he was a CIA agent, that his home contained a museum and "ancient library," and several other strange things. At one point, when Albrecht insisted from the witness stand that he really was a CIA agent, Smith quipped, "The only CIA men I know are you and Mr. Kleasen." The courtroom erupted with laughter.

Besides Albrecht, Ganne and Bays put five other witnesses on the stand, including Kleasen. Each limited his testimony to the defense team's being unaware of this testimony the previous May. After that the state pounced.

Smith and Craig brought in twenty-two witnesses who each said Albrecht had a bad reputation in the community for telling the truth. It wasn't so much that people thought he was dishonest, they just thought he was nuts. He told everyone his CIA stories and that he was in the Foreign Service. An FBI agent, Howard Riley, related Albrecht's regular complaints against those who he believed were communist spies in the Austin area. Another witness related Albrecht's claim that as an undercover agent he had discovered that President Franklin Roosevelt was really poisoned in 1945 by a Russian artist. Bob Smith put himself on the stand to testify that he had known of Albrecht's claims during the trial and that he had disclosed them to the defense. He angrily accused Ganne and Bays of lying in their sworn affidavits saying they had not known about the witness.

The defense had subpoenaed one of the jurors, Cynthia Bartlett, who they hoped would testify that she would not have found Kleasen guilty had she heard Albrecht's testimony about seeing the missionaries on October 29. After sitting through Albrecht's testimony, however, she was not called to the stand. "I just couldn't have testified that it would have changed my mind," she told a newspaper reporter.

At the conclusion of the testimony, Smith argued that the new defense witness was "old, eccentric, and senile." At the end of the four-hour afternoon hearing, Judge Blackwell ruled that Albrecht's testimony was "just not believable" and denied the "Motion for New Trial." He defended Ganne and Bays to reporters, saying they had offered the testimony legitimately "because the defense has the duty to grasp at any straw."

As soon as the hearing was over, Kleasen was loaded into a sheriff's department cruiser and taken back to Huntsville. His return to Austin had lasted less than twelve hours. Now everything rested on his appeal.

TWENTY-EIGHT

O N JUNE 4, 1975, KLEASEN ARRIVED AT THE TEXAS MEN'S DEATH row at the Ellis One Unit outside Huntsville. Travis County deputies drove him there less than three hours after his sentencing.

When Texas went to a centralized state execution system in 1924, state authorities began numbering death sentenced inmates starting with No. 1. Kleasen was No. 527.

The Texas electric chair almost immediately acquired the name "Old Sparky." It was first used at the Walls Unit located in downtown Huntsville on February 8, 1924. Five black men were put to death in less than two hours. Charles Reynolds was executed at 12:09 a.m., quickly followed by Ewell Morris, George Washington, and Mack Matthews. Melvin Johnson had been scheduled for execution that night but received a last-minute one-hour reprieve from Governor T. W. Davidson that was not further extended. Johnson became the fifth execution when he was pronounced dead shortly after 2:00 a.m.

Until a 1995 change in Texas law, executions were carried out after midnight but before dawn.

Death sentenced men were held at the Ellis One Unit about ten miles outside town, but they were brought to the Walls Unit for executions. They passed their final hours in a small steel-wire cell just off the death chamber. This remains the practice, but in 1982 lethal injection replaced the electric chair.

Kleasen arrived at the Ellis One Unit about the same time as "The Candy Man," Ronald Clark O'Bryan. O'Bryan was inmate No. 529, sentenced to death for the Halloween 1974 poisoning of his eight-year-old son Timothy with cyanide-laced candy. His Houston trial and death sentence were handed down about the same time as Kleasen's.

O'Bryan's case made him even less sympathetic in the public's mind than Kleasen. An optician by trade, O'Bryan had dug himself a deep financial hole, owing as much as $100,000 to various creditors. By the fall of 1974, he was selling the family home to pay debts and still juggling bills. He took out $20,000 insurance policies on the lives of each of his two children. In August 1974 he ordered cyanide from his employers to clean gold frame glasses. This in spite of the fact cyanide had not been used in the optical business for over twenty years. His employer refused, but O'Bryan eventually secured it through a chemical supply house. O'Bryan also asked, out of "curiosity" he said, about doses fatal to humans as well as about how cyanide was detected in deceased persons. In October 1974 he began telling friends and creditors he expected a large sum of money very soon.

After taking his children trick-or-treating on Halloween night, O'Bryan, or so a jury believed, gave his son Timothy candy laced with cyanide. He encouraged Timothy to eat all of it even though the child complained that it tasted funny. The boy got sick almost immediately and was dead within an hour. An autopsy discovered levels of cyanide almost twice as high as are required to kill a person. A police search of O'Bryan's home later produced additional Halloween candy which had been tampered with. A key witness in O'Bryan's trial was Harris County medical examiner Dr. Joseph Jachimczyk.

O'Bryan had been represented at trial and on appeal by Houston defense lawyer Marvin O. Teague. Teague was a prominent criminal defense lawyer and civil liberties champion. A 1961 graduate of the University of Houston Law School, he was the in-coming president of the Harris County Criminal Lawyers Association. While many Texans didn't care for Teague's commitment to civil liberties, few could resist his broad smile, sense of humor, and love of people. His charm was effective at containing difficult clients like O'Bryan. If a client were especially unsympathetic, as many charged with capital crimes were, he would use his personal warmth to deflect some of the public hostility. He was a lawyer's lawyer who threw himself completely into his cases. Colleagues were always amused by the deep layer of papers that buried his desk.

O'Bryan and Kleasen were in individual cells next to each other. The other inmates wouldn't speak to O'Bryan because of his crime, but he and Kleasen became friends. Boredom is a constant burden for men on death row, and Kleasen complained of having nothing to do but play Dominoes in the day room. Most inmates' time is devoted to endless rehashes of their trial and appeals.

O'Bryan bragged about the sharp lawyer he had. Kleasen, never shy about changing lawyers, was impressed. Ganne and Bays realized Kleasen needed more experience than they possessed for his appeal and actively encouraged Teague to take the case. Kleasen wrote Teague, who traveled the 85 miles from Houston to visit him. It's hard to say what Teague thought of this delusional man, but he was impressed with the legal issues in Kleasen's case. Soon he was on board as Kleasen's attorney for the mandatory appeal to the Court of Criminal Appeals (CCA).

Teague immediately saw the trailer search as a potential winner. He often praised Ganne for making certain it figured in the record of the trial. "I learned from Teague that the most effective appellate lawyer was the trial lawyer who preserved the issue," Ganne now recalls.

O'Bryan would not be as lucky as Kleasen. The CCA affirmed his sentence in 1980 making him the third person put to death in Texas during the post-*Furman* era. Charles Brooks was executed for a Ft. Worth murder on December 7, 1982, followed by James Autry's execution on March 4, 1984, for a Port Arthur convenience store robbery-murder, then O'Bryan on March 31, 1984.

Once the Erie County, New York, district attorney's office confirmed Kleasen's conviction and death sentence, they dismissed the thirty-eight firearms counts arising from the 1971 ATF raid of his Victoria Street home.

As part of routine death row paperwork, Kleasen was interviewed about his life and the facts of his crime by a prison parole officer. His January 1977 report recited what Kleasen said about his life without attempting to verify facts. Kleasen acknowledged that he had been arrested repeatedly since 1968, but claimed that "all of these arrests occurred because of harassment he was receiving from the Central Intelligence Agency because of his involvement in the anti-Vietnam war movement." He refused to discuss his capital conviction other than to say that "all the evidence presented at his trial was manufactured by the Central Intelligence Agency." He claimed to have lived all over the world from 1952 to 1968 while he was a CIA agent.

Kleasen explained that his CIA "cover" was as a "professional student and school teacher." As a result he taught school in "different places throughout the world," most recently in 1973 at the "American School for American Studies" in Zahle, Lebanon. Kleasen claimed an 80 percent hearing loss as the result of injuries received when Israeli troops attacked the school in Zahle. He also claimed to have two master's degrees, one in education from the University of Stockholm, the other in sociology from the University of Copenhagen. At this point he still claimed to be Mormon, albeit excommunicated as a result of this conviction. The officer concluded his evaluation:

> Mr. Kleasen is an emotionally unstable person of above average intelligence who displays considerable evidence of a severe psychological disorder involving delusional thinking. His thought processes are disorganized to the extent that any factual information reported by Mr. Kleasen and included in this report must be viewed with extreme skepticism. His delusional system centers around the belief that he was at one time a high ranking member of the Central Intelligence Agency and his belief that the Central Intelligence Agency manufactured all the evidence used to convict him in an attempt to persecute him. Mr. Kleasen apparently believes that everyone connected with his conviction for the instant offense were either CIA agents or acting under instructions from the CIA. The nature of his delusional thinking and his conviction for the instant offense indicate that he is an extremely dangerous person who would constitute a threat to society if ever released from the institution and would constitute a threat to prison inmates and officials if ever released to the general inmate population.

Pat Ganne visited Kleasen once on death row. He had a parole revocation hearing in Huntsville and called the Ellis One Warden to schedule time with his former client. They talked less than thirty minutes, but Ganne was shocked at what he saw. In just a few months,

Kleasen's hair had turned completely white and he had put on more weight. It was a pattern that would balloon Kleasen out considerably during the next few years.

TWENTY-NINE

UNLIKE MOST STATES, TEXAS HAS A TWO-TRACK APPELLATE
system. Since 1876 the Texas Supreme Court has limited itself to
civil matters while the Court of Criminal Appeals handles criminal
cases. Among Texas lawyers, the criminal court is known as the CCA.
The actual number of judges and the way in which they consider cases
before them have changed over the years, but the two-track appellate
system was a well established fact of Texas judicial life by the time
Kleasen's appeal came along.

Teague's brief is still legendary among Travis County lawyers. It
ran into hundreds of pages. Folklore in the legal community holds that
the Kleasen brief finally got the CCA to introduce a rule limiting how
much lawyers could file. It argued over a hundred points of error,
many of which targeted the death penalty's still uncertain status and
specific legal problems with the new Texas statute. Most claims had
stacks of attached transcript excerpts, copies of relevant court opinions, and sometimes short essays setting out information that appeared
nowhere in the trial record.

From the beginning Teague had seen the search of Kleasen's
trailer as the issue which would win a new trial for his client. The argument was that the affidavit provided the federal magistrate by ATF
agent Dale Littleton was inadequate to support a search warrant. It did
not set out sufficient "probable cause," the legal buzz word for adequate suspicion, for the magistrate to decide if a search was justified.
Consequently, it was argued, Judge Blackwell should have granted
Kleasen's Motion to Suppress the "fruits" of the search.

The district attorney countered by arguing that Kleasen had no
right—called "standing"—to challenge any search of the trailer because it wasn't his. You may only complain about the search of a place

where you have a legally recognized personal expectation of privacy. Kleasen lived in a trailer which he either stole or knew was stolen, prosecutors argued. His mere occupation of the trailer for over a year did not alter its character as stolen property. The only person who had a reasonable expectation of privacy in the trailer was the legal owner, Odell Bowen, or the Allstate Insurance Company which had paid his claim after it was stolen. They also noted that Kleasen did not own any of the surrounding land and structures. Taxidermist Lem Rathbone did, and he had given permission for the searches. Much of the most damning evidence had come from areas under Rathbone's control. When a property owner gives police permission to search, a warrant is not needed. The damning band saw had been secured with Rathbone's permission.

The CCA issued its opinion on November 23, 1977. It was a bombshell. The court discussed only one issue, the search of Kleasen's trailer, and reversed the conviction on a finding that the warrant lacked probable cause. After summarizing the evidence, the court observed that the search had produced "Mormon bibles, a Seiko watch identified as belonging to the deceased, a key ring and keys which opened locks to the car and apartment of [Mark Fischer] and [Gary] Darley, and a manuscript which detailed the means of disposing of the carcasses of illegally killed deer."

As the court saw it, the determining question was whether Kleasen had "standing" to claim a right to privacy in the trailer. If the record established he had stolen the trailer, or had knowledge of its stolen character, then he could not complain about the search. In denying the Motion to Suppress at trial, Judge Blackwell had written that "there is no question in the Court's mind that the trailer house was stolen. The defendant did not have the consent or permission from the owner to be in it or to use it, irrespective of who stole it. That's immaterial. He has no standing to complain about the search." Teague did not dispute that the trailer was stolen in April 1973. Instead he argued that Kleasen did not know it was stolen or, at least, that the prosecution hadn't proven this. The CCA agreed: "There was no evidence adduced tending to show how appellant acquired the trailer, or that he was in any way connected to the theft of the trailer." In a footnote the court wrote that Kleasen had testified during his punishment phase "that he had bought the trailer from a former work associate." Judges did not comment on the seemingly incredible nature of Kleasen's story.

The court went on to say that in order to challenge the search Kleasen had to show "a possessory interest in the trailer." They seemed impressed that he had lived in it "for nineteen uninterrupted months." In order to defeat Kleasen's claim of a "protected possessory interest," the court seemed to say, prosecutors would have to prove Kleasen stole the trailer, which they had not done. Consequently, the defendant "had a reasonable expectation of privacy sufficient to warrant protection by the 4th Amendment."

From there the court moved to the federal magistrate's November 5, 1974, search warrant. In order to be lawful, the warrant would have to be adequately supported by the law enforcement affidavit submitted to the magistrate at the time. Agent Littleton had provided the two-paragraph document. After describing the trailer, its location, and the .22 Browning rifle Littleton expected to find there, the affidavit said only that he had been informed of the rifle's presence "by a reliable citizen who lives near ROBERT KLEASEN that he has seen KLEASEN shooting a firearm of this same general description on the premises ..." Kleasen could not lawfully have purchased or possessed the weapon because of his outstanding New York charges and prior psychiatric hospitalization, but in a critical omission the affidavit failed to set that information out.

This was far from adequate, the court said. "The affidavit is based upon the hearsay statement of an unnamed informant. There are no facts in the affidavit from which the magistrate could have determined the informant's reliability. The informant was unnamed. There is no allegation that the affiant investigated the reliability of the informant or why the affiant considers him trustworthy. A mere statement that the source of the hearsay is reliable or credible offered the magistrate no substantial basis for crediting the hearsay." Judges went on to note that the affidavit on its face "shows no probable cause" because it did not allege any facts to say that Kleasen had committed a crime by possessing the rifle.

The Court of Criminal Appeal cited only one prior case as a basis for their ruling, the 1964 U.S. Supreme Court decision called *Aguilar v. Texas*. Once the court determined that Kleasen had a reasonable expectation of privacy in the trailer, the facts of his case seemed almost identical to *Aguilar*. There two police officers sought a search warrant from a state magistrate to look for drugs. The officers presented affidavits, but all they contained were the claim that they had "reliable information from a credible informant," who was not otherwise identified, that drugs would be found. The Supreme Court threw out the conviction, saying the results of the search could not be introduced against the defendant.

Without additional analysis, the Court of Criminal Appeals reversed Kleasen's conviction and sent the case back to Travis County. The court did not direct that Kleasen should be set free, but said he must be retried without the use of evidence seized in the trailer search.

Local Mormons and the families of the murdered missionaries were stunned at the decision. Kelle Darley, Gary's brother who had testified at trial, was furious. He told an *Austin American-Statesman* reporter: "The man has killed, he has a history of it, and he will kill again." The reporter had tracked down twenty-six-year-old Darley in Santaquin, Utah, seventy miles south of Salt Lake City, where he ran a small motel. "My only feeling is he was obviously guilty. You can definitely say I'm sorry the death penalty wasn't carried out. It would not be a matter of revenge, but protection of society. I feel sorry they didn't execute him right away." Like most lay people, Darley couldn't understand the reversal. "The bulk of the evidence, I thought, was not generated from that trailer. I don't know how they got into the taxidermy shop, which is where they found the blood and the hair on the band saw," he told the reporter.

Austin area Mormons who did not understand how the law worked feared that Kleasen would be released immediately. Many worried that he would then track down individual church members, especially those who had testified against him, and take revenge.

Reporters interviewed attorney Pat Ganne. "Personally, I find it comforting to realize that everything I did, I did correctly and properly," he said. But Ganne also told reporters that he had "mixed emotions," that he felt "kind of ambivalent about the whole thing." Ganne had stayed in touch with Kleasen during his time on death row. "I could not believe what death row has done to him," the young lawyer said. He described the forty-four-year-old Kleasen as looking like a man in his seventies. His thick black hair had gone completely white. He'd seemed to shrivel up, to have lost all his vitality.

Judge Blackwell, whose decision on suppressing the trailer evidence was reversed by the Court of Criminal Appeals, was tight lipped. He called the decision "very unfortunate. I don't criticize it, but it is unfortunate." He added: "There ought to be some other way to ensure the defendant's constitutional rights while guaranteeing that guilty persons are not set free on technicalities."

Back in Buffalo, Dick Murphy was as stunned as anyone. Now working as an investigator at National Fuel, a public natural gas utility, he contacted the Erie County district attorney's office and urged them to dust off their 1972 firearms prosecution against Kleasen. He was told too much time had elapsed, Kleasen would never stand trial.

The Travis County district attorney's office was noncommittal when they first learned of the CCA's decision. Smith had been succeeded by Ronald Earle in 1976. Earle had left the state legislature to run for district attorney when Smith ran unsuccessfully for judge. Charlie Craig had also left the DA's office. Assistant district attorney Charles Hardy, who had handled the appeal, told reporters, "We're going to do our best not to let him walk." Earle promised to retry the case "if we can. But we can't retry a case if there isn't any evidence."

A team of prosecution lawyers was assigned to file a motion for rehearing. There was some hope of changing the court's mind, as well as buying some time to consider their chances at retrial. In a strident eighteen-page motion, four government lawyers tried to show that there was circumstantial evidence Kleasen stole the trailer and that they were not required to prove he was the thief in order to defeat his claimed right to privacy in it. They stressed that Kleasen had failed to register the trailer as required by Texas motor vehicle law, evidence that he probably had not acquired it honestly.

The new district attorney assembled the interested parties to discuss the situation, among them Mormon bishop McCullough and departed prosecutor Charlie Craig. Earle also assigned Richard Banks and a deputy sheriff to reinvestigate the case. Banks had come from the Dallas DA's office and had a reputation as a bulldog. One Austin defense lawyer said of him, "He is ruthless in the pursuit of a conviction. He is smart and uncompromising. If anyone could have put the Kleasen case back together and gotten a new death sentence it was Richard Banks."

Banks had a theory that Kleasen had disposed of the body parts in a vacant lot next to the old Lamar Avenue location of the taxidermy studio. Kleasen likely had keys to the old, vacant building. He could have stored the tires there until he could retrieve them. Banks and a deputy dug up a good portion of the lot without finding anything. He also tried to secure infrared aerial photographs of the rural areas searched by hand back in November 1974. Banks hoped that buried and decomposing bodies could be detected It was eventually determined that too much time had passed to hope for results.

The Court of Criminal Appeals closed the book on the first trial when it denied the DA's motion for a rehearing on February 8, 1978. The court did not address the DA's motion for rehearing, although one judge dissented and two other newly elected judges did not participate.

Earle immediately announced there would be no retrial, saying he would dismiss the charges within a week. He felt he lacked sufficient evidence to secure a conviction. Smith, by then in private practice in Austin, stormed over to the DA's office to protest. He was adamant the case could be retried. His protests fell on deaf ears.

Kleasen was free.

THIRTY

FOR THE FISCHERS, THE MOST DIFFICULT STRUGGLES FOLLOWED the 1975 trial. Mark and Gary's apartment was cleaned by church members who mailed Mark's things home. These included the University of Texas t-shirts he had bought for his brothers and sisters the day he was killed. After the trial someone mailed them Mark's name tag, with the bullet hole, and his watch, the gift from Barbara Bakewell, with flecks of blood on it.

Melissa Fischer—"Mis" to Mark—wrote a child's poem for her brother as part of her personal therapy. It was constructed as a dialogue between a little girl and her big brother:

"Mark, are you going on one of those missions for the church?"

"Yes, Mis, I am. Why?"

"Well, because ... because I don't want you to go."

"Well, let me tell you something Mis. Going on a mission is part of the Lord's plan. And I want to have a part of that plan."

"But Mark, why ... I don't want you to go. I ... I need you to protect me like big brothers should and ... and Mom needs you to run to the store for her, and Dad does too. He needs help to fix the cars. Matt, Mike and Mart need you to wrestle with. Please don't go. We all need you."

"I want you to listen to me Mis. I know how hard it's going to be for everyone, but I have to go, and besides its only two years. And when I come home, I'll protect you all you want."

"But Mark, what happens, I mean, what if you don't come home, what if ..."

"I want you to know that I'm going to miss you more than I will Matt, Mike, and Mart. You're the best little sister in the whole world and don't you forget that. I'm very lucky to have you."

Melissa went on to write that the day Mark left for his mission was "the hardest day of my life" and that she wished she "could really understand."

"Mark, could I please have a hug but, only could we make this special just between you and me," she wrote of the day he left.

Melissa ended her poem with "Well, Mark never did make it home. He was killed just one month after he left. I'm sure he is much happier where he is now. And his memory still remains and always will, till that final day when we will be reunited."

Jim and Cathy Fischer had battled the angry feelings of some that they had contributed to Mark's death by allowing him to serve as a Mormon missionary hundreds of miles away. Some strangers even sent them sick and accusatory mail over the incident.

In the months after Mark was killed, Frank McCullough had arranged for the Fischers to meet Spencer W. Kimball, president of the Mormon church who had earlier met the Darleys. Kimball had been deeply affected by the murder of these two young men and was anxious to express his personal best wishes for their parents. The Fischers also met with Vaughn Featherstone, the church official who had first warned Texas Mormons of Kleasen's unsavory past. These meetings did not replace their son, but the Fischers were thrilled.

Less than a year after Mark was killed, their next eldest son, Matthew, announced he was ready to serve a mission. His parents were a little surprised. Their pleasure at his commitment was tempered by a fear that they could lose another child. Cathy had the hardest time letting go. But they said little of their fears. "If you want to go, Matt, we'll support you," they told their son. "And if you don't want to go, we'll support you in that decision too." Matthew eventually served a routine mission in Las Vegas, Nevada, from 1977 to 1978, where his mission president kept an especially watchful eye on him. By 1978 Jim and Cathy's son Mike was serving full time in Honolulu, one of six young people in the Milwaukee First Ward on missions then.

By sheer coincidence, shortly after Matthew's Nevada mission, Kelle Darley moved to the state and attended an LDS ward where the younger Fischer had spoken of his brother in church meetings. Both

Kelle and other members of the ward were jolted to realize they shared this sobering connection.

Jim and Cathy Fischer were no different from other parents who have lost a child to murder. They grieved deeply in their own personal ways. The loss strained their marriage. Everyone in their ward had been supportive, but the deep hurt remained with the family. Finally they began seeing a counselor. It helped that he was a stranger, someone who found it easier to say things that friends and family members could not. There were times when Cathy was furious with him for the things he pulled out of them, but the process brought them closer to peace.

Because they had been denied even the closure of a burial, Cathy finally devised one of her own. She collected a few of Mark's things—not things that were so dear to her she could not part with them, but things that she associated with him—and buried them in a private place.

Gradually the hurt subsided. The loss of a good son was always with them, but they reached a point where they could move on with their lives. They had several other good children who married and had children of their own, so there was the joy of grandchildren to envelop them.

Today Cathy and Jim can recall the exact moment when they came to forgive Bob Kleasen. A peace came over them, a calming spirit, that signaled the end of their anger. They no longer hated him, no longer feasted on their fury with him, no longer allowed him into their lives to destroy things. It was then, they felt, that Kleasen lost all power over their family.

To this day Jim and Cathy keep many things that once belonged to their son—his missionary notebook, name tag, letters to him which were returned after his murder, his high school diploma, and many others. A black and white photograph of Mark in a suit, one of the last taken of him, hangs on their apartment wall. They keep these because they will always love him.

Kelle Darley struggled as well to rid his life of Bob Kleasen. For a long time after the murders, Kleasen stalked through his worst nightmares. Kelle finally spoke of this gaping wound in a class at Brigham Young University, confessing that he hated Kleasen for what the man had done to his family. Afterwards the teacher took him aside and encouraged him to try to forgive Kleasen, advising that he would never be able to get on with his life until he had done so. Kelle had to work hard at it, but gradually he forgave and the nightmares stopped. While he didn't think he'd ever share a meal with Kleasen, he knew he'd never again let the man's twisted spirit dominate his life.

THIRTY-ONE

WITH THE CCA'S REVERSAL OF KLEASEN'S CONVICTION, THE U.S. Attorney initiated prosecution for his 1968 federal Firearms Act violations. A month before the Travis County district attorney's Motion for Rehearing was denied in the Court of Criminal Appeals, a federal bench warrant was issued with a $100,000 bond. In the meantime, New York had also asked to prosecute him on the 1971 assault charge.

The Texas feds charged Kleasen with purchasing three firearms in Austin and San Antonio in June and August 1974. Anyone who purchased a firearm was required to fill out a form—with "yes" or "no" answers—attesting to the fact that he or she was not under indictment for or previously convicted of a felony, was not a fugitive, nor had ever been committed to a mental hospital. It was illegal for persons to possess a firearm under these circumstance. Kleasen answered "no" to each in spite of bold type on the form warning that "an untruthful answer may subject you to criminal prosecution." In at least one instance, Kleasen used a fake Texas driver's license to purchase a .22 Walther Hornet rifle in San Antonio using the name Richard Raadt.

Finally Kleasen had a lawyer whose counsel he was willing to follow. Teague was appointed on January 20, 1978, to represent the indigent Kleasen in U.S. District Court. Teague was paid $20 an hour for out of court work, and $30 an hour for courtroom time. The lawyer entered a not guilty plea to all six counts. While awaiting trial, the prisoner was held in the Bastrop County Jail just east of Austin.

U.S. district judge Jack Roberts looked and sounded like state district judge Blackwell. Roberts was a 1931 graduate of the University of Texas law school who had earlier been both a state prosecutor and state district judge. He was appointed to the federal bench in 1966 by President Lyndon Johnson. The federal appointment realized his greatest ambition. Roberts was from a family of lawyers and regarded it as the most honorable profession. Attorneys who practiced before him did not regard him as a legal scholar—"Not a bookworm," one said—but he knew the law and loved to preside over trials.

While being held in Bastrop, Kleasen again encountered Pentecostals ministering to inmates, one of them, an Austin cook named Mark Finger, with whom he would correspond for many years. Rev. Kenneth Phillips of the World of Pentecost Church also came to know Kleasen. Many regarded Kleasen as an intelligent man who sincerely embraced their religious beliefs. It is unclear if Kleasen ever formally became a member of the church, but many people approached him as one.

With the murder charges disposed of, Teague tried to get Kleasen released for the first time in three and a half years. His Motion for Release on Personal Recognizance Bond urged that the government was not acting in good faith. Kleasen wasn't going anywhere should he be released, Teague wrote the court.

At a February 9, 1978, hearing, Teague called the recent indictment on the firearms charges nothing but a "harassment measure" by the government. The U.S. attorney had dismissed the original charges in 1975 following his conviction for capital murder, Kleasen complained, and only revived them when his conviction was ruled to have been improper.

In his written response, San Antonio assistant U.S. attorney Jeremiah Handy insisted he was acting in good faith and that Kleasen had never been pressed for trial on the charges. He argued the defendant had a proven record as a flight risk, had no ties to the community, and that in view of his love of firearms he should be considered dangerous. Finally, he urged the court to consider Kleasen's earlier Travis County murder conviction as evidence of his character, pointing out that the reversal was not based on an insufficiency of the evidence but rather on the search and seizure issue.

Judge Roberts refused to release Kleasen on his own recognizance. If he wanted out, he would have to come up with a $20,000 bond. Given Kleasen's financial situation, it might as well have been a million dollars. For his part, Kleasen wearily complained to Roberts, "I am very, very sick and need a doctor very badly. I suffered very, very much on death row, suffered from malnutrition."

Mindful of his past history, Judge Roberts just before trial ordered that Kleasen again be examined by a psychiatrist on his competence to stand trial. Dr. Coons was brought back to see the defendant. Kleasen remembered full well Coons's earlier testimony, and the encounter was icy—"Mr. Kleasen recognized me immediately and conveyed to the Marshal that he refused to speak with me"—but the psychiatrist had no doubt of Kleasen's competence. The doctor's March 24 letter to the court noted, "Though he refused to answer my questions, I was able to observe his conversation with the U.S. Marshal." The letter sets out information on this and past mental status exams of Kleasen and concluded: "He is presently competent to stand trial in that he is able to understand the proceedings against him and to properly assist in his own defense." Kleasen's mental competence would not resurface in any court.

It took one day on March 27, 1978, to select an eight-woman, four-man federal jury from a pool of 104. Surprisingly, few said they recalled any publicity about Kleasen or knew who he was.

Teague filed another Motion to Suppress, again alleging that the November 5, 1974, search of the trailer was unlawful in that the warrant was issued without probable cause. Once again he challenged the sufficiency of Littleton's accompanying affidavit. Teague hoped to dispose of the federal charges on the same grounds as the murder charges. The motion was heard right after the jury was selected on March 27, 1978. This time prosecutors were ready.

Where the record in support of the search warrant in the murder trial emphasized the stolen character of the trailer, here the focus was on the probable cause investigators had developed in support of the warrant. On direct examination, Handy lead ATF agent Dale Littleton through a lengthy description of his role in the investigation and how several pieces of reliable information came together to establish Kleasen's illegal gun purchases. Littleton told Judge Roberts how local ATF officers routinely established files on suspicious gun possessions and purchases with information they secured from local law enforcement. They had one on Kleasen. By October 1973 they had a list of five firearms he possessed from various encounters with game officers.

When Kleasen came to their attention again as a result of the missing missionaries, Littleton began tracing the guns Kleasen reportedly had. He explained ATF's going through the Washington, D.C., based National Tracing Center. Using the description and serial numbers from the gun they began with, the manufacturer tracked the gun to the retailer, and they then located the sales records. Part of these records were the required disclosure forms where Kleasen indicated he was not a fugitive and had no psychiatric history.

Within twenty-four hours, the ATF had confirmed his purchasing the Browning .22 rifle on August 11, 1973, from McBride's Gun Shop in Austin. Having already verified Kleasen's being a New York fugitive, they now had probable cause for the search warrant and went to U.S. magistrate-judge Phil Sanders for it. Littleton emphasized that without the search warrant they would not have searched Kleasen's trailer that day. The next day, after Kleasen's arrest, Littleton got verification on the second gun purchase, a Colt Trooper .357 magnum pistol bought on June 27, 1973, from an Austin Montgomery-Ward's.

Sometime after Kleasen's arrest, the ATF investigation connected Kleasen with a San Antonio gun purchase under the alias Richard Raadt. They probably saw the Raadt identity papers in Kleasen's trailer and started searching that name as well. After securing the forms the purchaser filled out, they had been able to verify through handwriting experts that it was Kleasen who went to Don's Gun Sales at 3329 Fredrickson Road on August 25, 1973. He bought a Walther .22 Hornet rifle with a Texas driver's license under the name Raadt. Littleton also related sketchy information about Kleasen's 1971 run-in with the ATF in Buffalo.

The ATF officer then described the November 4, 1974, search of Kleasen's trailer, and his arrest in Burnet with more guns within easy reach in his car, including the Hornet .22 he purchased as Richard Raadt.

Teague vigorously cross-examined Littleton but could not budge him. Judge Roberts denied the Motion to Suppress with little comment. All the evidence collected in the trailer search could go to the jury.

At this point the jury was brought to the courtroom and the actual trial began. Prosecutors then methodically presented their case, leaving Kleasen and Teague no room to squirm. The government presented the records custodians from the three gun shops, introducing the falsified forms through them. None had an independent recollection of the sales, they merely recited what the paperwork showed. Another witness traced the guns from the manufacturers to Texas wholesalers, establishing that they had traveled through interstate commerce. Then came Ralph DeGelleke, clerk of the Wayne County, New York, Court where the assault charges were still pending. He testified that the 1971 charge was still outstanding.

New York State trooper Ernest Sanett testified next, reviewing his investigation of the case and arrest of Kleasen. He described the offense as a class D felony carrying a maximum sentence of seven years under New York law. Sanett made it clear to the jury that Kleasen had not surrendered himself as he would often claim—"It wasn't a surrender situation, no sir"—and that he jumped bail.

On cross-examination Sanett verified that Texas governor Dolph Brisco had refused to extradite Kleasen to New York in 1973. He made it clear that New York still wanted to prosecute Kleasen and was again seeking to extradite him to Wayne County.

Then Agent Littleton returned to the stand to repeat a small part of his testimony from the suppression hearing. He explained the ATF Form 57-a, the personal history form he had Kleasen fill out a day or two after his arrest. He was followed by Phillip White, an ATF handwriting expert, who matched the known samples of Kleasen's writing with that on the forms completed at the three firearms purchases, including those as Raadt. With that, the government rested.

The defense then rested without putting on any testimony. Kleasen's Motion for a Directed Verdict of not guilty was denied. After a short break, both sides gave closing arguments.

Teague told the jury that none of the circumstantial evidence had been proven. The forms were a mere formality, he argued, which sales people often filled out for the customers and which no one paid much attention to. There was no intent to deceive, he said, because Kleasen had a good faith belief that his New York charges were no longer outstanding after Texas refused to return him for trial. "Knowingly" was the key word, Teague emphasized.

Curiously, Teague never addressed the gun purchased as Raadt or Kleasen's psychiatric hospitalization. There really wasn't a defense that could be offered to explain away the fake driver's license.

The jury was not taken in. After hearing instructions, the panel took about two hours to convict Kleasen of all six counts.

A disappointed Teague spoke with reporters after the verdict. "I sort of anticipated something along these lines," he said. "There will be an appeal, hopefully on several points."

Roberts pronounced his sentence on April 28, 1978. First, however, Kleasen read the court a lengthy written statement. His lawyer, no doubt mindful of Kleasen's disastrous testimony in the capital murder trial, had insisted that he write out his remarks. Kleasen complained that he was "not permitted to speak during this trial." "I want to say a word or two about my life," he began. Kleasen then launched into a rambling recital of imaginary academic accomplishments, professed his complete innocence of the murders, and claimed he had never read the federal forms which had resulted in this prosecution. He denounced "the hoax of the capital murder case, which was unanimously overturned." Darley and Fischer "are no doubt alive today," he told Roberts. "I have no reason to believe that they are dead at all, and no one can prove they are dead." He complained bitterly about the "sensationalism or the trash written in the press."

Unconvinced, Roberts sentenced Kleasen to a total of nine years in prison without commenting on the defendant's speech. He handed out two and three years on each count, some running consecutively, some concurrently. Kleasen did not get any credit for the time he had been in prison on the capital murder charges. Still, county prosecutors were disappointed in what they regarded as a light sentence. They thought Kleasen should have received as much time as Roberts could throw at him. Outside the courthouse, Teague told reporters his client was "disappointed, but he's in good spirits."

Kleasen appealed his conviction to the federal Fifth Circuit Court in New Orleans, with Teague again at his side. This time the conviction was affirmed without an opinion on May 8, 1979. By not publishing anything, the Fifth Circuit avoided having to explain the conflict with the Texas Court of Criminal Appeals decision on substantially the same facts.

Kleasen served some of his federal sentence at the same Springfield, Missouri, psychiatric facility which had evaluated him before the 1975 murder trial. He was moved to several federal institutions around the country before facing his New York charges.

In April 1979, Kleasen was forwarded to New York state where he was finally tried on his eight-year-old Wayne County assault charges. On April 16 he made an initial appearance before Judge Harold Stiles. Ron Valentine, the local public defender, was appointed; Kleasen objected. A prominent local criminal lawyer, Robert Zecher of Sodus, was later appointed as a special public defender. The case was prosecuted by district attorney Carmen Parenti.

Lawyers took four hours to pick a twelve-women jury in Lyons, New York, on June 4, 1979. During two days of testimony, jurors heard William DuBois again recount how Kleasen shot him in the foot eight years earlier. The jury convicted Kleasen of second-degree assault.

Kleasen's old nemesis, probation officer David Williams, was there to update the 1972 presentence investigation. He interviewed Kleasen in the Wayne County Jail a week after the jury verdict. Williams heard the story about Kleasen's travels in Europe, his academic accomplishments in Sweden and Denmark, and his teaching school for three months in Lebanon before being bombed out by Israelis. Kleasen neglected to mention his Danish assault conviction and expulsion from the country, but Williams was fully aware of those events. Kleasen also claimed his third wife, Irene Fredriksson, had been killed in a Swedish auto accident in 1977.

In his report to Judge Stiles, Williams summarized the last few years of Kleasen's extraordinary life. He noted that New York had tried to extradite Kleasen on the charges earlier. "However, on June 5, 1974, Governor of the State of Texas blatantly refused extradition on the spurious basis that Kleasen would not receive fair treatment in the State of New York."

Williams concluded by setting out Kleasen's future plans. "When he completes his sentences he plans to make his home in the Corpus Christi, Texas, area. Supposedly, he met a fellow on death row in Huntsville, Texas, and has corresponded with the man's elderly mother, Juanita Bird. He claimed that he has shipped some of his belongings to her for safekeeping. He eventually hopes to be able to teach college level courses." Kleasen was probably talking about Jerry Joe Bird, Texas death row inmate #512 who was executed on June 18, 1991.

Williams's report closed by recommending a maximum sentence. "We again emphasize that Kleasen has continued to exhibit erratic and irrational behavior, which the Federal authorities are attempting to modify with drug therapy. However, we believe Kleasen to still be a very dangerous individual who has not as yet reached a criminal menopause."

On June 29, 1979, Judge Stiles sentenced Kleasen to four to seven years in prison to run consecutively with what remained of his federal sentence. Kleasen appealed and again lost. At least now his prosecutions had come to an end.

THIRTY-TWO

BY OCTOBER 1983 KLEASEN HAD COMPLETED HIS FEDERAL sentence and was turned over to New York authorities. He was first assigned to the Attica Correctional Facility, scene of the infamous prison riot in 1971, then to the Auburn Correctional Facility. Almost immediately he petitioned the New York Parole Board for discretionary release.

Kleasen still refused to accept responsibility for his crimes. A report prepared for the board stated: "Kleasen denies his culpability in the instant offense indicating that he was the subject of harassment by authorities." He again told how he had been beaten by ATF agents. He said they used the butt of a Thompson sub-machine gun on him in front of his wife Irene Fredriksson during the September 1971 raid of his home. He again claimed Fredriksson was so terrified by the ordeal that she returned to Sweden and was not available to testify on his behalf in the assault case. As Kleasen phrased it, he "decided to go to Europe instead" of appearing for his 1972 trial date. He also claimed the gun collection seized in 1971 by the ATF was worth a million dollars. With each retelling, the collection's value increased. The parole board asked about the Texas murders. He said the murders were never proved and "that no people ever died."

A few months earlier the Wayne County district attorney had written the parole board to oppose Kleasen's release. The board appreciated who they had and how controversial his early release would be. "Your positive achievements are noted and considered," the board blandly wrote Kleasen. "However, all factors considered your release would not be in the best interest of the community." They urged Kleasen to continue with prison psychotherapy and set the next parole review twenty-four months off.

Kleasen was transferred from Auburn to Attica briefly, then in April 1986 to Sing Sing. He wanted out of Attica because of what he called "brutal conditions." He also suffered a heart attack there while carrying heavy materials, so his first month at Sing Sing was spent in a hospital ward. By then other inmates were calling the fifty-four-year-old Kleasen "Pops."

Kleasen set his sights on his next parole possibility in 1987. Seeking to impress future parole boards at Auburn and Sing Sing, he participated in forty-five-minute psychotherapy sessions every two weeks. He continued to take the antidepressant Desyrel prescribed by psychiatrists for what he described as a "nervous condition." Kleasen also suffered from a long-standing angina condition and took nitroglycerin tablets. He walked with a cane. Prison officials described him as overweight and he complained of a hearing loss in both ears "due to an accident."

Kleasen refused vocational training, telling prison officials he did not need it thanks to his extensive "higher education." He worked in the prison as a typist for $1.30 an hour. Not surprisingly, his favorite recreation was writing letters to friends. One of those pen pals was an Auburn inmate serving a life sentence for murder.

Kleasen had only two minor disciplinary infractions, one for smuggling, which was dismissed, and one for not having his inmate identification card on his person.

He tried again for parole in 1987. At the time he had no money to help him get established on the outside. He claimed all his holdings had been "seized" for back taxes. His inmate account showed a balance of $126.06. He also told the board he had completed a master's degree in June 1986 while at Auburn prison and was about to begin a Ph.D. No verification was produced.

While at Auburn Kleasen had applied for admission to the University of Buffalo's American Studies Department which apparently was available to inmates. He met with program administrator June E. License. A brief autobiography was required of each applicant, but Kleasen wrote twenty-eight pages. It was filled with stories of flying jet missions in Vietnam, meeting the queen of a Scandinavian country, and living on the Texas death row. Only the last subject had any basis in fact. License remembered thinking Kleasen either lived an incredible life or had an incredible imagination. She later told newspaper reporters that "the parole people have a real challenge." However, Kleasen did undertake some graduate courses while in prison.

If paroled in 1987, Kleasen hoped to return to Austin, Texas, where he could live with his friend Mark Finger, a short-order cook. Finger was a Pentecostal who met Kleasen in 1978 when his church visited federal prisoners in the Bastrop, Texas, jail. They had corresponded about once a month for years and Finger promised to help him find a job in Texas.

Once again the parole board declined to release Kleasen, writing to him, "The panel notes your institutional progress but considering all factors cannot recommend discretionary release." They notified Texas authorities and urged Kleasen to continue with therapy and medication.

Only twice during his time in New York custody did his records reflect any visitors other than for legal matters. Once a Quaker representative called on him, and once an unknown friend.

Kleasen continued to write his pen pals. One newly acquired one was a woman in Northern Ireland he met through a London-based International Pen Pals outfit. She was Ann-Eliza Young (not her real name). He explained his various prison addresses by saying he had a Ph.D. and was hired to teach college courses to inmates. He also wrote that his parents were Dutch-German, but that he was an English duke and his mother a duchess.

When Kleasen was sentenced in Wayne County, New York law required that an inmate who had served two-thirds of his sentence be paroled. Kleasen would reach that point on May 8, 1988.

Kleasen still wanted to be released to the Austin area, which was possible if Texas agreed to supervise him. Not surprisingly, Texas was not the least bit interested. A spokesman in Austin later told reporters, "He didn't fit any of our criteria. He's not a resident, he didn't have a job in Texas, and he didn't have any family here." Kleasen wrote Mark Finger that "his heart was broken because they wouldn't let me live in

Texas." So it would be somewhere in New York.

New York parole officials were as alarmed as anyone at the prospects of his release. Robert J. Purcell, a parole officer working out of the Auburn Correctional Facility wrote a March 25, 1988, "Threat Documentation Report" in which he called Kleasen "an extremely dangerous individual with a great deal of underlying hostility." Purcell went on to note that the soon-to-be released inmate had the "potential, as well as the capability, of carrying out any veiled threats" because he was a "master marksman and an explosives expert."

Four days later a Syracuse area parole supervisor, Chester G. Fritz, wrote another report saying Kleasen was "an extremely dangerous individual with so many unresolved psychosocial problems that it is almost inevitable he will once again act out in a violent fashion at some future date." Fritz's office normally supervised inmates paroled from Auburn. He urged that New York and Texas authorities be given detailed information about Kleasen so his "movements may be known to everyone at the earliest possible time."

A month before his release, the LDS church-owned *Deseret News* in Salt Lake City reported the impending parole in Utah under the headline "Man once sentenced to death for murdering LDS missionary to be paroled May 9 in New York." New York Division of Paroles executive director Edward Elwin would only say that Kleasen was to be paroled to "an undisclosed city in New York."

Texas authorities were notified of the impending release. Travis County prosecutors added to the growing hysteria in their interviews with New York press. "I wouldn't feel comfortable if he was in the neighborhood. And, of course, the jury answered that question 12 or 13 years ago when they found he would continue to be violent," Bob Smith, long retired as district attorney, told reporters. "This guy is probably the most dangerous person I've ever met." Smith was further quoted as believing that Kleasen had no conscience whatsoever. In another interview he said, "I think once he gets out, he would have the propensity to try and do whatever he wanted. He lived for violence. His background indicates he's a walking time bomb." "It was a terrible murder," added assistant county district attorney Phil Nelson, noting that "a jury said that, and it's always a shame to see a case come apart, but they do, and this one did."

As Kleasen's release neared, the parole board prepared another law enforcement advisory dated April 26, 1988. Continuing with the same tone, it warned that Kleasen had "pent-up hostility and a great potential for extreme violence." It went on to say Kleasen "believes there are no innocent people and that all of society is responsible for what has happened to him in his life. He also is a master marksman and an explosives expert."

Parole board officials quietly sounded out rural Wayne County as a release site but quickly dropped the idea after a heated response. The only connection Kleasen still had with Wayne County was the shooting; the family farm had been sold and Kleasen had no friends or acquaintances there.

Next they planned to place Kleasen in Rochester at the Cadillac Hotel. When hotel manager Donald Stubbs realized who Kleasen was, he refused him, later telling the *Austin American-Statesman*, "He was a walking time bomb, every police officer on the Rochester force was carrying his picture." In fact, Rochester police chief Gordon Urlacher and other law enforcement had been tipped off about Kleasen's possible arrival. They raised such an alarm that the parole board was forced to drop Rochester as a placement. "I think it's outrageous that this man can be assigned into this community without any input from local officials," Urlacher complained. Happy now that Kleasen would not be his problem, he told reporters, "If you yell loud enough, they'll hear you. I feel bad for Buffalo, but I feel pretty good for Rochester."

So it came down to Buffalo. About a month before his scheduled release date, Kleasen had told his parole officer Robert Purcell he now preferred his hometown as a placement. No one appreciated what a circus was in store for them. Kleasen could not help but become aware of the controversy over his release. "I didn't bother watching TV," he would later say, but added, "I heard most of the TV reports from the guys in the prison yard."

Buffalo greeted him like a leper with open sores. The local newspapers were soon comparing his situation to that of California ex-convict Lawrence Singleton who was run out of several communities after his parole from a sentence for the rape and mutilation of a teenage girl. The screaming began a couple days before his actual release.

On Friday, May 6, the *Buffalo News* first announced his arrival in a headline: "Convict With Record of Violence Will Spend His Parole in Buffalo." That day Kleasen was driven from the prison at Auburn down the New York State throughway to Buffalo by three state parole officers. They left early in the morning, stopping only when they accidently hit a deer—a strange omen for a man who had previously loved poaching. By late morning, they pulled up to the General Donovan Building in downtown Buffalo. State parole offices were located on the fourth floor.

The specific conditions of Kleasen's parole were that he be in his approved residence from 11:00 p.m. to 7:00 a.m., that he not leave the county without prior permission or enter Canada which had expelled him years earlier, and that he make weekly office reports to his parole supervisor. He also had to comply with all the mental health treatment requests of parole officials including medication.

At the Donovan Building no one had planned for the army of television trucks and reporters that laid siege the instant they figured out Kleasen's whereabouts. The parole office was paralyzed while they tried to figure out how to sneak him out of the building. Albany was called but had nothing to offer. Through the day Kleasen rambled incoherently about how the most important thing was for him to visit his late mother's Buffalo area grave as Mother's Day approached.

Kleasen was smuggled out of the office building in the afternoon. They first took him to a Seneca Street rooming house, but there the owner withdrew his offer of shelter when he figured out who Kleasen was. Kleasen would later recall that when they arrived in Dunkirk a Channel 7 television truck was already camped out waiting for them, so the party did a 180-degree turn and headed back into Buffalo's center city.

Finally he was deposited in the rundown Main Street Towne House Hotel. State officials came to the hotel office and told the clerk they wished to register a "guest," not an uncommon procedure because of the nearby state hospitals.

Several plainclothes officers were stationed at the hotel, both to keep an eye on Kleasen and to protect him. The officers shadowed his every move. "Whenever he went anywhere, we followed him and kept him out of hardware stores," police commissioner Ralph Degenhart joked.

That night reporters caught one exhausted parole official on his way home, regional director Peter K. Blaauboer. He refused to say where Kleasen was. "I'm not saying anything further," he snapped. "I'm exhausted after two days of this, and I'm going home."

Later that evening more television reporters showed up outside the Towne House Hotel. They told employees a "walking time bomb" was inside. For a while hotel workers thought this was a decoy operation and that the infamous parolee was really elsewhere. The next morning at 6:00 a hotel clerk dialed Kleasen's room. A groggy man answered, obviously dragging himself out of a deep sleep.

The siege was on and continued through Saturday. Kleasen ventured out of the hotel at 8:30 in the morning, walking to a post office to mail a letter and then to a convenience store looking for breakfast. He was followed all the way by a herd of plainclothes police and newspeople who later reported what he bought as well as the store clerk's reaction to being in his presence. "I wasn't scared, I made myself ready for him," clerk Mana N. Alasri told a *Buffalo News* reporter. Kleasen also claimed that a Channel 7 television crew shadowed him as well.

One night of this circus was enough for the hotel. They told parole officers to get Kleasen out. An indignant clerk at the hotel told a reporter, "As a citizen and someone from Buffalo, I would not want a man who killed other people here. For the safety of our guests, the management asked him to leave." One roomer had jokingly asked if guests would be issued chain saws while they stayed, a reference to the erroneous link between Kleasen and the movie *The Texas Chainsaw Massacre*. Hotel managers did admit that Kleasen had not actually been a problem.

Kleasen was in his room getting ready to take a bath when parole officers, among them Richard Low, and police told him to get dressed because they had to check out. Kleasen was told he was going to a hospital. Parole officers were trying to buy time to secure a placement while hoping the public outcry would diminish. "We got to check you out," Kleasen was told. "But I have already been checked out," he protested. Low then told him he was under arrest and handcuffed him. It seemed to Kleasen forty armed law enforcement officers looked on through the motel room door.

An unhappy Kleasen was taken in a car to the Meyer Hospital where he was briefly examined by three psychiatrists. The parolee was not impressed. "They got three shrinks there and they talked to me for about three or four minutes and then they signed some papers. The next thing I know, they put me on a gurney, strapped me down, and put me in an ambulance," he later said. He was taken to the Erie County Medical Center's emergency psychiatric unit at 400 Forest Avenue.

Parole officers had used Kleasen's past psychiatric history and what they described as his incoherent ramblings to persuade the necessary two physicians to involuntarily admit him for evaluation. A psychiatric center official at first told the press, "Based on what we're seeing, we have determined he needs treatment."

In order to hold Kleasen for an extended period, the evaluation would have to find that he was mentally ill and that as a result of his illness he would be a danger to himself or others. It is not enough to be just emotionally disturbed.

At first hospital spokesmen said Kleasen would remain with them at least two weeks; parole officials breathed a sigh of relief. "There is no decision we can make on this case until we know about his stability and whether he is on the appropriate medication," Elwin told the press after an Albany staff meeting on the snowballing controversy. "This we will only find out after they have done a workup at the Buffalo Psychiatric Center."

Elwin stood by the decision to hospitalize Kleasen. "While he did not do anything unusual, he was being followed around town by the press and TV, and we felt that with the added pressure it would be wise to have him looked at," Elwin said. "It's just a general concern. There was no acting out on his part." Kleasen, he acknowledged, had not been very happy about it. "He didn't make any objection. But it was not a completely voluntary thing."

"We don't know what the doctors will do," said Donald Gawronski, a regional parole board administrator. "It's in their court now."

Local law enforcement were only mildly placated by the involuntary hospitalization. "Do you want him living next to you?" asked Erie County sheriff Thomas F. Higgins. "That's what it boils down to. I'm supposed to say he's rehabilitated, it's all right for him to live here. But if I don't want him as my neighbor, what right do I have to foist him upon you?" Police commissioner Ralph V. Degenhart was likewise unpersuaded by the hospitalization. "We want nothing to do with him here," he said, adding that he hoped the parole board would "put him on an island some place."

Among the precautions undertaken was assigning police to guard the home of a retired officer, Sergeant John C. Rapp. Seventy-two and retired from the force since 1967, Rapp had served on the homicide squad and was a polygraph operator. He had known the parolee for nearly fifty years, beginning when Kleasen was a small boy growing up on Victoria Avenue. He moved about seven houses down from the Kleasens in 1940. Rapp had arrested or participated in arrests of Kleasen at least three times. In one of those encounters in 1958 or 1959, Kleasen had reportedly threatened to kill him and his family. The retiree recalled Kleasen to reporters as "a genius no matter what he does." Rapp was on vacation in Texas when Kleasen was paroled, but police protection was assigned to his home even while Kleasen was hospitalized.

There were other rumors that Kleasen had threatened various court officers in Wayne County. A parole board advisory went to the sheriff there, spreading the paranoia.

About the only good news for Kleasen at this point was a Sunday morning newspaper article stating that he had not been the inspiration for the cult movie classic *The Texas Chainsaw Massacre*. At least two Buffalo television stations had presented this as fact and accompanied their news coverage of his release with clips of the leatherfaced protagonist from the movie revving a chain saw.

Once Kleasen became the subject of involuntary hospitalization proceedings, he had a right to counsel to defend against them. If he was indigent, as Kleasen was, the court would appoint a lawyer for him. David Jay, a tenacious and well-known Buffalo civil rights lawyer, was assigned the case. He quickly proved to be a vocal champion for his client.

Jay immediately went on the offensive. He told a clamoring press that Kleasen was a "public relations hostage" who was committed to the psychiatric center because state officials wanted him off the streets. Public officials were "stirring up hatred" to prevent anyone from being released from prison, Jay said. "If people don't like these parole laws, they should change them," he challenged.

But Jay went on to express confidence in the system. "I believe that the legislators and the people who implement parole have their heads on straight and can withstand populist uproars and demagoguery from whatever quarter." More important, Jay challenged his client's involuntary hospitalization and a court hearing was scheduled.

Then suddenly the hospital released Kleasen. "After an extensive evaluation by staff physicians at the Buffalo Psychiatric Center, it was determined Mr. Kleasen no longer met the standards for involuntary retention," a Buffalo Psychiatric Center spokeswoman said, adding that the parolee was no longer dangerous to himself or the community. Jay was convinced the release had more to do with the scheduled hearing than any change in Kleasen's condition.

With Kleasen's discharge, parole officials had few options left. By Thursday, May 12, Kleasen was placed in the downtown City Mission which provided shelter and food for over 200 transients. The City Mission was run by Rev. Bob Timberlake, who was deeply committed to serving the unwanted and volunteered to take this man who had few friends. Parole officials now acknowledge that the City Mission "really did us a favor."

Bob Kleasen, the crazed band saw murderer as portrayed by the media, was a long way from the pathetic, worn-out man now living in the City Mission. During his prison years, Kleasen had ballooned to over 300 pounds. His steady diet of prescribed anti-depressants had had the unfortunate side effect of contributing to his weight gain. This didn't mean he couldn't still be dangerous, but he certainly didn't look the part.

Kleasen had refused to talk to the press during the chaos that preceded his coming to the City Mission, but his first day there he was trapped in another siege. He decided to let himself be interviewed for a couple of hours in a conference room. He would talk to the media one at a time, no tape recorders or cameras allowed. Jay had not yet arrived to talk him out of it.

Kleasen told reporters he hoped his answering questions would get them to leave him alone, which indicates just how out of touch he was. "I just want to end this monster business," he said with real feeling.

Reporters described him as looking much older than fifty-five with gray hair growing out in a brush cut. He walked with a cane and talked of his heart attack at Attica during which he fell backwards over a steel staircase. He wore dark blue pants, a white t-shirt, and a dark green jacket for the interviews. He described the media feeding frenzy as "a very traumatic experience," adding, "I'm free now. I don't want you chasing me all over the place. I just do not want people chasing me about." Asked if the hysteria over him was justified, Kleasen said, "People who know me need no explanation, and the ones who are my enemies—no explanation is possible."

But the delusions were still there. He told reporters he had a master's degree from SUNY-Buffalo and a Ph.D. from the University of Copenhagen. "I would like to have a low profile job," he went on to tell the *Buffalo News*. "If there is anybody out there who would like to offer me a job ..." Kleasen wanted to leave Buffalo. "If a job was offered to me and agreeable to the Parole Commission, I would leave immediately," he said. He claimed to be a teacher by trade. "I want to live a productive life," he said. He emphasized that he would serve out his two years of parole "to the letter."

Again he was asked about the murdered missionaries and again he dismissed the matter. The evidence was circumstantial and no bodies or witnesses were ever found, he said. "How can you say people are dead? I don't know anything about it." Kleasen did add that he felt sorry for the missionaries and their families.

"Texas is not a benevolent state," he continued. "I was a Yankee in Texas. If there was any validity to the charges, I would have died on death row." Perhaps he was thinking of his death row friend Ronald O'Bryan who was executed in 1984. Nor did he claim to be a Mormon. He told reporters he had been a Quaker for twenty years, having joined the Society of Friends in Denmark.

Sheriff Higgins, hoping to get a "feel for the situation," also paid Kleasen a visit that day with two deputies in tow. "Really looking at him, I personally couldn't have any problem with him myself," he told reporters. Higgins described the real Kleasen as a "middle-aged fat man with a big belly." "I don't think he could run very fast. I don't think he could do many things physically that a normal person could do. I don't know if his physical capabilities would allow him to do many things," the sheriff explained. "Am I personally in fear of him? No. I can't tell other people not to be. I wouldn't worry about him myself," the sheriff said. He later opined "I don't think he will do anything to jeopardize his parole. He is not stupid."

Jay finally arrived and ended all the interviews.

Kleasen was not immediately popular with Mission residents. Reporters fanned out to interview anyone who would talk and found plenty who resented Kleasen's being there. "It does kind of bother me," one said. "I'm all for kicking him out of Erie County." But others were sympathetic. "He served his time," one told the *Buffalo News*. "I know how the man feels. They should leave him alone." One Mission administrator, Rev. Jerry Spaeth, said, "When they come to the City Mission and they behave themselves, we allow them to stay. It's quite a hard thing for a fellow to go through." Bob Kleasen had found a home.

Kleasen had the misfortune of being paroled during television sweeps weeks when Buffalo stations were prepared to do just about anything for ratings. Kleasen was followed everywhere by reporters of every stripe. His every move, no matter how inconsequential, was reported at 6:00 and 11:00 each evening.

In an especially inflammatory twist, two local stations accompanied their coverage with film clips *The Texas Chain Saw Massacre*. Stern-faced anchors claimed Kleasen was the inspiration for the film. In fact, the movie had no connection to Kleasen and Buffalo television news departments had made no attempt to document a link. A *Buffalo News* television critic, while not defending Kleasen, castigated the coverage in a Sunday commentary a week into the episode, calling it "an absolute disgrace." The critic, Jeff Simon, said, "Watching the Kleasen story on TV news was like having someone throw lit cherry bombs in your lap every night." Simon also pointed out the *Texas Chain Saw Massacre* error.

While Kleasen was hospitalized, reporters had tracked down the Fischers in Milwaukee. Cathy Fischer told the *Austin American-Statesman* she was opposed to the death penalty but wished Kleasen were serving a life sentence. "It's too late for us, but he's going to do this again and some other family will have to go through what we went through," she told the reporter. "Somebody's got to be aware of what he's capable of doing. I know he's going to be under supervision, but no one can watch him all the time. He ran off once from New York. What's going to stop him from doing it again?"

The following week the *Buffalo News* called Cathy who expressed the same concerns. "My fear is that he's going to get out and do this again." She told the reporter of her ordeal sitting through the 1975 trial until she fled in tears, unable to listen to any further testimony. Her pain remained. "He never paid the price. It's like my son had no rights. Mark paid the price, we're still paying the price." But she made it clear she did not want revenge. "I really am against the death penalty, I didn't want that to happen to him," she said. "But I also don't think he should be let out on the streets either. There has to be something else that can be done." Cathy, who worked at a midwestern hospital at the time, doubted that Kleasen's mental illness ever would be safely contained. "Schizophrenia is not a disease you treat with a 10-day supply of antibiotics and it's over with," she told the *Buffalo News*. "I just can't see that man out on your streets again."

By now Kleasen had become a political issue and public office holders of Erie County scrambled on board the media band wagons. It probably didn't help that New York governor Mario Cuomo vetoed a bill to restore the death penalty that week. It was his sixth veto of such a bill. His predecessor Hugh Carey had also vetoed death penalty bills six times.

Erie County executive Dennis Gorski publicly demanded an explanation from state officials as to why Kleasen was dumped on his county instead of another. Gorski was incensed that Rochester had succeeded in driving Kleasen out of Monroe County and into Buffalo. He demanded to know "why the citizens of Monroe County are entitled to any greater protection in their homes than are the citizens of Erie County." He decried Erie County being used as "a testing grounds for Kleasen's mental health."

Buffalo mayor James Griffin addressed another public letter to the parole board protesting Kleasen's release to his community. In what seemed more like a press release, he wrote that Kleasen had "been diagnosed as having an anti-social personality disorder, along with schizoid personality disorder, and is on medication. ... Mr. Kleasen did not respond to treatment in jail and should be considered extremely dangerous. It is felt that because of his fascination with guns that he will attempt to obtain some type of weapon, and he is considered a master marksman and explosives expert. We do not want this person in our city."

New York State assemblyman William Hoyt, a Buffalo Democrat, told reporters, "It's as if the criminal justice system has gone amok. I'm going to do everything I can to see this decision reversed."

Buffalo politicians decided to sue the state in an effort to rescind Kleasen's parole to the community. The suit had more to do with politics and providing a release for public anxiety than with winning. "Politicians do political things," Jay said when told of the suit. "All it's doing is stirring up hatred and a feeling in the population that maybe parole is bad and that all people should stay in jail." After telling reporters that Kleasen had served his time and state law required his supervised release, Jay further pointed out that his client was from Buffalo. He was not arbitrarily dropped in the community. If people don't like those laws, legislators should change them, Jay said.

After Erie County filed suit, Jay went on the offensive with a suit of his own. He filed against county executive Dennis Gorski and Sheriff Higgins for, in Jay's words, orchestrating a campaign of "hate and disinformation which has made a mockery" of Kleasen's legal rights. They sought $500,000 in damages. The efforts of local politicos to force Kleasen out of Buffalo had gone "beyond the bounds of common decency" and were aimed at "whipping up public opinion," Jay told reporters. Kleasen had paid his debt to society and was entitled to a presumption of no new wrong doing since his release, Jay said.

Parole board documents on Kleasen had been leaked so regularly to the press that few things had not been exposed during the public debate. Jay challenged this practice as well. For his part, while going into court Kleasen told reporters, "I just want to live in peace. I have every faith in the court and every faith in my lawyer."

New York Supreme Court judge Vincent E. Doyle, Jr., was assigned the cases. (The Supreme Court is a local trial court in the New York system.) Doyle promised to rule quickly on Kleasen, whom he called "a man without a city." Doyle observed, "I share their apprehension" about Kleasen, but said he was from Buffalo and "has more ties to this area than anywhere else."

On Wednesday, May 19, 1988, Doyle threw out the Buffalo suits and ruled that Kleasen could stay. He noted that under New York law Kleasen was "entitled to release from the state correctional facility." In denying the injunction sought by the county executive and sheriff, Doyle wrote: "Mr. Kleasen's danger to the community is not at issue, nor is the right of a community to bar certain individuals from its area at issue. Likewise, past crimes attributed to Mr. Kleasen by the media, but for which he stands innocent in the eyes of the law, are not at issue. What is at issue is the legal capacity of the plaintiffs here to challenge the discretionary action of the New York State Parole Board. The wisdom of the Parole Board's actions is not for this court to review and where public outcry is made against the agency's policies, representatives of the legislative branch should be pressed to enact appropriate legislation. While this court sympathizes with the public concern and the motivation of petitioners to protect the citizens of Erie County from possible harm, nevertheless this court must follow the law, even where controversial issues are raised." Doyle also dismissed Kleasen's $500,000 countersuit.

Jay explained to reporters that Doyle's decision meant Kleasen was "entitled to be here as long as he wishes. He's basically free to do anything he wants." He also said he was recommending that his client refile his civil rights suit in federal court.

With Doyle's decision things began to settle down. Law enforcement made a show of intense surveillance of Kleasen for a while but soon wearied of it. For his part, Kleasen never acted like the demon he was supposed to be. "I'm perfectly happy with the decision the judge made because it's the law," said retired police sergeant Rapp whose home had been guarded for a time. "He has a right to live the way he should live. Let him live in peace, but let everybody else live in peace as well."

THIRTY-THREE

CITY MISSION RESIDENTS EVENTUALLY GOT USED TO KLEASEN'S presence and decided he was not such a menace after all. As he had done so many times before, Kleasen embraced the religious mores of his audience and gained acceptance, or, in the words of one Mission observer, "gave himself to Jesus."

Kleasen secured privileged living space in the basement of the building rather than the large dormitory area where over 200 other transients lived. He usually got first pick of the donated clothing that came into the Mission, though at 300 pounds he could not find much that fit.

Kleasen continued to see himself as a privileged person deserving of more than others. On July 11, 1988, this resulted in a nasty confrontation with an eleven-year-old boy who volunteered as a food server with his family at the Mission cafeteria. The boy served him the usual portion given to all residents, but Kleasen angrily insisted he was entitled to more. He finally threatened to throw his plate in the boy's face. The incident earned him another round of unflattering television news coverage.

Aware of Kleasen's toxic public image, the parole division investigated the matter. He later admitted the threat to his parole supervisor, saying, "It was hot and I was tired and hungry because I had skipped breakfast trying to lose weight." He claimed the youth had been "shorting" him food for a month. The resulting report noted the incident "showed the darker side of his nature." After concluding the matter was relatively trivial, the investigator observed it was not helped by Kleasen's being "infantile, a bully of nasty temperament, and without remorse." As predicted, the matter blew over.

Kleasen made his weekly visits to a parole officer in the Donovan

Building a dozen blocks from the City Mission. He talked about the Texas murders, always insisting that the two missionaries were still alive and hiding from the Mormon church in Mexico. He let on that they had confided their fears of the church to him. He had been railroaded at the 1975 murder trial, Kleasen insisted. Kleasen said Texas District Court judge Tom Blackwell—the national guard general—had once been his commanding officer in Southeast Asia. He claimed Blackwell had sent him on a number of secret "black bag jobs" which would embarrass the government. Kleasen claimed to know of atrocities Blackwell had orchestrated against various Asian peoples and insisted he had reported these to the World Court at The Hague. Kleasen claimed the death sentence was Blackwell's payback for his having revealed the ex-general's dirty secrets. Today Blackwell just laughs when told of these new Kleasen delusions.

During the last few months of his parole, Kleasen managed to qualify for New York welfare benefits. He used the income to move out of the City Mission and into the Hotel Lafayette some five or six blocks closer to the Donovan Building. The hotel was once one of Buffalo's elegant addresses. It was completed in 1904 at the corner of Washington and Clinton streets near Lafayette Square. At the time it cost $1 million, boasted 350 rooms, was billed as "fully fireproof," and was said to be one of the finest hotels in New York. It would later be expanded to 500 rooms. But when Kleasen moved there in late 1989, it had become a typical big city transient hotel inhabited by welfare recipients, parolees, and poor retirees. About 100 people lived there full time. In many instances their rents were paid directly to the hotel owners by the state of New York.

The Erie County Public Library was across the street, probably an attractive feature for Kleasen. The City Mission was an easy walk and many other Lafayette residents also took their meals there. The Donovan Building with its parole offices was a few blocks in the opposite direction. No doubt, the hotel was a more elegant sounding address for his pen pals, among them Ann-Eliza Young in Northern Ireland.

Mrs. Hung Nyguen, a short, friendly Vietnamese woman, ran the hotel with her husband. She could be found just about every day behind the hotel's long first floor registration desk, a wall of mail slots behind her and a large cage of chirping parakeets before her in the lobby. Like everyone else in Buffalo, she had been bombarded by television accounts of Kleasen's parole. She did not know what he looked like, but was aware that he was supposed to be a demon.

One day a huge fat man with a cane slowly approached her at the registration desk and asked if she had a room. "Of course," she said, and then began to register him. He told her he was Bob Kleasen and she froze, recognizing the name. But he hardly looked like a crazed killer, more like a broken down old man who appeared much older than his fifty-five years. She was afraid of having Kleasen as a guest, both for safety reasons and because she feared other tenants would move out if they heard he was now living among them. But she had already told him she had rooms so she was also reluctant to turn him down.

Mrs. Nyguen registered Kleasen in a room in the middle of the sprawling hotel. She explained her concerns and urged him not to reveal where he was living because if it hit the news she would have to ask him to leave. Kleasen agreed. He rarely spent his days in the hotel, but left early in the mornings and stayed out until after eating dinner at the Mission.

Reporters did find out, but by then Kleasen had become an accepted and appreciated member of the Lafayette Hotel community. Mrs. Nyguen came to regard him as a nice man who was always courteous, treated everyone else well, and never showed any of the pathological killer he was made out to be. At one point assistant hotel manager Peter Stegura told a reporter Kleasen was "one of the nicest guys we have here. He's on the preferred customer list, as far as I'm concerned. He doesn't bother anyone here. In fact, if you ever need a hand, he's happy to provide it." The owner of the hotel bar, The Tapp Room, also spoke to reporters. Robert McCarthy said, "Since the initial shock of him moving here, it's become no big deal."

Kleasen had his quirks, one of which was his refusal to allow maid service. He wanted to clean his own room, and Mrs. Nyguen's periodic inspections suggested he was an adequate housekeeper. The room was filled with papers arranged in no particular order. New York parole officers also inspected the room from time to time.

Mrs. Nyguen still calls him "Dr. Kleasen," accepting his stories of graduate degrees and scholarship without question. He told everyone in the hotel he was writing a book and that the mountains of papers he kept in his room were part of his research. Most residents had the good sense not to challenge his grandiose claims. His crimes were not often discussed, but when they came up, Kleasen maintained his complete innocence, saying he was framed. He did not often mention the CIA.

Detective Murphy, who maintained a cautious, professional interest in Kleasen, no longer worked for law enforcement. He was mildly alarmed to learn Kleasen had moved into a hotel close to the downtown public utility whose security operation he ran. He made a point to find out if Kleasen had a room in the center of the Lafayette, as opposed to an outside room with a window opening onto his place of business. The two never encountered each other.

David Jay did refile Kleasen's 1988 civil rights complaint in U.S. District Court and the matter finally came to trial in late January 1990. Kleasen was asking for $2.5 million in damages against Erie County executive Dennis Gorski and sheriff Thomas Higgins. The two prepared for trial in Jay's downtown office not far from the hotel. Both were convinced they would win.

During a brief press conference before the trial, Kleasen said he had been living "in hiding" since his 1988 parole, and that he had no social life and no activities he enjoyed. "You've all spread so much poison about me," he said of the local press. "There's no way I'll ever have a normal life." "Buffalo hasn't exactly been the City of Good Neighbors to him," Jay added.

On the third day of the trial, Kleasen took the stand. He used a cane to hobble slowly to the witness stand. He denied any involvement in the Texas murders and complained that his parole officers "didn't seem to believe me" when he said this. Asked about his ordeal following his release from prison in May 1988, Kleasen said, "I was shocked. I thought my dilemma was over with, and here it started all over again. The poison is there no matter how many times they're told the chain saw massacre thing did not happen. It sticks in people's minds."

His parole officer, Richard Low, who was the first witness to testify, was now seated in the courtroom. As Kleasen's delusions began to pour out, Low could not help but grin. He had heard most of them already and knew how they sounded.

On the fourth day of the trial, testimony concluded. Attorneys for the county then moved to dismiss the case as being unproven, thus taking it away from the jury. Judge John T. Curtin agreed. Even if all the facts as presented by Kleasen were true, Curtin said, he still could not find that he had been wronged. "I find nothing here to indicate there was any malicious prosecution or malicious intent by either Gorski or Higgins," the judge said.

"I was denied a jury trial," said a disappointed Kleasen. "I was denied my constitutional rights." Asked if he was now prepared to put the dispute behind him, he replied, "That all depends on the accuracy of the news media which hasn't been very accurate to date."

Gorski and Higgins were delighted and offered no apologies to Kleasen. Asked if he thought Kleasen presently posed a threat, Higgins said, "He's still on parole, still under observation by the parole office. They do a competent job and I'm sure they'll keep an eye on him. You never know if a person is going to act out. There's always a potential for danger."

Back in Jay's law office, Kleasen took the decision with uncharacteristic good grace. Jay had earned his trust and respect so he wasn't ready to blame his lawyer. Besides, he only had to serve a little over seven more months of parole and he would finally be a free man again.

In September 1990 Kleasen completed his parole. He pestered parole officers to release any holds on his passport and made plans to leave the country. Kleasen had been corresponding with at least three women—Young in Northern Ireland, another in England, and one in Australia. He settled on the English lady, showing her photograph and a ring to his friends at the hotel. He said they planned to marry.

Kleasen would not give Mrs. Nyguen a forwarding address, saying he did not want to put her in a compromising position. He did give a Mission friend, a young cook, an address and put him in charge of shipping much of his stuff to South Humberside, England. The boxes mostly contained his papers, but Mrs. Nyguen and her guests jokingly speculated as to which boxes contained body parts.

Kleasen's parole supervision was terminated on September 8, 1990. He received a certificate of "Final Discharge" reading, "This is to certify that KLEASEN, ROBERT has this day been discharged from further supervision of the Board of Parole in accordance with the provisions of law." By his fifty-eighth birthday on the 20th, he was gone.

Investigator Murphy made sure that Interpol and British authorities knew of Kleasen's departure and intended destination. (Interpol, the International Criminal Police Organization, has no arrest or investigative powers of its own but is comprised of 176 nations that exchange information.)

No doubt Kleasen continued to churn out letters, but none of the people I interviewed received any. In 1992 Buffalo lawyer David Jay received a postcard from Kleasen from England. Around Christmas, Marvin Teague, by then a judge on the Texas Court of Criminal Appeals in Austin, received another English postcard from Kleasen. He brought it to the Texas Chili Parlor, a popular watering hole for Travis County lawyers, and showed it to Pat Ganne.

Kleasen continued to write to Young in Northern Ireland for two or three years but never visited her. He told her he married the English woman in a big church wedding shortly after arriving in 1990. They lived in a "lovely antique home." Kleasen claimed he had become active in a local gun club. His new wife worked in a craft shop she owned. He had previously boasted to Young that he was an English duke and his mother had been a duchess.

THIRTY-FOUR

DICK MURPHY HAD MADE A POINT OF SECURING FROM KLEASEN'S Buffalo City Mission buddies the address he'd asked them to ship his possessions to. The boxes were sent to a Marie Longley in Barton-upon-Humber, South Humberside, England. In 1996 I wrote to Kleasen in England but received no response. Through friends, I checked some British public records, but this also failed to provide any leads. Given his claims of poor health, I thought he might be dead, since I didn't believe he could go long without getting into trouble again. Then in early September 1999, I received a call from Bennett Loudon, a reporter for the Rochester *Democrat Chronicle*. Loudon had just learned that British authorites were starting to ask questions about Kleasen.

Humberside County is a business and fishing center with around 900,000 people and about 2,000 law enforcement officers located about 150 miles north of London on the British east coast. According to Humberside police, Kleasen had been allowed to own and deal in firearms. The permitting process required disclosure of past criminal or psychiatric history. Kleasen had "given a number of narratives regarding his past history in the U.S.A.," and police finally decided to check him out. "Much of what has been related by Kleasen ... about his past has been disbelieved," the police told Interpol. "Because of the nature of the (inquiry) and the important need to establish his suitability to hold the above position as a dealer in firearms and explosives, details of his history in the U.S.A. is requested as a matter of urgency."

I told Loudon what I knew of Kleasen's history and he broke the story on September 7, 1999, under the headline "Wayne convict surfaces in England." I contacted Humberside County law enforcement, identified myself as Kleasen's biographer, and shortly faxed them newspaper accounts and other documents. The police inspector who took my first call seemed surprised to hear that Kleasen had never been associated with the U.S. military or the CIA. As one article with a photograph of Kleasen came across his fax machine, another officer exclaimed, "That's him all right, he looks just the same today."

Other reporters soon followed Loudon. Shortly thereafter, I began hearing from a friend of Kleasen's terrified fourth wife, the former Marie Longley, who knew nothing about his real past. For the next three months, I gathered information from these and other sources and was able to construct the following narrative of Kleasen's life since September 1990.

While in the New York prison system, Kleasen had corresponded with women he had met through a seemingly reputable Irish pen pal organization. Besides Ann-Eliza Young in Northern Ireland, he'd written women in Finland, Taiwan, and other countries. Beginning in 1986, Kleasen wrote Marie Longley, a widow his age living in South Humberside. They corresponded about once a week. Kleasen would grow impatient if she did not respond weekly. He apparently cultivated each woman as a possible partner and finally selected Longley. She was an attractive widow who had a house of her own, few family members, and a small independent income. She had enjoyed pen pals since she was a school girl and accepted Kleasen's stories about being a college professor hired to teach New York state inmates.

Kleasen had first announced plans for a "short visit" in 1988 but delayed the trip because of "work." He ran into problems getting a passport because he'd never repaid the federal government for repatriating him from Lebanon in 1972 or 1973, but he finally managed to borrow the money from a friend. Kleasen arrived in England a week after his parole ended in September 1990, flying out of Toronto. Marie had been led to believe Kleasen was coming for a friendly visit, but his Buffalo City Mission boxes began arriving at her house before he did.

Today Marie recalls that her impression of Kleasen was of a man who never stopped talking about himself and had no interest in anyone else. After about six weeks, she finally told him they were not suited for each other and asked him to go. He responded that he'd burned his bridges in the United States and would not leave. At the time, he was otherwise considerate and tried to be helpful around the house. Marie remembers that she began to feel sorry for him and was finally manipulated into marrying him on January 11, 1991. Kleasen made a point of wearing his fake medals at the ceremony, including what he said was a Congressional Medal of Honor. The next day Kleasen insisted they travel to London and meet with a British immigration office to have his visa extended to a year's residency.

Within weeks, Kleasen reverted to his old habits. Shortly after their marriage, he tried to get a job teaching at Hull University but was turned down. He did secure temporary jobs as a security guard in a food store and as a joiner, but never worked for long. He began borrowing money from Marie for tools and other wants. He felt she had an obligation to support him and ran up substantial household debts. Marie had to work as a cleaner to keep them afloat. Kleasen's temper again surfaced, and, just as in his previous marriages, he became increasingly violent and controlling. In 1994 he beat Marie then refused to let her go to a hospital for treatment. She discussed divorce several times, but he wouldn't consider it. During one especially angry confrontation, he told her, "If you try to leave me, I'll hunt you down and kill you." Marie stayed, and gradually resigned herself to a miserable marriage, believing that Kleasen could always convince others he was the offended party deserving of sympathy.

Marie's few friends regarded Kleasen as a bore and a braggart. Kleasen ran many of her friends off, leaving her increasingly isolated. Marie came to see what she believed were the symptoms of a paranoid mental illness in Kleasen. She lived upstairs, he downstairs. Sometimes Kleasen told his pen pals she was a maid. She left the house only for domestic chores and to walk Ri, her golden labrador retriever. The dog had been abused by a previous owner and rescued by the couple, but when Ri proved to have no desire to hunt, Kleasen lost interest in it.

With the Atlantic Ocean seemingly insulating him from the truth of his own life, Kleasen again claimed a fantastic past. Over the years, he told anyone else who would listen that he was the son of the archduke of Rotterdam and that his parents had owned paint and art stores in Buffalo. He was raised speaking German and did not learn English until age nine which made his life in the Buffalo school system miserable. He told his new wife that his strict parents had forced him to participate in the "Hitler Youth in America" during his childhood. He claimed that during World War II his parents would retreat to the attic of their Buffalo home to listen to radio broadcasts by "Uncle Adolph."

At age eighteen, he said, he began working on an assembly line at a Bell Aircraft plant near Niagara Falls. (Kleasen had briefly worked as a file clerk there but had never been on the assembly line.) His genius was quickly recognized, he claimed, leading to a job as an assistant to rocket scientist Wernher von Braun and test pilot "Chuck" Yeager in New Mexico. He claimed to have been the youngest person in the United States with an FAA pilot's license. Kleasen said he was a captain in the air force and flew combat missions during the Korean War, practically winning the Battle of Inchon single-handedly and earning the Congressional Medal of Honor. After the war, he began flying U2's for the CIA. When a U2 pilot was shot down by the Soviets in 1960 and exchanged for a Russian spy two years later, Kleasen claimed it was he who escorted the pilot back to freedom in a divided Berlin. Later his CIA assignments had him conferring with Chairman Mao Tse-tung in Red China. He claimed to have worked with U.S. presidents Harry Truman, Dwight Eisenhower, and Richard Nixon, and said former president Lyndon Johnson had been a hunting partner in Texas.

When he decided he didn't like his Chinese assignment, Kleasen claimed he returned to the United States and enrolled as a college student in Buffalo where he was actually a CIA operative spying on the peace movement. While a "student," and while married to his first wife, he was promoted to CIA "Sphere Chief" in charge of all Latin American operations. It was during this period that he converted to the cause of peace and became an embarrassment to the CIA. From that point on, Kleasen said, the CIA was responsible for all the miseries in his life.

Some people in England believed him. Kleasen was invited to speak about his flying career to a Rotary Club and to local women's groups. He was interviewed on a local radio program about his life and on another occasion was asked to give awards to a youth Air Training

Corps which he was happy to do while wearing his Congressional Medal of Honor. A few law enforcement officers even consulted with him on firearms and ballistics matters.

In 1993 he cultivated a young man named Joe Fawden (not his real name). When the youth showed no interest in guns or hunting, Kleasen dropped him, but his mother, Vera Fawden (not her real name), became a close friend of Marie's. Fawden was the daughter of a psychiatric nurse and had taught special education. She saw in Kleasen's spelling indications that he was dyslexic. Ultimately it would be the Fawdens who rescued Marie from Kleasen's influence.

Armed with his marriage to a British citizen, Kleasen took advantage of generous public health coverage to have major surgery on his knees, claiming they had been shot up in the Korean War. He then secured British disability benefits which he enjoyed for years. These included a car and a monthly cash allowance. For a few months after arriving in England, Kleasen conspired with an accomplice in the United States to continue collecting social security disability benefits which he was not entitled to. When he reached retirement age, Kleasen began to collect regular social security benefits, and by 1997 was apparently drawing $400 a month from that source.

His gun fetish, restricted by incarceration and parole supervision since 1974, remained as well. Among the possessions he had shipped from Buffalo were books on firearms, all stamped as property of the Buffalo Public Library. As soon as he was legally able, Kleasen applied for and received a permit to own a firearm. Armed again, he joined a local gun club called the Wildfowlers Association which required an initial year of probation. The next year, 1993, he received a permit for another firearm.

In 1996 Kleasen received a permit to deal in explosives and firearms. In each instance he was required to fill out applications which asked about his past criminal history. Kleasen represented that he had none; he also boasted of holding a doctorate in education. As Kleasen had hoped, the permits were issued with little or no background check. He took the business name of Kleasen's Rifling Services in spite of the fact he had none of the necessary equipment to service firearms and had to farm out his own guns for such work.

One condition of his dealer's permit was that the guns be kept in a building with security protections specified by British law. Kleasen wanted to keep his guns in Marie's 200-year-old home. Such old historic buildings are protected by English preservation requirements. This meant the necessary alterations could not be accomplished without damaging the building's historical and architectural integrity. Kleasen was undeterred. He persuaded police to water down the required security in his case, then set about wrecking the inside of the home to accommodate his guns.

At Marie's home, Kleasen would clean and baby his guns by the hour. In a chilling reprise of the experience of some Texas Mormons, Marie would often look up to find him sighting down at her head. It was intended to intimidate her and it succeeded.

Kleasen joined various other local gun clubs where he bragged about his past as a decorated war hero, CIA operative, Olympic marksman, and educated gentleman. Kleasen's anger was always close to the surface, especially if someone dared to question his claims. One 1993 confrontation with another gun club member was reported to the police after Kleasen threatened him with a gun. The incident resulted in Kleasen's being kicked out of his first gun club as well as being fined a year-long peace bond. In fact, Kleasen made himself so obnoxious that he was expelled from one gun club after another.

Soon a legitimate British firearms dealer, Tony Fox, checked with the Congressional Medal of Honor Society in Washington, D.C., to verify Kleasen's story. The society responded that "Mr. Kleasen is not a Medal of Honor recipient" and asked if he possessed such a medal. If he did, they wanted it back. Joe Fawden later also found evidence of Kleasen's U.S. criminal convictions, while Fox demanded that Kleasen resign from their gun club, which he did. Fox went to the police, who began their own investigation which eventually reached Interpol.

As Kleasen's fantasy life unraveled, he slid into what sounds like another clinical depression. He spent nearly all his time in Marie's house. He refused to bathe or clean himself. His wife remained a fastidious housekeeper and kept his clothing and linens clean in spite of his bad hygeine. Kleasen also concealed firearms, knives, and a black-jack throughout the house.

On April 27, 1999, Marie returned home to find several police vehicles parked outside. The officers showed her documents confirming Kleasen's U.S. convictions. Inside Kleasen sat sobbing with two officers beside him and others searching the house. "They're taking my guns away," he cried. Kleasen begged to sit on a favorite couch where he had weapons concealed within reach; the police told him to stay in the kitchen. They collected forty-four guns including a Thompson sub-machine gun and ammunition. Kleasen was ordered to present himself at the police station for questioning, but it was weeks before he appeared. After the confiscation of his guns, his wife recalled him crying and moaning repeatedly about the loss of his "children."

At this point, Fawden asked her son, a computer whiz, to investigate Kleasen on the Internet. At one point in the past, Joe had volunteered to secure photographs of the fighter planes Kleasen claimed to have flown in the Korean War. Instead of being pleased, Kleasen had exploded. This time Joe found Kleasen on New York and Texas websites listing criminal convictions as well as a December 1997 article I published about him in *Sunstone* magazine.

Fawden brought Marie the findings and, after several hours of pleading, persuaded her to leave. Five days later, on September 28, 1999, Marie packed a few possessions and crept out of the house with Ri to Fawden's waiting car. Kleasen was rarely up before mid-morning. A neighbor reported Marie missing and the police began to investigate, finally locating her at Fawden's where she recounted her ordeal. Once Marie was safe, Fawden contacted the LDS mission office in London to warn them of Kleasen's presence.

Armed with Kleasen's U.S. criminal history, the police returned on October 5. A search of his home produced two unregistered .22 handguns, one with a silencer. A firearms dealer who knew Kleasen had the weapons called them "assassination pistols." Kleasen was then arrested on four charges: obtaining pecuniary advantage by deception, roughly a fraud charge with a maximum prison sentence of five years; possession of prohibited firearms and ammunition with a maximum sentence of five years; being a prohibited person possessing firearms and ammunition, with a maximum sentence of five years; and threatening to kill his wife Marie, which carries a possible ten-year sentence. The British don't make the same distinction between misdemeanor and felony charges that the United States does, but all four counts roughly translated to felonies and carried maximum individual sentences of five to fifteen years in prison.

In spite of his history of flight to avoid prosecution, Kleasen was released on what amounted to a personal recognizance bond with the requirements that he report to the police department regularly and not contact witnesses. This included Marie who was in hiding with the Fawdens. Kleasen continued to reside in Marie's home, and police kept a close watch on him. One visitor to the home said it was a "wreck" and that Kleasen looked like "a caged animal."

Shortly thereafter the British Home Office served notice of its intention to deport Kleasen at the conclusion of his prosecutions and possible incarceration. Kleasen had secured resident alien status with his marriage to Marie but this did not prevent him from being deported.

In the meantime, Marie divorced him but declined to pursue allegations that Kleasen had threatened to kill her. She was terrified that he would try to carry out his threats especially since he remained free on bail.

In mid-March 2000, Kleasen's fabricated world came to an end. He reluctantly entered a guilty plea to four of the firearms charges against him. The judge warned him not to interpret his release on bail as assurance that he would not be sentenced to prison. The British press is prohibited from discussing a case prior to a guilty verdict, but with his plea Kleasen became a sensational news story, with headlines screaming "Secret of Death Row" and "Public Concern that 'Anyone Can Come to England.'"

One gun club member told reporters that his group came to call Kleasen "Odd Bob." Kleasen, he continued, "had a very colorful manner. The man had delusions; first of all he had an obvious obsession with guns and he used to remark about his work in various American CIA-type organizations. I don't think he is the weak old frail man he appears to be in court."

Still free on pre-trial release, Kleasen tried to persuade friends to help him slip out of the country. He was caught late one afternoon at the King George Docks in Hull and taken into custody. Police found more prohibited ammunition in his possession and new charges were leveled against him.

Grimsby Crown Court Judge Michael Heath is, according to one observer, "no softie." He too was unpersuaded by Kleasen's claims that he was merely sending his possessions to the continental mainland. Kleasen was ruled a flight risk and he landed in jail.

Meanwhile, as one British newspaper headline put it, "Alarm bells rang at the highest level." Kleasen's case was discussed in the House of Commons where promises were made to tighten British gun laws and immigration policy.

On June 2, 2000, Kleasen appeared in Heath's courtroom in a wheelchair. The judge ordered him to walk to the dock. Kleasen then fired his barrister, repeating a life-long pattern of trying to manipulate the judicial process. After two hours with another barrister, Kleasen returned to the courtroom to face sentencing. When asked what explanations he had to offer, Kleasen again claimed to be a retired CIA supervisor and U2 pilot, to hold a Ph.D. from the University of Buffalo, and to be misunderstood by his accusers. His barrister advised the court: "He was abandoned in ill health and in desperate mental condition because of depression."

Judge Heath sentenced Kleasen to a series of two- and three-year concurrent sentences with credit for the six weeks he had already served. He could have been sentenced to ten years each on two counts and five years each on the others. The judge observed, "You have displayed utter contempt and disregard for the laws governing firearms in this country. I consider you still to be an intelligent and devious individual likely to commit further offenses."

Kleasen first underwent psychological and risk evaluations before going to prison for the remainder of his sentence. With good behavior, he could serve about two years, after which he will be deported to the United States.

THIRTY-FIVE

THE AUSTIN TAXIDERMY STUDIO CONTINUES TO OPERATE AT ITS
1974 location just outside Oak Hill, Texas. *Lem Rathbone* has retired and the business is now run by his son *Jimmy Byrd*. They don't
easily talk about Bob Kleasen and the 1974 murders.

Richard Banks was later an assistant U.S. attorney in Houston,
Texas, where he was one of the office's more aggressive prosecutors.

David Bays and *Pat Ganne* still practice criminal defense law in
Texas, Bays in San Antonio, and Ganne in Austin.

Tom Blackwell retired from the bench in 1982. However, as a
senior judge, he presides over as many Austin trials as ever. He is
also a co-author of the three criminal law volumes of West Publishing's *Texas Practice* series, along with his daughter Betty Blackwell and Texas Court of Criminal Appeals former presiding judge
Mike McCormick.

Richard Coons still practices psychiatry in Austin, Texas.

Charlie Craig is an Austin criminal defense lawyer with an office
a few blocks from Pat Ganne's office.

David K. Darley, Gary's father, still lives in Simi Valley, California. Gary's mother, *Jill*, died in 1994. Gary's siblings *Kelle*, *Clark*,
Todd, *Beverly Duncan*, and his twin sister *Gay Page* all live in California not far from their father.

Eddie Davis still lives in Austin, Texas, where he sculpts military
history themes and is an active Mormon.

Ronald Earle was elected to his sixth four-year term as Travis
County district attorney in 1996.

Vaughn Featherstone is a general authority of the LDS church,
serving in the First Quorum of the Seventy since 1976.

Former Austin police investigator *Doug Ferris* is in the private security business in Austin, working primarily with polygraph examinations.

Cathy and *Jim Fischer*, Mark's parents, continue to be committed Mormons in Milwaukee, Wisconsin. Their sons *Matthew* and *Michael* live in Centerville and Provo, Utah. Their daughter *Melissa* and son *Martin* live near their parents in suburban Milwaukee.

Ed Guyon has a solo law practice in Salt Lake City, Utah.

Not long after the Kleasen trial, *R. Roscoe Haley's* drinking reached a point where he could no longer function as a lawyer. In February 1976 he was arrested for receiving stolen property in a sting operation, but the charges were dismissed when it became obvious he had been entrapped. Later two clients brought complaints before the bar over his failure to return monies he held in his trust account and over his writing another client a bad check. In November 1976 Haley voluntarily resigned from the Texas bar for two years. Other complaints surfaced again in 1982; this time Haley acknowledged he was no longer capable of practicing law and surrendered his license for good.

Max Hartmann was a Texas game warden stationed in the scenic Hill Country community of Fredericksburg. In 1995 he was elected a Gillespie County justice of the peace.

Norm Henk is still a Texas game officer in Fredericksburg, Texas.

Joseph Jachimczyk retired in 1995 after thirty-five years as Harris County's chief medical examiner. He had become a fixture in Texas criminal law and for years directed his office through growth and technological advancements. The last few years of his administration, his office was plagued with allegations of mishandled autopsies, inattention to filing reports, and unauthorized office policies.

David Jay still practices law in downtown Buffalo, New York.

Colon Jordan retired in 1991 after thirty-seven years with the Austin police department. He still lives in Austin. His son Sam now works for APD.

Hans Kindt, the LDS stake patriarch who spoke movingly at Mark Fischer's memorial service, is now president of the Milwaukee Stake. He and his brother immigrated to Milwaukee from Germany in the

1950s. Today he runs his own tailoring business.

The Texas Court of Criminal Appeals's decision in *Kleasen v. State* has virtually disappeared. It has almost never been cited as a precedent for any Texas search and seizure question since it was issued in 1977.

Former Texas San Antonio LDS mission president *Ron Loveland* was called as an Area Authority Seventy at the April 2000 general conference of the LDS church.

Richard Low is still a senior state parole officer in Buffalo, New York.

Frank McCullough continues to teach at the University of Texas in Austin. He serves in the Austin Texas Oak Hill Stake presidency of the LDS church.

Dick Murphy lives in the Buffalo suburb of Orchard Park where he runs a private consulting service. He was on the Buffalo police force from 1957 until moving to the district attorney's office in 1971. In 1972 he moved from the D.A.'s office back to the Buffalo police department. In 1979 Murphy retired and became director of security for National Fuel, a public natural gas concern, for the next fifteen years.

Phil Nelson continues to serve as a Travis County assistant district attorney.

U.S. district judge *Jack Roberts* retired in May 1980. Newspaper accounts at the time called him "the most powerful man in central Texas."

Phil Sanders is now a municipal judge in Austin, Texas.

Bob Smith gave up the district attorney's office to run unsuccessfully for Travis County, Texas, 98th District Court judge in 1978. He then practiced law until he was appointed to a vacancy on the Texas Third District Court of Appeals in Austin. He was defeated when running for a full term in 1980. He died in Austin on September 27, 1990, at age sixty-eight.

Bruce Smith is now on the agriculture faculty at Brigham Young University in Provo, Utah.

Marvin O. Teague was elected to the Texas Court of Criminal Appeals in 1980. There he became a respected liberal voice on the court with considerable influence on Texas criminal law. He died of cardiac arrest in Austin on February 20, 1991, half way through his third term on the court.

Ron Valentine is still the public defender in Wayne County, New York.

Glen Wilkerson continues to practice law in Austin, Texas.

David Williams is still a senior probation officer in Wayne County, New York.

CONCLUSION

I am often asked what conclusions could be drawn from the foregoing events. Did Kleasen do it? Was he insane? Was the Texas Court of Criminal Appeals correct when they reversed the conviction in 1977? Was the district attorney wrong not to reprosecute in 1978? What can Mormons and members of other churches do, if anything, to prevent this sort of tragedy from happening again? Was Kleasen the serial killer that so many people believed he was?

Given the record, Kleasen's story that Gary Darley and Mark Fischer are still alive but have secretly fled some sinister plot by the Mormon church is unbelievable. His alternative claim that the CIA is responsible for their deaths is also a fabrication. I believe Kleasen killed these two young missionaries. While much evidence has been lost since 1974, nothing suggests someone else did this. I admit, however, to still wondering what exactly motivated him. Kleasen was a man filled with rage and he certainly had a grudge against all authority figures in the LDS church.

But young missionaries were the one group of Mormons who consistently gave him the kind of attention he craved. So why kill them? Rage and impulse? Kleasen was mentally ill. His control mechanisms were so diminished that it took little to provoke him. There are indications that Kleasen's illness was in an escalating state in late October 1974, giving him even less control over his dark impulses. The stealing was incidental. Kleasen was just a scavenger.

I suspect that the missionaries, probably Darley, the senior companion, went to Kleasen's home having decided this would be the last visit. Darley's missionary journals indicate he was growing weary of the man. In the course of the evening, they may have told Kleasen they could not return, that they were going to restrict or even end the relationship. That pushed one of Kleasen's buttons and in a moment of rage he shot them. (If he shot them at his outdoor shooting range where Fischer's name tag was found, this suggests some premeditation, not a sudden flash of anger.) From that moment on, it was a matter of covering up his crime, however ineptly.

Kleasen's mental illness did not render him legally insane. Insanity, according to mental health experts, covers a wide range running to mostly shades of gray. It is a condition which fluctuates from day to day. It is the legal profession that imposes an artificial line of sane/not sane. Like many things the law does, it's arbitrary and not always well connected to reality. In my opinion, Kleasen was capable of knowing right from wrong and, thus, was legally competent to stand trial.

The question of what he did with the bodies remains a mystery. Nothing has ever surfaced in spite of considerable effort by prosecutors and law enforcement to locate the remains. Kleasen's denial is complete and he has never offered any clues. It seems evident, however, that he cut the heads up on the taxidermist's band saw. This is one of the more compelling arguments for Kleasen's being both mentally ill but legally sane. I have often thought of him holding a dead man's head, especially the head of someone he knew, against the long blade of a band saw and cutting it up for disposal. Certainly, the gruesome horror of such an act points to someone whose control mechanisms are almost completely overridden by illness.

At the same time, Kleasen seems to have known that his actions were wrong for he apparently took steps to conceal them. If one is so ill he doesn't appreciate the criminality of what he's done, he doesn't go to extreme lengths to hide the evidence of his crime. In spite of the evidence against him, Kleasen always denied any knowledge of the missionaries' disappearance. Under the standards adopted by our legal system, he was sane enough to be responsible for his acts.

I still wonder why the bodies were apparently dismembered with so little care. Logically, because of his law enforcement background, Kleasen knew how to dispose of evidence to avoid being caught. With some damning evidence, like the bodies and fingerprints, he was successful. But what kind of person then squirrels away so much of the personal property of the victims in and around his residence? The car tires and jack, the license plates, the watches with blood on them, and the religious teaching materials. How could Kleasen not think he would be a suspect and subject to a search?

Retired Buffalo police investigator Dick Murphy recalls being told of a comment Kleasen allegedly made: "no corpse, no case." If Kleasen ever said that, or something like it, perhaps his sloppiness was simply overconfidence.

I'm not sure I share district attorney Bob Smith's theory that Kleasen liked to keep trophies of his kills. And surely Kleasen appreciated the potential of the band saw as evidence.

For me, the best explanation is Kleasen's mental state. While not legally insane, he surely was "nuts" in the colloquial sense. In my opinion, he was, and remains, a mentally ill person.

Was Kleasen a serial killer? Several people have since reported hearing that he was suspected in other killings and that various police agencies had found evidence of this. I looked for that evidence but never found any. Such gossip appears to be a natural human reaction to conduct which by itself is so horrible that it repels everyone. We sometimes feel a need to demonize such people even more, to attribute conduct to them that makes them less human, less like ourselves.

Besides, Kleasen was too unstable to get away with multiple killings, even for a short time. He was identified almost immediately as the suspect in the murders of Darley and Fischer and was so sloppy that he left plenty of evidence pointing directly to himself. I don't believe he had the mental capacity to kill multiple victims and evade detection for long.

Dick Murphy, who probably knows more about Kleasen than anyone, disagrees with me. I've never met Kleasen, Murphy has had considerable contact with him. He also has a twenty-two-year law enforcement career to guide his conclusions. Murphy feels Kleasen is a serial killer with other victims in his wake. He believes the Wayne County, New York, victim was saved only because witnesses were present. Murphy also feels Kleasen was caught for the missionary murders because so many people were closely involved in the victims' lives. He agrees with Bob Smith that Kleasen kept trophies of human kills which accounts for the watches and other objects found in the trailer. Murphy believes other victims—as yet undiscovered—are people who did not have close ties to friends or family members who would have raised an alarm when they disappeared.

Was the Texas Court of Criminal Appeals right to reverse his conviction? Even as a committed defense lawyer, I see this case as a close call, but given the specifics of the search warrant, I think the reversal was justified. We must remember that in 1972 the U.S. Supreme Court had held the Texas death penalty law, as well as that of every other state, to be unconstitutional in *Furman v. Georgia*. Kleasen was tried in 1975 under a new death penalty law that still had not been heard by the Supreme Court. Many legal scholars believed the court would not find any death penalty statute constitutional. The court would not approve the Texas death penalty statute until 1976 in *Jurek v. Texas*. The Texas Court of Criminal Appeals heard Kleasen's appeal against this uncertain legal backdrop. It is probable that they were bending over backwards to be cautious. That same court today is not at all defense-oriented and never relies on the *Kleasen* decision when considering search and seizure cases.

To my mind, the more troubling question is why a proper search warrant was not obtained. The state had sufficient information to support a search, they just neglected to make it part of the court record. I suspect that officers at the time still hoped to find the two boys alive and therefore rushed ahead because of that.

What about the decision not to retry Kleasen? The district attorney's office has misplaced or lost the file so it is impossible to review their thinking and reasons. (A lost file this old on a crime that was last investigated in 1978 doesn't necessarily suggest anything sinister.) After two decades, memories fade and people are unable to fully reconstruct the decision. A lot of intensely held views on this can still be found in the Austin Mormon and legal communities. (Assistant district attorney Richard Banks supervised a new search for the bodies in 1976, without success.) Other factors not generally discussed on the record very probably influenced the decision not to retry the case.

Kleasen was facing other prosecutions in cases that were easy "slam-dunks" for the government and received unusually heavy sentences in those instances. Everyone knew he wasn't going to walk away. Finally, the decision was a judgment call—one, I'm sure, made after much thought. To his credit, Ron Earle has always taken full responsibility for his decision.

Some Mormons have asked me if I thought anti-LDS prejudice had anything to do with the decision not to retry Kleasen. I have seen nothing that suggests such a possibility. I have found considerable sympathy and respect for Mormons in the Travis County district attorney's office. If anything, prosecutors looked to protect the church from what they saw as unsavory attacks on Mormons by Kleasen or his defense attorneys.

Could the Mormon church have done anything to prevent this tragedy? Frankly, no. Like many religious communities, Mormons consider themselves to be an evangelizing church. They send missionaries out to save souls and win converts. Unless the church takes the attitude that investigators must establish their fitness to become Latter-day Saints with background checks and fingerprints, they will encounter their share of predators. Even so, the LDS church did take clear steps to alert local Mormons of the need to look closely at Kleasen. No one at the local level acted improperly or recklessly. I don't mean to suggest that these events could not have been avoided, because I believe they could have, but I realize this is possible to say only from the benefit of hindsight.

As I worked on this book, I struggled to find positive messages. This is, after all, a story of enormous tragedy. Not just the murders themselves, but the unsatisfying final result in the criminal justice system. I include Bob Kleasen in that list of tragedies, as unsavory as he may be. His life was something no one would ever want to experience.

Still, there were heroes in the midst of enormous pain. The parents of Mark Fischer, Cathy and Jim, and David K. Darley, Gary's father, deserve our respect. Their great anguish has not left them; they shed many tears when they talk about their sons. Cathy Fischer once wrote me: "It's difficult telling you about the Fischer family in 1974 because that family doesn't exist anymore." But their loss has been tempered by their religious faith, their dignity, and their love of family. Never once did I detect even a trace of bitterness from any of them.

During an interview with the single surviving prosecutor, Austin attorney Charlie Craig, he turned from answering my questions to talking about what fine people the parents of both victims seemed to be. He asked me what the Mormon faith said on the death penalty. I explained that the LDS church does not object to the death penalty and that there is strong support for it in Mormon culture. My own personal opposition to capital punishment is unusual.

Craig then said he wondered because both sets of parents had been highly unusual family members in a murder case. The families of murder victims are normally intensely interested in exacting their pound of flesh, often demanding a death sentence. In public statements, "justice" often translates to revenge. Not the Fischers or the Darleys. They cooperated fully with prosecutors, but revenge never seemed to motivate them. Craig believed they had forgiven Kleasen even before his conviction.

At another point defense lawyer Pat Ganne remembers Cathy Fischer emotionally embracing Kleasen in the courtroom even while the evidence that he had murdered her son was being presented. Cathy does not recall this, but the fact that such a possibility sticks in Ganne's memory is revealing of his impression of the family.

Rather than leave them alone in a hotel, former LDS bishop Frank McCullough and his wife put the Fischers up in their Austin home as events unfolded in 1974 and 1975. The Darleys stayed with Bruce Yarborough and his wife. McCullough still marvels at the spirituality of the Fischers. He also believes they had forgiven Kleasen while the rest of the Mormon community in central Texas had come to loathe him. The pain and sorrow remain, but the Fischers have never allowed the seeds of bitterness to take root.

Over the years, as Kleasen popped up in the news again, reporters tracked down the Fischers for interviews during his controversial New York parole. Not surprisingly, they were opposed to his release from prison, expressing concern that his untreated mental illness might lead him to further violence. But still there was no bitterness. Cathy Fischer went out of her way to express her personal opposition to the death penalty, saying they had never wished for Kleasen's execution.

It is not unusual for the parents of murdered children to divorce. It is an enormous blow to any marriage and parents often handle the grief in such different ways that it can destroy a relationship. The Fischers were not immune to such strains, but the same faith they drew upon in other areas preserved their marriage as well. Instead of surrendering to the tragedy, they continued to live lives centered on raising their children. After Mark was murdered, brothers Matthew and Michael served their church in Nevada and Hawaii. Jim was a stake missionary and served in a number of local ward callings over the years. Cathy taught Sunday school and junior Sunday school, and was Primary president. Daughter Melissa taught Primary along with her mother.

David Darley's family reacted much the same way, sending other sons to serve LDS missions after Gary's murder. Besides the Texas mission service of Gary's older brother Kelle, younger brothers Todd and Bruce served. Todd was in Australia in 1982 and 1983, Bruce in Spokane, Washington, in 1984 and 1985.

Here are ordinary people visited by the worst kind of human tragedy for no reason whatsoever. Drawing upon their faith and personal integrity, they refused to give in to bitterness and blame. They held fast to the convictions which had guided their lives before tragedy struck and they were somehow enlarged as human beings. It is easy to display such virtue when faced with the kind of mild crises we all encounter in the routine course of our lives. But to live by forgiving principles in times of enormous loss and grief and pain demands complete faith.

As a final thought, I would like to quote from Maxwell Anderson's 1946 play, *Joan of Lorraine*, which was paraphrased at Mark Fischer's memorial service on November 23, 1974. In this closing scene, Joan of Arc bravely faces both her inquisitors and her imminent death by fire:

[I]f I give my life … I know this too now: Every man gives his life for what he believes. Every woman gives her life for what she believes.

Sometime people believe in little or nothing; nevertheless they give up their lives to that little or nothing. One life is all we have, and we live it as we believe in living it, and then it's gone. But to surrender what you are, and live without belief—that's more terrible than dying—more terrible than dying young. … To live your life without faith is more terrible than the fire.

No one can look at the lives of Mark Fischer and Gary Darley, compare them with that of Bob Kleasen, and not be struck by the contrast in values, accomplishments, and relationships.

Sources
(Arranged Alphabetically)

INTERVIEWS

K. C. Anderson: March 18, 1996.

Richard Banks: January 5, 1996.

David Bays: April 6, 1996.

Judge Thomas Blackwell: September 11 and 15, 1995.

Joe Butler: March 1, 1996.

Jimmy Byrd: May 29, 1995.

Dr. Lance Chase: May 21, 1996.

Dr. Richard Coons: November 13, 1995.

Charlie Craig: May 25 and 29, 1995, February 26 and March 5, 1996.

David K. Darley: January 23, 1999.

Kelle Darley: January 22, 1999, and documents provided by him.

Eddie Davis: June 1, 1995.

Larry Doty: February 7, 1996.

Joe Fawden [not his real name]: Numerous times between September and November 1999.

Vera Fawden [not her real name]: Numerous times between September 1999 and June 2000.

James and Catherine Fischer: August 2, 1995, and numerous times thereafter, and documents provided by them.

Martin Fischer: July 15 and 16, 1995.

Milton Fischer: August 1, 1995.

Pat Ganne: March 18, 1996.

Paul Griffiths: October 1999.

Ed Guyon: July 6-7, 1995.

Max Hartman: February 12 and March 1, 1996.

Norm Henk: March 1, 1996.

David Jay: July 26, 1995.

Dr. J. B. Jones: 1996.

Colon Jordan: September 18, 1995, and documents provided by him.

Marie Longley Kleasen: Numerous times in October and November 1999.

Don Lefevre: July 6, 1995.

Richard Low: March 2 and July 15, 1995.

Jerry Mack: July 12 and 16, 1995.

Frank and Norma McCullough: Numerous interviews beginning June 7, 1995, through April 2000.

Dick Murphy: Numerous interviews beginning July 28, 1995, and 1999, and documents provided by him.

Eric Neal: June 28, 1995.

Phil Nelson: 1995, and documents provided by him.

Haun Nyguen: July 26, 1995.

Richard and Lynn Odell: September 13 and 14, 1995.

Melissa Fischer Pietrzak: July 15 and 16, 1995.

Don Price: July 28, 1995.

Ruth and Bruce Smith: August 9 and 13, 1995.

Ronald C. Valentine: July 28, 1995.

Ann-Eliza Young [not her real name]: 1995.

Paul Wain: Several times between October 1999 and June 2000.

Caleb West [not his real name]: July 7-8 and August 14, 1995.

David Williams: July 28, 1995, and documents provided by him.

MATERIALS FROM THE
FISCHER AND DARLEY FAMILIES

Mark Fischer's missionary journals.

Tape recording of the Fischer memorial service in the Milwaukee Stake Center on November 23, 1974. [Courtesy of James and Catherine Fischer.]

Gary Darley's missionary journals.

TRIAL TRANSCRIPTS, COURTHOUSE FILES, AND OTHER LEGAL DOCUMENTS

Agular v. United States, 378 U.S. 108 (1964).

Blanco County, Texas, County Court file for case nos. 131-A (felony 1970) and 716 (misdemeanor 1969). Blanco County Courthouse in Johnson City, Texas.

Erie County, New York, Probate File on Elmer Kleasen, case #68-4403. Erie County Courthouse in Buffalo, New York.

Federal Court file in *Kleasen v. Frank and Mansell et al.*, case no. A-75-CA-65, United States District Court, Western District, Austin Division. Branch federal archives in Ft. Worth, Texas.

Jurek v. State, 522 S.W.2d 934 (Tex. Crim. App. 1975), aff'd, 428 U.S. 262 (1976).

Robert Kleasen deposition dated August 15, 1988, taken as part of *Kleasen v. County of Erie*.

O'Bryan v. State, 591 S.W.2d 464 (Tex. Crim. App. 1979), cert. denied, 446 U.S. 988 (1980).

Opinion in *Gorski and Higgins v. Division of Parole*, No. 04611/88 by Supreme Court Judge Vincent F. Doyle, dated May 19, 1988.

Texas Court of Criminal Appeals, appellate files in *Kleasen v. State*, case no. 56073, reported at *Kleasen v. State*, 560 S.W.2d 938 (Tex. Crim. App. 1977). Austin, Texas.

Transcript of January 23, 1975, Travis County, Texas, Justice of the Peace Inquest by JP Jim McMurtry.

Travis County, Texas, 167th District Court files on *State v. Kleasen*. Travis County Courthouse, Austin, Texas.

Wayne County, New York, Court files for case no. 71-51, *People v. Kleasen*. Wayne County Courthouse, Lyons, New York.

Wayne County, New York, real property records on the Brasser/ Kleasen farm. Wayne County Courthouse, Lyons, New York.

LAW ENFORCEMENT, CRIME LAB, AND PRISON FILES

Austin Police, various reports by Lt. Colon Jordan, Sgt. Albert Riley, Lt. Harold Bilberry, Sgt. Doug Ferris, Sgt. A. P. Lamme, and others.

New York Parole Board Files for 1985, 1987, and 1988.

Texas Department of Criminal Justice death row file on Robert Kleasen, inmate #527.

Texas Department of Public Safety crime lab files on their investigation.

LDS CHURCH ARCHIVAL MATERIALS

Local unit records for Milwaukee, Wisconsin, First Ward and Santa Susana, California, Third Ward.

"Material concerning homicide of Gary S. Darley and Mark Fischer, 1972-1975." Four folders.

NEWSPAPER AND MAGAZINE ARTICLES
(Arranged Chronologically)

"YOUTH FIRES SHOTGUN IN MEYER, TERRIFIES NURSES AND VISITORS," *Buffalo Evening News*, December 26, 1950 ("second section"), pg. 17.

"Two Missionaries Reported Missing," *Austin American-Statesman*, November 4, 1974, pg. 1.

Wendell Fuqua, "Missing Missionaries' Stripped Car Located," *Austin American-Statesman*, November 5, 1974, pg. 1.

"Missionaries Missing; Foul Play Suspected," *Daily Texan*, Wednesday, November 5, 1974, page number unknown.

Crispin James, "Missing Pair's Friend Is Held," publisher unknown, Wednesday, November 6, 1974, page number unknown, in LDS Archives.

Wendell Fuqua and Billie Veach, "Suspect to be interrogated on missionaries' disappearance," *Austin American-Statesman*, November 6, 1974, pg. 1.

"Group combs brushland for missionary clues," *Austin American-Statesman*, Wednesday, November 7, 1974, pg. 15.

Tim Ater, "Man Questioned In Disappearance of Missionaries," *Daily Texan*, Wednesday, November 7, 1974, page numbers unknown.

"Rain May Hinder Search For Two Missionaries," publisher unknown, Wednesday, November 7, 1974. [In LDS Archives and Texas Court of Criminal Appeals files.]

"LDS join search for missionaries," *Deseret News*, Wednesday, November 7, 1974, pg. B4.

"Aerial Search Due for Two Missionaries," publisher unknown, Wednesday, November 7, 1974, page numbers unknown. [In LDS Archives.]

"Mormon missionaries volunteered for service," *Austin American-Statesman*, Thursday, November 8, 1974, pg. A8.

"Pair Still Missing One Missionary Apprehensive," *San Antonio Light*, November 8, 1974.

"Father of Missionary Assists Search For 2 Thought in West Austin Hills," *Daily Texan*, November 8, 1974.

"Rain hinders missionary search," *Austin American-Statesman*, November 8, 1974, pg. A8.

"Mormons' Tires Reported Found," *Austin American-Statesman*, November 9, 1974, pg. 14.

"Hundreds of LDS hunt for evidence," *Deseret News*, November 9, 1974, pg. 4A.

"Despite Continued Rain, Yearly Total Still Low," *Austin American-Statesman*, November 9, 1974, pg. 8.

"Mormons Search For Pair," *Austin American-Statesman*, November 10, 1974, pg. A15.

"Volunteers Hunt Missionaries," publisher unknown, November 10, 1974. [In LDS archives.]

"Hundreds of LDS in Texas Seek Clues, Search for 2 Missing Missionaries," *Deseret News*, November 10, 1974.

"Police Search Old Settlement For Mormons," *Austin American-Statesman*, November 11, 1974, pg. 7.

Robert Fulkerson, "Search Continues No Sign of Missing Mormons," *Daily Texan*, November 12, 1974, page number unknown.

"Missionary Search Data To Be Studied By Police," *Austin American-Statesman*, November 12, 1974, pg. 10.

Wendell Fuqua, "$50,000 in Counterfeit Accidently Discovered," *Austin American-Statesman*, November 13, 1974, pg. 19.

Wendell Fuqua, "Slain Mormons Praised for Mission Work," *Austin American-Statesman*, Thursday, November 14, 1974, pg. 7.

"Charges Filed In Deaths of Missionaries," *Austin Citizen*, November 14, 1974, pg. 1.

Wendell Fuqua, "Man Charged in Slaying of Pair, Parts of Two Missionaries' Bodies Found," *Austin American-Statesman*, Thursday, November 14, 1974, pg. 1.

"Austin man charged in missionary deaths," *San Antonio Express*, Thursday, November 14, 1974, pg. 20A.

"Charged in Slaying of Pair Parts of Two Missionaries' Bodies Found," publisher unknown, Thursday, November 14, 1974. [In LDS Archives.]

Wendell Fuqua, "Kleasen's Strange Odyssey, How Suspect in Mormon Deaths Came to Austin," *Austin American-Statesman*, November 15, 1974, pg. 1.

"2 Missionaries Blood, Hair Among Discoveries," *Austin American-Statesman*, Friday, November 15, 1974, pg. 13.

"2 Missionaries' Bodies Feared Unrecoverable," *Austin American-Statesman*, Saturday, November 16, 1974, pg. 1A.

"Deaths and Funerals in the Milwaukee Area Mark Fischer," *Milwaukee Journal*, Sunday, November 17, 1974, pg. 11.

"The Mormon Murders: Letters From The Accused," *Texas Monthly*, January 1975, pgs. 12-15.

"Trial Set May 19 In Kleasen Case," *Austin American-Statesman*, March 25, 1975, pg. 8.

Robert Heard (AP), "Kleasen Says CIA to Blame for Murder Charges," *Austin American-Statesman*, March 30, 1975, pg. A13, jump to pg. A14.

John Sutton, "Kleasen Innocence Reassert Lawyer Rules Out Raising Sanity Issue," *Austin American-Statesman*, March 30, 1975, pg. 1.

"Jail Food Spurs Kleasen Suit," *Austin American-Statesman*, April 23, 1975, pg. 1.

"Inmate Disputes Kleasen's Food Story," *Austin American-Statesman*, April 25, 1975, pg. A11.

Carol Fowler, "Kleasen Lawyers May Seek TRO," *Austin Citizen*, April 25, 1975.

Robert Heard, "Motive to be factor in Monday Kleasen trial," *Austin American-Statesman*, Sunday, May 18, 1975, pg. A10.

John Sutton, "Attorneys pick housewife for Kleasen trial jury," *Austin American-Statesman*, Tuesday, May 20, 1975, pg. 6.

John Sutton, "Kleasen jurors now at 5," *Austin American-Statesman*,

Wednesday, May 21, 1975, pg. 17.

John Sutton, "Kleasen protests county jail treatment 9 jurors selected for trial," *Austin American-Statesman*, Thursday, May 22, 1975, pg. A20.

John Sutton, "Kleasen trial testimony to begin," *Austin American-Statesman*, Friday, May 23, 1975, pg. 1.

John Sutton, "Handful of people hold Kleasen's fate How long a road to 'market place?,'" *Austin American-Statesman*, Sunday, May 25, 1975, pg. A9.

John Sutton, "Kleasen jurors see bloody pants," *Austin American-Statesman*, Tuesday, May 27, 1975 [evening edition only], pg. 1.

"Maneuver fails in Kleasen case," *Deseret News*, Tuesday, May 27, 1975, pg. 14A.

John Sutton, "Kleasen trial, Youth's mother quotes slayer: 'I loved Gary, too,'" *Austin American-Statesman*, Wednesday, May 28, 1975 [morning edition only], pg. 1.

John Sutton, "Kleasen's death talk reported," *Austin American-Statesman*, Wednesday, May 28, 1975 [evening edition only], pg. 1.

"Kleasen cried, witness said," *Deseret News*, Wednesday, May 28, 1975, pg. 17A.

John Sutton, "Kleasen 'belief' of deaths told," *Austin American-Statesman*, Thursday, May 29, 1975 [morning edition only], pg. 1.

John Sutton, "Bandsaw test, Blood, hair, 'human,' jury told," *Austin American-Statesman*, Thursday, May 29, 1975 [evening edition only], pg. 1.

"Texas' star witness to tell of hair samples," *Deseret News*, Thursday, May 29, 1975, pg. 4B.

John Sutton, "Bandsaw was used only on heads, witness says," *Austin American-Statesman*, Friday, May 30, 1975 [morning edition], pg. 1.

John Sutton, "Kleasen prosecutors rest," *Austin American-Statesman*, Friday, May 30, 1975 [evening edition only], pg. 1.

"Kleasen prosecution rests," *Deseret News*, Friday, May 30, 1975, pg. D10.

John Sutton, "Final Kleasen witness due Monday," *Austin American-Statesman*, Saturday, May 31, 1975 [both editions], pg. 1.

John Sutton, "Kleasen defense nears end," *Austin American-Statesman*, June 1, 1975, pg. B1.

John Sutton, "Jury declares Kleasen guilty Slayer faces either death or life imprisonment," *Austin American-Statesman*, Tuesday, June 3, 1975 [morning edition], pg. 1.

John Sutton, "Kleasen begs for life," *Austin American-Statesman*, Tuesday, June 3, 1975 [evening edition], pg. 1.

"Kleasen convicted of murder, jury to decide life or death," *Deseret News*, Tuesday, June 3, 1975, pg. B1.

John Sutton, "Kleasen jury decided 'inconceivable' case," *Austin American-Statesman*, June 5, 1975, pg. 1.

John Sutton, "Kleasen thankful for 'reprieve'," *Austin American-Statesman*, Thursday, August 28, 1975 [Evening Edition], pg. A14.

Mike Cox, "Kelle Darley sure of guilt," *Austin American-Statesman*, November 23, 1977.

"Murder conviction reversed; warrant invalid," *Houston Post*, November 24, 1977, pg. 1.

Rosemary Beales, "Kleasen murder conviction erased," *Austin American-Statesman*, November 24, 1977, pg. 1.

"Brother Jolted: "Kleasen 'has killed, will kill again,'" *Austin American-Statesman*, November 24, 1977, pg. 1B.

"Kleasen must stand trial again," *Austin American-Statesman*, February 8, 1978, pg. B2.

"No retrial in slaying of 2 missionaries," *Salt Lake Tribune*, February 9, 1978.

John Sutton, "Kleasen pleads not guilty," *Austin American-Statesman*, February 9, 1978, pg. 1.

"First verdict overturned, Court affirms death sentence," *Houston Post*, February 9, 1978, pg. 28C.

Mark Kirkpatrick and John Sutton, "Kleasen transfer pressed," *Austin American-Statesman*, February 10, 1978, pg. 1B.

Rosemary Beales, "Jury chosen for Kleasen trial," *Austin American-Statesman*, March 28, 1978, pg. B3.

Rosemary Beales, "Kleasen firearms case set to go to jury today," *Austin American-Statesman*, March 29, 1978, pg. B2.

"Closing arguments begin today, No defense offered by Kleasen in federal firearms trial," *Houston Post*, March 29, 1978, pg. 11A.

Rosemary Beales, "Kleasen guilty of violating firearms laws," *Austin*

American-Statesman, March 30, 1978, pg. 1.

Rosemary Beales, "Kleasen guilty on gun charges," *Austin American-Statesman*, March 30, 1978, pg. 1.

"Jury declares Kleasen guilty on federal firearms charges," *Houston Post*, March 30, 1978, pg. 1B.

Rosemary Beales, "Kleasen draws 9-year sentence in firearms case," *Austin American-Statesman*, April 29, 1978, pg. A1.

Steve Crosby, "12-Woman jury picked to hear shooting case," *The Finger Lake Times* (New York), June 5, 1979, pg. 8.

Warren White, "Kleasen goes on trial for shooting," *Rochester Democrat and Chronicle*, June 5, 1979 [Regional Edition], pg. 1B.

Warren White, "Judge denies Kleasen mistrial over news article," *Rochester Democrat and Chronicle*, June 6, 1979 [Regional Edition], pg. 1B.

Lucius Lomax, "Judge Roberts takes semiretirement status," *Austin American-Statesman*, Thursday, May 1, 1980, pg. B1.

John C. Henry and Linda Anthony, "Death Watch Witnesses call O'Bryan execution quick, painless," *Austin American-Statesman*, Sunday, April 1, 1984, pg. B2.

Louise Hoffman, "More Jail Time For Murder," *The Finger Lake Times* (New York), November 26, 1985.

Michael Beebe, "Convict With Record of Violence Will Spend His Parole in Buffalo," *Buffalo News*, May 6, 1988, pg. 1A.

John Harris, "Man once accused of slayings freed Parolee feared to be dangerous," *Austin American-Statesman*, May 7, 1988, pg. B1.

Tom Buckham, "Parolee With Past Of Violence Settles In Secret City Site," *Buffalo News*, May 7, 1988, pg. A1.

Charles Azalone, Thomas J. Dolan, and Mike Vogel, "Kleasen Committed To Psychiatric Center," *Buffalo News*, May 8, 1988, pg. B1.

"Kleasen Case, Cult Film Seem Unconnected," *Buffalo News*, May 8, 1988, pg. 1B.

"Feared convict apparently back in Buffalo area," *Houston Post*, May 8, 1988, pg. 7A.

Susan Schulman, "Threat by Kleasen Prompts Watch on Ex-Officer's Home," *Buffalo News*, May 9, 1988, pg. 1A.

Michael Beebe and Dave Ernest, "State's Kleasen Decision Awaits Psychiatric Tests," *Buffalo News*, May 9, 1988, pg. 1A.

"Missionary's Killer, 'A Walking Time Bomb,' Goes Free," *Salt Lake Tribune*, May 9, 1988.

John Harris, "Parolee will remain in N.Y. hospital," *Austin American-Statesman*, May 10, 1988, pg. B1.

Michael Beebe, "Confine Kleasen, Victim's Kin Urges," *Buffalo News*, May 10, 1988, pg. A1.

Michael Beebe, "Kleasen Seeking to Gain Release," *Buffalo News*, May 11, 1988, pg. A1.

Susan Schulman, "Ex-Officer Told Police Of Threat by Kleasen," *Buffalo News*, May 11, 1988, pg. A6.

Gene Warner, "Rights Advocate Says Kleasen Puts Parole System to Test," *Buffalo News*, May 11, 1988, pg. B1.

Matti Gryta and Barbara O'Brien, "Memo on Kleasen Saw Violent Acts in Future," *Buffalo News*, May 12, 1988, pg. A1.

Barbara O'Brien, "Kleasen: I'll Leave if I get a Job, Says He'll Move From City if He Can Find Work; Gorski Pursues Removal," *Buffalo News*, May 12, 1988, pg. A1.

Dave Ernst, "Cuomo Kills Bill To Bring Back Death Penalty," *Buffalo News*, May 13, 1988, pg. A2.

Michael Beebe and Matt Gryta, "Cook in Austin Says Kleasen Is Welcome, But Texas Barred Him," *Buffalo News*, May 13, 1988, pg. C1.

"Ex-convict Kleasen wants a life without 'monster' image," *Austin American-Statesman*, May 13, 1988, pg. B3.

Matt Gryta, "Griffin to Decide Whether to Join Effort to Force Kleasen From Area," *Buffalo News*, May 15, 1988, pg. C4.

Jeff Simon, "The Robert Kleasen case is a Sweeps Week disgrace and brings to the fore choice pieces of blockheaded local TV sensationalism," *Buffalo News*, *TV Topics*, May 15, 1988, pg. 2.

Matt Gryta, "Kleasen Suing Gorski, Sheriff Over Effort to Oust Him From Area," *Buffalo News*, May 17, 1988, pg. B1.

Matt Gryta, "Doyle Promises to Rule Quickly On Plea by 'Man Without a City'," *Buffalo News*, May 18, 1988, pg. B1.

Matt Gryta, "Court Order Allows Kleasen To Remain in Buffalo Area," *Buffalo News*, May 20, 1988, pg. 1A.

"Ruling Satisfies Former Officer," *Buffalo News*, May 20, 1988, pg. A6.

Dan Herbeck, "Trial begins in $2.5 million Kleasen suit against county officials," *Buffalo News*, Monday, January 22, 1990, pg. 1B.

Dan Herbeck, "Hotel official has kind words for ex-inmate, $2.5 million suit claims Kleasen was thwarted in effort to start anew," *Buffalo News*, Tuesday, January 23, 1990, pg. B4.

Charles Anzalone and Dan Herbeck, "Kleasen claims he was hounded after his parole, Tie to Texas massacre was sought, he testifies," *Buffalo News*, Wednesday, January 24, 1990, pg. 1B.

Dan Herbeck and Charles Anzalone, "Kleasen's lawsuit dismissed by court Curtin says he didn't prove case," *Buffalo News*, Thursday, January 25, 1990, pg. 1A.

"Judge Marvin Teague dies of cardiac arrest," *Houston Chronicle*, Thursday, February 21, 1991, pg. A21.

Alicia L. Locheed, "The Development of The Court of Criminal Appeals," *Texas Bar Journal*, November 1992, pgs. 1052-1056.

Vern Anderson, "Trail of Missionary Killer Went Cold," *Salt Lake Tribune*, Sunday, September 10, 1995, pg. A-1.

John L. Hart, "Over half LDS now outside U.S.," *Church News*, March 2, 1996, pg. 3.

Hank Stuever, "99 Minutes, 30 Years Later," *Austin American-Statesman*, July 29, 1996, pg. A1.

Katy Kelly, "Mormons on mission to grow," *USA Today*, Tuesday, October 21, 1997, pg. 1D.

R. Scott Lloyd, "Mormons in Milwaukee," *Church News*, December 5, 1998, pgs. 8-10.

Bennett J. Loudon, "Wayne convict surfaces in England," *Rochester Democrat and Chronicle*, Tuesday, September 7, 1999, pg. 1-A.

Greg Burton, "Is Suspect in LDS Killings a Gun Dealer?," *Salt Lake Tribune*, Friday, September 10, 1999, pg. A-1.

Michael Beebe, "City native's past arouses suspicion in England," *Buffalo News*, Monday, September 13, 1999, pg. B1.

Bennett J. Loudon, "Convict with Wayne ties faces counts in England," *Rochester Democrat and Chronicle*, Saturday, October 30, 1999, pg. 1-A.

"Death Row Man In Dock," *Grimsby Evening Telegraph* (England), March 17, 2000.

"This feeble old man with a house full of guns," *Grimsby Evening Telegraph* (England), March 17, 2000, pg. 1.

Lisa Bingham, "Bail for death row defendant," *Grimsby Evening Telegraph* (England), March 17, 2000, pg. 5.

"Ex-wife unaware of his past," *Grimsby Evening Telegraph* (England), March 17, 2000, pg. 5.

"Home turned into arsenal of weapons," *Grimsby Evening Telegraph* (England), March 17, 2000, pg. 5.

"Obsessed with guns," *Grimsby Evening Telegraph* (England), March 17, 2000, pg. 5.

Kevin Cantera, "Kleasen's Violent Saga May Be Near End," *Salt Lake Tribune*, March 18, 2000, pg. 1.

"Kleasen must be deported, says MP," *Grimsby Evening Telegraph* (England), March 20, 2000.

"Man accused of ammunition charge," *Grimsby Evening Telegraph* (England), April 11, 2000.

"Man suspected in 1974 missionary slayings tries to flee from Britain," *Orem Daily Journal*, April 12, 2000.

Richard Woodward, "Kleasen case alerts Home Office to dangers Gun Law Tighter," *Grimsby Evening Telegraph* (England), April 19, 2000, pg. 1.

"American may face a retrial," *Grimsby Evening Telegraph* (England), April 19, 2000, pg. 1.

"Kleasen: The whole story?" *Grimsby Evening Telegraph* (England), April 19, 2000, pg. 3.

"Jack Straw has power of deportation," *Grimsby Evening Telegraph* (England), April 19, 2000, pg. 3.

Ian London, "Essential Evidence?" *Grimsby Evening Telegraph* (England), April 20, 2000, pg. 1.

"Kleasen ordered into the dock," *Grimsby Evening Telegraph* (England), April 20, 2000, pg. 1.

"Complaints over police conduct," *Grimsby Evening Telegraph* (England), April 20, 2000, pg. 4.

"'Ecstacy' at ruling," *Grimsby Evening Telegraph* (England), April 20, 2000, pg. 4.

"Force hits back at criticism," *Grimsby Evening Telegraph* (England), April 20, 2000, pg. 4.

Bennett J. Loudon, "Murder case gets 2nd look," *Rochester Democrat and Chronicle*, April 21, 2000, pg. 1B.

Kevin Cantera, "U.S. Gun Zealot Alters U.K. Law," *Salt Lake Tribune*, May 8, 2000, pg. B1.

REFERENCE BOOKS

Gorton Carruth, *The Encyclopedia of American Facts and Dates.* 10th ed. New York: Harper Collins, 1997.

Deseret News 1993-1994 Church Almanac. Salt Lake City: Deseret News, 1992.

Deseret News 1995-1996 Church Almanac. Salt Lake City: Deseret News, 1994.

Deseret News 1997-1998 Church Almanac. Salt Lake City: Deseret News, 1996.

Deseret News 1999-2000 Church Alamanac. Salt Lake City: Deseret News, 1999.

James W. Marquart, Sheldon Ekland-Olson, and Jonathan R. Sorensen, *The Rope, the Chair, and the Needle.* Austin: University of Texas Press, 1994.

Armand L. Mauss, *The Angel and the Beehive: The Mormon Struggle with Assimilation.* Urbana: University of Illinois Press, 1994.

William Mulder, *Homeward to Zion: The Mormon Migration from Scandinavia.* Minneapolis: University of Minnesota Press, 1957.

Polk's Buffalo City Directories for 1907, 1911, 1919, 1921, 1925, 1931, 1936, 1937, 1938, 1939, 1948, 1951-52, 1953, 1955, 1959, 1963, and 1969.

Bernard Salzman, *The Handbook of Psychiatric Drugs.* New York: Henry Holt and Co., 1991.

Social Security Administration, "Your Payments While You Are Outside the United States," June 1997.

SELECTED LETTERS TO THE AUTHOR

Central Intelligence Agency Information, Privacy & Classification Review Office, letter dated August 4, 1995.

Edward Kimball, letter dated January 15, 1998, enclosing materials from the diaries of Spencer W. Kimball, and e-mails of various dates.

Index

Gibbons, Bob, 122, 123, 124, 125, 135

Gillespie County, 84, 85, 174; courthouse, 83, 250; jail, 83

Gilmore, Gary, xi, 129

Gines, Tim, 7, 9

Gladewater, Texas, 88

Gorski, Dennis, 231, 232, 237, 238

Gowanda State Hospital, 40, 44, 49, 53

Graff, Mike, ix

Graff, Tracy, ix

Greene, Rollo, 2

Gregg v. Georgia, 129

Griffin, James, 231

Grote, Frederick, 84

Guadalupe Street, 3, 146

Guevara, Che, 89, 183

Guyon, Ed, 7, 8, 9, 136, 158, 250

H

Haendiges, Phillip, 38

hair, cuts, 23, 94, 107, 111, 160; samples, 18, 21, 23, 94, 95, 96, 97, 160, 161, 164

Haley, Roscoe, 134, 135, 140, 143, 146, 150, 154, 155, 160, 171, 172, 175, 176, 177, 181, 184, 186, 189, 190, 191, 250

Hampton, Kerrie Lynn, 106, 107, 153, 154

Handy, Jeremiah, 119, 120, 211, 212

Hanson, Keyte, 32

Hardcastle, Conrad Brent, 2, 3, 21, 107, 152, 153

Hardy, Charles, 204

Harrington, Eden, ix

Harris County, Texas, 97, 132, 163, 196, 250; Criminal Lawyers Association of, 196

Hartman, Max, vii, 83, 174, 250

Haslam, Linda, ix

Hayes County, Texas, 21, 25, 191

Heard, Robert, 135, 137-38, 181

Hearst, Patty, xi

helicopter plant, *see* Bell Aircraft

Henk, Norm, vii, 84, 174, 250

Henzy, Frank, 20, 94, 152

Higgins, Thomas, 226, 232, 237, 238

Hill Cumorah, 45, 185

"Hitler Youth in America," 243

Hoffa, Jimmy, xi

Hoffman, Mark, 101, 165

Hohman, Alfred, 21

Holmes, Samuel M., 133

home teachers, 81, 90, 109, 186

Hood, Karen, 145

Hornet, car, *see* American Motors

Hornet .22 rifle, 75, 101, 213

Hotel Lafayette, vii, 235, 236, 237

Houston, Texas, vii, 10, 23, 24, 78, 89, 97, 132, 147, 163, 191, 195, 249

Hoyt, William, 231

Hull University, 242

Humberside, viii, 240

Hunter, Howard W., 184

42-43; marries Mexican woman, 43; as Erie County deputy sheriff, 43-44; divorces, remarries, 44-45, 46; mother's farm near Hill Cumorah, 45; graduates college, 47; kills buffalo 48-49; psychiatric treatment, 49; meets Fredriksson, 50-51; shoots DuBoise, 52-53; home raided by ATF, 54-55, 56; beats Fredriksson and mother, 57, 58; forces Fredriksson to write embassy, 58-59; in bathtub with deer carcass, 59, 178; flees the country, 61–62; in Copenhagen 63-65; writes Jensens from Copenhagen jail, 66-69; in Lebanon, 69-70; expelled from Canada, 70, 71, 72, 73; steals camper trailer, 74; buys guns, 75; joins LDS church, 79; asks bishop to write Jensens, 80, 81, 82; buffalo shooting, 83-85; letters to Elder Bell, 86-87, 88, 89; invites Darley and Fischer to dinner, 90, 91, 92, 93, 94, 97, 99, 100, 101, 102; psychiatric evaluation of, 114-18, 119, 120, 121; Texas competency trial of, 122-25, 127, 128, 129, 130, 132, 133; hires Haley, 134-35; Associated Press interview, 135-38; "centipede sandwich," 138-39; court trial, 146-65, 166-69, 170-71, 172, 187-89; sentencing of, 173-75, 189, 190; testimony of, 175-87; motion for new trial for, 191-194; on death row 195-99; appeal, 200-203; conviction of reversed, 203-205, 207, 208, 209; convicted of: firearms charges, 210-16; of assault, 216-17; in prison, 218-23; paroled, 223-33; lives in City Mission, 234-35; in England 240-48, 253, 254, 255, 256, 257, 258, 259; as "American Citizen," 65

Owens, David, 148

Wallace, George, xi

Walls Unit, 195

Walther .22 Hornet rifle, 17, 25, 150, 210, 213

Warney, Lynn, 52

Warnock, Christopher, 2, 90

Washington, D.C., 12, 70, 97, 120, 213, 245

Washington, George, 195

watches, Seiko, 15, 26, 94, 97, 111, 157, 201, 206; Voumard calendar, 22, 26, 97, 106, 154, 156, 160

Watergate, xi, 79

Watt, Ronald, ix

Wayne County, New York, vii, 13, 45, 47, 52, 53, 55, 59, 60, 61, 63, 117, 214, 216, 218, 220, 222, 226, 240, 252, 255

Wayne County Jail, 56, 57, 216

weapons, *see* Colt .357; firearms; revolver; rifles

Weathermen, 136

Weed and Company, 39

West, Caleb, vi, 77, 78, 151

West Mary Street, 2, 4, 22, 94

Whipple, Clifford, 115, 116

White, Mark, 85, 86, 185

White, Phillip, 214

Whitman, Charles, 30

"Whore Master," 67

Wildfowlers Association, 244

Wilkerson, Glen, 121, 122, 135, 252

Williams, Bobby, 163

Williams, David, vii, 61, 62, 216, 217, 252

Williamson, April, ix

Williamson, John Townstead, 15, 35, 41, 63-64, 65, 66, 68, 69, 70, 73, 74, 80, 153, 154, 183, 186, 187

Williamsville, New York, 52, 69, 117

Willis, Richard G., 144

Wilsolite Corporation, 46

Wise, Carol, 11

World Court at The Hague, 235

World of Pentecost Church, 211

World War II, 84, 126, 144, 243

Wright, Amos, 2, 7, 8, 24, 87

Y

Yarborough, Bruce, 6, 7, 8, 9, 10, 12, 147, 158, 191, 192

Yeager, Chuck, 243

Young, Ann-Eliza, vii, 220, 235, 238, 239, 241

Young, Brigham, 66

Z

Zahle, Lebanon, 69. *See also* Lebanon; Salah; Sale

Zanett, Ernie, 53

Zecher, Robert, 216

Zilker Park, 26